HAND BOOK OF ADHESIVES WITH THEIR FORMULAES

WITH DIRECTORY OF MANUFACTURERS/SUPPLIERS OF PLANT, EQUIPMENTS & MACHINERIES, RAW MATERIAL SUPPLIERS/ DEALERS AND PRESENT MANUFACTURERS/SUPPLIERS OF GLUE, ADHESIVES & SEALANTS

HAND BOOK OF ADHESIVES WITH THEIR FORMULAES

WITH DIRECTORY OF MANUFACTURERS/SUPPLIERS OF PLANT, EQUIPMENTS & MACHINERIES, RAW MATERIAL SUPPLIERS/ DEALERS AND PRESENT MANUFACTURERS/SUPPLIERS OF GLUE, ADHESIVES & SEALANTS

Written By

EIRI Board of Consultants and Engineers

ENGINEERS INDIA RESEARCH INSTITUTE

4449, Nai Sarak, Main Road, Delhi - 110006 (India)
Ph: +91-11-23918117, 23916431, 45120361, 23947058, 64727385
* E-Mail: eiribooks@yahoo.com & eiriprojects@gmail.com
*Website: www.eiriindia.org & www.industrialprojects.in

PRINTED & PUBLISHED BY

ENGINEERS INDIA RESEARCH INSTITUTE

4449, Nai Sarak, Main Road, Delhi - 110006 (India)
Ph: +91-11-23918117, 23916431, 45120361, 23947058, 64727385
* E-Mail: eiribooks@yahoo.com & eiriprojects@gmail.com
*Website: www.eiriindia.org & www.industrialprojects.in

Distributors:

EIRI Project Consultants and Publishers
Roop Nagar, Delhi-110007
and
Industrial Technologies, India
Nai Sarak, Delhi-110006

ISBN: 9788186732342

2nd Edition

Printed in New Delhi (INDIA)

₹ 900/-

Printed & Published by Sudhir Gupta for "Engineers India Research Institute", 4449 Nai Sarak, Main Road, New Delhi -110006

Preface

An adhesive is any substance applied to the surfaces of materials that binds them together and resists separation. The term "adhesive" may be used interchangeably with glue, cement, mucilage, or paste. Adjectives may be used in conjunction with the word "adhesive" to describe properties based on the substance's physical or chemical form, the type of materials joined, or conditions under which it is applied.

The use of adhesives offers many advantages over binding techniques such as sewing, mechanical fastening, thermal bonding, etc. These include the ability to bind different materials together, to distribute stress more efficiently across the joint, the cost effectiveness of an easily mechanized process, an improvement in aesthetic design, and increased design flexibility. Disadvantages of adhesive use include decreased stability at high temperatures, relative weakness in bonding large objects with a small bonding surface area, and greater difficulty in separating objects during testing.

Adhesives may be found naturally or produced synthetically. The earliest human use of adhesive-like substances was approximately 200,000 years ago. From then until the 1900s increases in adhesive use and discovery were relatively gradual. Only since the last century has the development of synthetic adhesives accelerated rapidly, and innovation in the field continues to the present.

In India adhesive & glue are not very prevalent probably because man hour is cheap in country & the time factor has not much impact on the mind of people. In developed countries adhesives & glues are extensively used in the wide spectrum of daily life and are very fast replacing the mechanical fastening methods.

The book 'Hand Book of Adhesives with their formuleas' covers almost all the basic and advanced details to setup own unit of Adhesives & Gums etc. The Chapters covering in this book are adhesives concept & terminology, selecting an adhesive, hot melt adhesives, pressure sensitive adhesives, water based adhesives, testing of adhesives, adhesive materials, formulations

& applications, EVA emulsion adhesives, rubber based adhesives, butly & poly isobutylene rubber adhesives, nitrile rubber adhesives, SBR adhesives, thermoplastic rubber based adhesives, polychloroprene adhesives, polysulphide sealants & adhesive, epoxy resin adhesives, polyurethane adhesives, acrylic adhesives, cyanoacrylate adhesives, anaerobic adhesives, polyamide adhesives, silicone adhesives, natural resin based adhesives, dextrin based adhesives, acid modified or thin-boiling starch adhesive, casein glues, soyabean adhesives, animal glues, rosin adhesives, various other types of adhesives, blood albumen glues, pressure sensitive tapes & labels, performance & application of adhesives, test methods & standards, the major chapters for the benefits of new as well as established entrepreneurs & existing manufacturers have also been added up i.e. manufacturers & suppliers of machinery & equipments and suppliers of raw materials & chemicals used in adhesive, glues & sealants industries. Apart from these, present manufacturers, dealers & suppliers of glue & adhesives have also been provided.

The book has been written for the benefit and to prove an asset and a handy reference guide in the hands of new entrepreneurs & well established industrialists.In this area it is found a series of articles which explain the fundamental basis for understanding the origin, nature and functioning of adhesives, glues and sealants, once we know how to operate with adhesives, we will be able to understand any kind of union made with them, as well as designing them.

In this book you will find information about different types of adhesives, glues and sealants available today, also you will learn about its chemical composition, physical and chemical properties. It can also be found various applications where the adhesive is used.

Director

ENGINEERS INDIA RESEARCH INSTITUTE

4449, Nai Sarak, Main Road, Delhi - 110006 (India)

Ph: +91-11-23918117, 23916431, 45120361, 23947058, 64727385

* E-Mail: eiribooks@yahoo.com & eiriprojects@gmail.com

*Website: www.eiriindia.org & www.industrialprojects.in

CONTENTS AND SUBJECT INDEX

1

ADHESIVES CONCEPT AND TERMINOLOGY

I. INTRODUCTION

A knowledge of basic concepts and terminology is helpful in deriving the maximum benefit from the use of adhesives and facilitating communication between designers, users, and producers.

II. SURFACES

Surfaces are complex and dynamic. They are never flat despite the best attempts at polishing. Industrially bonded surfaces often have a surface roughness of 50-100 microinches (12,700-25,400 μm) or more.

Rough surfaces are neither automatically good nor bad for bonding. The smoother the surface, the fewer crevices and microvoids are present to retain trapped air and prevent good contact of the adhesive with the surface. On the other hand, a rough surface provides more actual surface area for contact with the adhesive and may even allow some mechanical interlocking as the adhesive solidifies.

The most important property of a surface, as far as bonding is concerned, is cleanliness. Unless surfaces are clean, that is, free of loosely held foreign material, the bond may fail unexpectedly and/or at low loads for no apparent reason. Typical surface contaminants include dirt, oil, grease, mold release, oxides, moisture, gases, and lubricants.

Surfaces are dynamic in the sense that their chemical composition is frequently subject to change with time. Some metals may oxidize (corrode) by reacting with atmospheric moisture and oxygen which permeate the bondline. Occasionally, plastic surfaces may become coated with chemicals that migrate from the interior of the part or which reach the surface from the external atmosphere by diffusion through the bondline. In either case, a competition for attachment to the surface develops between the adhesives and the newly arrived chemical. Strong, long-lasting adhesives are generally those whose chemical. Strong, long lasting adhesives are generally those whose chemical structure is such that they can compete favorably for surface attachment sites with other chemicals which may find their way to the surface.

Surfaces also have a different composition than might ordinarily be expected. Most commonly, bonded metal surfaces exist, not as free metals, but as hydrated metal oxides. Freshly milled aluminum surfaces, for example, begin forming a transparent oxide layer immediately when exposed to the atmosphere. Iron and ferrous alloys do likewise. Applying adhesives to a metal-oxide surface is not necessarily bad. If the metal oxide is tightly bound to the metal and is cohesively strong and chemiçally stable, then the resulting adhesive bond may be both strong and durable. Aluminum, for example, is frequently oxidized under strictly controlled conditions (anodized) prior to bonding in order to provide the type of surface just described.

III. ADHESION

Adhesion is the phenomenon which allows two objects to retain surface contact nonmagnetically. Most theories of adhesion can be expressed in terms of electrical attractions. Essentially, certain minute locations on one surface possess or acquire positive or negative electrical charges which then align themselves adjacent to an oppositely charged location on the other surface. The ensuing unlike charge attractions result in adhesion of the surfaces. An adhesive is simply a material applied as a liquid, which allows the establishment of unlike charge attractions and then solidifies to provide the bond with significant internal strength.

IV. WETTING

Wetting refers to the ability of a liquid to intimately contact the surface over which it flows. Poor wetting is typified by water on a waxed surface. The water has a tendency to "bead up" because the water molecules are more vigorously attracted to themselves than they are to the waxed surface. Good wetting is essential for strong adhesive bonds. Adhesives may contain wetting agents, that is, chemicals which increase the ability of the adhesive to contact and be attracted to the surfaces being bonded. Wax, grease, oil, and fluorocarbons are notoriously difficult to wet. It is for this reason that most surfaces are subjected to some sort of degreasing treatment prior to bonding.

Surfaces which are not easily wet by water will be difficult to bond. The "water-break free" test is often used to determine the bondability of surfaces. Water is poured on the surface and observed to see whether it breaks up into droplets or remains as a single puddle. If individual droplets are formed, the surface is presumed to be contaminated with grease or oil. Some fluorocarbons, hydrocarbons, and silicones can not wet by water oven when they are clean. The test works well for nearly everything else, however.

V. BOND STRENGTH

Bond strength refers to the amount of force required to break the bond. It represents the force required to overcome either the adhesive strength of the bond or the cohesive strength of the adhesive material or of one of the bonded objects.

VI. FATIGUE LIFE

Fatigue life, which is usually expressed as the number of cycles required for failure, is the number of times a stress can be applied and released before the bond fails. The test is usually performed with an electrically driven instrument capable of subjecting the bond to tension or bending at a very high frequency. The underlying assumption is that the harmful effect of such stresses will be cumulative, and although they are performed at a very high frequency, it will still be possible to correlate the results with service conditions.

VII. HEAT LIMITATIONS

Most structural adhesives begin to lose strength significantly at temperatures above 300^0 F (149^0 C). A few are available which can tolerate continuous exposure at 400^0 F (204^0 C) or higher. The basic difficulty experienced by most adhesives at high temperatures is simply that the chemical bonds which are an inherent part of their structure begin to break down as the temperature increases. Invariably, those products which have extremely high heat stability also contain chemical bonds of unusual thermal stability. Sometimes heat-stable fillers can be added to the formulation in order to raise the service temperature.

VIII. DEBONDING

Debonding is the process by which an adhesive looses its attachment to a surface. Debonding usually occurs when water or some other chemical displaces the adhesive from surface attachment sites. the process is usually a gradual one although it may not be noticed until the adhesive and the adherend separate completely, and a catastrophic failure results.

IX. UNSTRESSED AGING DATA

Unstressed aging data describe how bond properties of interest, possibly impact or shear strength, change with time using speciments that have not been stressed prior to testing. Engineers frequently request that strength-retention data be collected for a particular adhesive bonding system. As a result, bonds are made and tested to failure at various times after joining. The results obtained frequently depend heavily upon whether the samples were simply stored under ambient conditions or whether they were cyclically stressed before testing. Since most adhesively bonded products will experience stresses in service, it is often misleading to base any decision concerning them on test results obtained from unstressed samples.

X. NONDESTRUCTIVE TESTING

Nondestructive testing refers to a number of tests for bond strength or durability which are performed on assemblies without destroying the bond. Nondestructive tests are often carried out by subjecting the bond to ultrasonic vibration or other physical stimuli and measuring the physical response of the system. Techniques range in complexity from a hammer-tap sound test to electronic frequency analysis.

XI. EXPANSION COEFFICIENTS

The expansion coefficient of a material is a number which indicates how the material changes dimensionally with changes in temperature. An expansion coefficient of 6 x 10-5 cm/cm/^{0}c means that a 1-cm segment will increase 6 x 10-5 cm in length for each degree Celsius of increased temperature. Similarly the part will shrink by the same amount for each degree of temperature decrease. This concept is important in adhesive bonding because adhesives are frequently used to join materials with dissimilar expansion behaviors. Furthermore, the adhesive itself undergoes expansion and contractions as the temperature rises and fails. When te mismatch of expansion behavior is too great, severe stresses result at the bondline, and a separation or fracture of the adhesive may occur. increasing the flexibility of the adhesive is a common technique for resisting expansion contraction failure. In general, flexible adhesives are better able to resist such stresses because they can shrink and stretch with the moving adherends. On the other hand, flexible formulations often have a greater tendency to creep. The expansion behavior of adhesives can often be modified by the addition of fillers or additives.

XII. CREEP

The tendency of any material to undergo a permanent change in dimension when subjected to mechanical stress is known as creep. Creep is particularly a problem with thermoplastic polymers. The tendency of a material to creep results primarily from the flexibility of its molecular segments. Creep may often be retarded or reduced to an acceptable level with fillers or small amounts of crosslinking.

XIII. THERMOPLASTIC

Polymers which soften when heated are called thermoplastic. With very few exceptions, they are also soluble in at least a few solvents. Thermoplastic materials usually have a tendency to creep under load, and they are generally not used for critical structural application.

XIV. THERMOSETTING

Plastics which do not deform readily under load and which resist solution in nearly all solvents are called thermosetting. The molecular chain segments of thermosetting materials are chemically bound to one another (crosslinked) in such a fashion that it is difficult for segments to move independently. In effect, the chain segments lock each other in place, and permanent deformation is difficult or impossible at ordinary temperatures. Solvents are also unable to dissolve thermosetting resins.

XV. SURFACE CONVERSION

Surface conversion refers to any process in which the surface to be bonded is changed from its condition as manufactured or assembled to one which is more suitable for bonding. More than simple cleaning is implied by surface conversion. Typically, a ferrous surface might be converted to zinc phosphate, or an aluminum surface to aluminium oxide. Phosphatizing, anodizing, chromating, and polymer oxidation are typical of conversion processes widely used industrially. The advantage of surface conversion is simply that the surface is changed from a more or less unknown condition to one of fairly well understood composition and behavior. Thus, some assurance is gained that the adhesive is always being applied to a uniform surface.

XVI. SCANNING ELECTRON MICROSCOPY

This is a surface observation technique using the a microscope which depends upon electron beams rather than light rays for magnification. It gives extremely high magnifications with excellent depth of field. Magnification up to 100,000 or more are achieved with relative ease. The equipment is expensive and somewhat sophisticated, but its acquisition

XVII. POT LIFE

The period of time after mixing a two -or-three component adhesive during which the mixture is still workable is the pot life. Once the pot life has been exceeded, the viscosity of the formulation becomes so great that spreading and wetting is difficult.

XVIII. VISCOSITY

Viscosity is the ability of a liquid to resist flow. In practical terms, solutions of high viscosity are difficult to stir, pump, and spray, Low-viscosity formulations, on the other hand, may be excessively runny and difficult to apply uniformly to vertical surfaces. This problem is often solved through the addition of thixotropic materials.

XIX. THIXOTROPY

A temporary decrease in viscosity upon stirring is called thixotropy. In more technical terms, it is accurate to say that the viscosity of thixotropic materials is shear-rate dependent. Thixotropic additives are often used to give an adhesive enough body to resist sagging on vertical surfaces and yet become runny enough to flow easily under the stress of brushing, rolling, or spraying during application.

XX. GLASS TRANSITION TEMPERATURE

The glass transition temperature Tg is the temperature above which an adhesive (or other polymeric material) becomes somewhat rubbery. At temperatures above the Tg, polymers point, they are often brittle. Adhesive formulators generally select resins having transition temperatures which are a compromise between flexible-rubbery and brittle-glassy structures. Adhesives design and for used on flexible materials almost always have transition temperatures below the anticipated use temperature to insure that the bondline will remain flexible in service.

XXI. SHELF LIFE

Shelf life is the period of time for which an adhesive may be stored without deteriorating to the point that performance will be unsatisfactory. Shelf life for reactive adhesives can usually be extended by refrigeration.

XXII. CURING

Curing is the process during which an adhesive changes from a liquid to a solid. Classically, curing means the formation of a crosslinked polymer film. More loosely, the term is sometimes used to describe any method of forming a solid adhesive film, including solvent loss and linear polymerization.

XXIII. SAG RESISTANCE

Sag resistance refers to the ability of the adhesive to stay in place on a vertical surface without running or "sagging" on the surface. Fillers are sometimes added to adhesives to give them more body and improve their sag resistance.

XXIV. RESIN

The major polymer or polymer-forming material used in an adhesive is the resin. Some resins are natural products such as starch or rubber. Other resins, such as epoxies and urethanes, are produced by chemical synthesis.

XXV. POLYMER

The plastic-like material which forms the bulk of most adhesive films is a polymer. Polymers are made by the repetitive joining of many small chemical units (molecules). The resulting high molecular weight material is known as a polymer. Most of the bulk properties of an adhesive material, such as heat resistance and tensile strength, are primarily due to the nature of the polymer used in the adhesive.

XXVI. MOLD RELEASE AGENT

Mold release agents are materials used to reduce the adhesion of a polymer to the mold in which parts are formed. Release agents are the opposite of adhesives. Their task is to reduce or prevent adhesion. Release agents may either be applied to a mold surface before it is filled (external release agents) or mixed into the molding material before it is used (internal release agents). In either case, it is essential that mold release agents be removed from surfaces before bonding is attempted.

XXVII. OUTGASSING

Outgassing is the formation of gas bubbles in an adhesive film while it is curing. This generally undesirable situation may arise because gaseous products are formed while the adhesive cures or because curing conditions, such as temperature, may cause bubbles of dissolved air to be released. In general, severe outgassing should be avoided.

XXVIII. CURING AGENT

Curing agents are chemicals which react with an adhesive to form a solid adhesive film. Curing agents are generally used in much larger amounts than catalysts. They may be considered coreactants with the adhesive resin since they are consumed during the curing reaction.

XXIX. HARDENER

Hardener is a term which is more or less synonymous with catalyst. Hardeners are mixed with adhesive resins in very small quantities to initiate the curing reaction.

XXX. FILLER

A material which is added to an adhesive formulation to influence its properties in some specific fashion is called a filler. Fillers are generally particulate materials, such as finely ground glass, metal, clay, or other inorganic chemicals. They are used to control such properties as impact resistance, heat stability, conductivity, sag resistance, etc.

XXXI. ADHESIVE FAILURE

Adhesive failure is the failure of a bond at the interface between the adhesive and the adherend.

XXXII. COHESIVE FAILURE

The failure of a bond within either the adhesive or the adherend, rather than at the interface between them, is known as cohesive failure.

2

SELECTING AN ADHESIVE: WHY AND HOW

1. INTRODUCTION

The selection of a specific adhesive for a specific application can be likened to the process of selecting a marriage partner. Successful completion of questionnaires, suitability tests, interviews, trial evaluations, and tentative commitments theoretically lead to a final and lasting union. In matching an adhesive to prospective substrates, influenced by design and performance requirements, the same procedures of consideration in mating apparent compatibilities and evaluating prototyes or working models is, of course, the correct engineering method to be employed. Unfortunately, as in some marriages, unforeseen stresses and unanticipated circumstances can nullify the best of our intentions and expectations.

One of the major problems in selecting an adhesive for any given application is the presence of so many attractive candidates. The number of adhesive variations available to the engineer today is fantastic. Adhesives offer such a broad range of mechanical and handling properties that it seems that there must be at least one which will be best suited for any potential bonding application. On the other hand, beneath the seemingly marvelous attributes of each adhesive type, there are inherent, if subtle, dehabilitating characteristics of which we must be aware.

Each category of adhesive has its individual appeal and appears to possess some unique property-such as highest mechanical performance,greatest ease of use, lowest unit cost, greatest longevity, etc. While any one of these claims may be valid for a tightly defined, totally controlled laboratory condition, in the real world of adhesive bonding, it is not unusual for the inadequacies of an adhesive to reduce its promise to the point of non usefulness. These inadequacies may not necessarily be technical in nature. For example, the solution or solvent-type adhesive which you have selected, after through and diligent examination, as the best and most economical for your application may have to be rejected because of new local legislation barring volatile solvent-containing materials. Similarly, the cost of hoods, vents, collecting towers, etc., necessary to comply with the law may suddenly price the selected adhesive out of consideration.

One prime fact must be borne in mind when submitting oneself to the rigor of selecting "the" adhesive for "the job": Maintaining rigid criteria of nonnegotiable design and mechanical performance greatly restricts the choice of adhesive and often imposes severe processing and/or cost penalties.

The engineer will recognize that logical compromises between design, performance, handling characteristics, cost, etc., are absolutely necessary to achieve profitable adhesive success.

II. ADHESIVES VERSUS OTHER FASTENING SYSTEMS

The first step in the adhesive selection process, which is often overlooked, should be the fundamental affirmation of the suitability of adhesive bonding, as opposed to other fastening methods, for your particular application. Threaded mechanical fastening, riveting, stapling, welding, brazing, and soldering are just a few alternative joining methods. These techniques are normally associated with metallic components and structures. Heat staking, ultrasonic welding, and solvent bonding are joining methods used for plastic materials, but they cannot really be considered as adhesive systems since the classic definition of adhesive bonding is one in which two substrates are attached by a distinctly separate material entity.

Also, there are combinations of fastening systems, such as weldbonding, in which a continuous bead of adhesive is periodically reinforced or secured in the "Fixturing" sense by a spot weld. The instantly stable spot weld holds the parts together while the adhesive cures. The resulting structure benefits from the brute strength of the weld and the fatigue-failure resistance of the adhesive. Another well established combination is anaerobic adhesives and screws or bolts to reduce vibrational loosening.

All fastening and joining systems, including adhesives, fall into one of three general categories which describe the primary and typical ways in which they are most successfully used.

Periodic. The attachment of two members by occasional placement of through fasteners or site unions typified by rivets, screws, nuts, bolts, spot welds, etc. This is the most widely used joining technique for structures which require high mechanical strength and a minimum of sealing or other nonstrength performance properties.

Linear. A continuous or occasional edge bead attachment which is best represented by welding.

Area. An attachment achieved by full-face contact and union between the two mating surfaces. Soldering, brazing, and adhesive bonding are examples.

Although adhesive bonding can be successfully employed in periodic or linear attachment applications, the main benefits and advantages of using adhesives are realized when they are used in "area" attachment designs.

Each manufacturer must determine the type of trade study needed when selecting a joining method and materials for a given assembly. Every new product, combination of materials to be joined, rate of production, etc. will cause priorities to differ. A typical example of a trade-off analysis comparing riveting (periodic type attachment), welding (linear attachment), brazing, and adhesive bonding (both area attachments) is shown in Table 1. Joining-method features are weighed against manufacturing and performance considerations. Obvious points, such as the impracticality of brazing ceramics or of using organic adhesives for prolonged exposure of at very high temperatures, would alter the study or preclude the consideration of certain materials and techniques. A numerical rating given to the elements of such an evaluation would indicate whether or not adhesive bonding could be used.

III. ADVANTAGES OF ADHESIVE BONDING

Many benefits accrue from the use of adhesive bonding. Some advantages, such as being able to attach components not otherwise joinable, are obvious, and their value is directly measurable. Other factors, such as eliminating corrosion between dissimilar materials, may or may not be of prime consideration in selecting a joining technique, but they definitely add a dimension to the worth of the assembly. A review of some of the more apparent beneficial aspects of adhesive use is provided below.

A. Fabrication of Smooth Exterior Surfaces

The fact that an adhesive is contained between joined surfaces eliminates the need for surface finishing, such as that required to grind down rivet heads, etc. Smooth exterior surfaces imply less drag and more efficient gaseous and fluid flow patterns over or around aerodynamic faces. This principle would apply to land, water, are of aerospace vehicles. External aesthetics are achieved which are of considerable sales importance to many product lines, such as appliances, furniture, musical instruments, etc. The absence of protruding bolt or rivet heads also signifies that there are no concentrated stress sites in the attachment area. Forces are dispersed over the entire assembly face.

Table 1. How Joining Methods Compare[a]

	Riveting	Welding	Brazing	Adhesive bonding
Preliminary machining	P	E	P	E
With thin metals	P	P	F	E
Limits on metal combinations	F	P	P	E
Surface preparation	E	G	F	P
Tooling	E	F	F	F
Need for access to joint	P	P	E	E
Heat requirements	E	P	P	F-G
Stress distribution	P	F-G	E	E
Sealing function	P	F	E	G
Rate of strength development	E	E	E	P
Distortion of assembly	F	P	F	E
Final machining	G-E	F	E	E
Final heat treatment	E	F	F	E
Solvent resistance	E	E	E	F
Effect of temperature	E	E	E	P
Ease of repair	G	P	P	F
Level of skill required	E	G	E	E

[a]E, excellent; G, good; F, fair; P, poor,

B. Protection Against Shock and Vibrational Failure

The elastomeric nature of most adhesives results in an energy-absorbing response to impact and fatigue forces. The ability of adhesively bonded structure to withstand significantly higher sonic-fatigue levels than mechanically fastened counterpart hardware in both subsonic and supersonic aircraft applications is a dramatic illustration of this property. Similarly, the transmission of sound itself is drastically reduced by passing through an adhesive interlayer. Since most polymeric adhesive systems are poor thermal conductors, they act to soak up stresses induced by thermal cycling, particularly in metallic structures. As mentioned earlier, the use of anaerobic adhesives as an interference fit material between threaded fasteners and the structures into which they are inserted or into which they are attached reduces or prevents vibrational loosening. The automotive and farm implement industries use adhesives to great advantage in this type of application.

C. Use of Light Gauge Materials

Stresses applied to a bonded structure are spread over a relatively large area (total facial contact area between mating substrates) compared to stresses directed to and through local sites, such as the bolts of a linear assembly. Thus, the total imposed force can be accepted by components having lower bulk strength per unit area because their cumulative load bearing-capability is probably greater than that possessed by a faw through fasteners. Coincidentally, facing materials have to be overdesigned in strength (made thicker and heavier) to compensate for the reduction in strength caused by the need to drill holes to allow for the passage of through fasteners.

The structurally efficient justification for using lightweight (thinner) surface materials in an adhesively bonded assembly is furthered by the possibility of broadening the function of the facing. A thin facing member may integrally incorporate a decorative exterior. Likewise, additional foil-thin top layers of specific-purpose material may be adhesively incorporated into a composite, achieving certain required properties, such as surface reflectivity, conductivity, insulation, corrosion resistance, abrasion resistance, etc.

D. Joining of Dissimilar Materials

Galvanic corrosion, which occurs when metals of differing electromotive force potential are in intimate contact with each other, is eliminated by an adhesive interlayer. Inherent properties of unmodified organic adhesives include good electrical insulation and poor thermal conductivity. Stresses caused by rapid thermal input or cycling are reduced by slow heat transfer through the adhesive. Dimensional distortion of the assembly, caused by different coefficients of thermal expansion, is reduced by the heat-sink action of the adhesive. This ability, of course, is limited by the adhesive strength achieved with the particular adhesive/substrate combination and by the cohesive strength of the adhesive. It follows, then, that if extreme thermal cycling is anticipated in a bonded assembly involving substrates of widely differing expansion rates, an elastomeric adhesive will be preferred. The trade-off is between a "giving: adhesive with limited strength retention as temperatures rise, and a thermally stable system depending on cohesive strength alone to resist the stresses as the temperature rises.

Since bonded assemblies derive their prime strength from the chemical interlocking of the adhesive with a substrate, the relative modulus (stiffness) and chemical nature (metal, plastic, glass, ceramic, etc.) of the attached surfaces do not have to be as closely matched as those of most mechanically attached components.

E. Simplified Joining of Contoured or Delicate Parts

Flat assemblies normally do not present mating problems even for mechanical fastening. Curvedor multicontoured surfaces present an entirely different situation. Surface loading of bonded assemblies transfers stress through a continuous, gap-filling, substrate membrane, which is connected to next-in-line components or faces. This fact allows the relaxation of fit tolerances. The reduced fit, or mating-gap tolerance requirement can often result in lower component-preparation costs and can simplify jig or fixturing setups.

Small sensing devices, such as strain gauges, are easily adhesively bonded to areas being monitored. Under these conditions no induced surface stresses or flow path-disruptions, such as might happen if the devices were mechanically attached, occur. The elasticity, or modulus, of the adhesive can be tailored to fit the particular test requirements.

F. Reduced Cost of Manufacture and Assembly

Frequently, a mechanically fastened assembly requires secondary operations, such as sealing or fillings gaps between fastener sites. Typical examples are storage bins, silos, water tanks, etc. Primary mechanical strength or holding-power considerations do not totally fill the functional requirements of the assembly. Adhesive bonding of such assemblies satisfies the requirements for both mechanical strength and end use. Similarly, the use of adhesives may eliminate the need for the auxiliary attachment of thermal or acoustic insulation. Savings of fabrication time and material cost by using adhesives in a dual role are readily apparent. As mentioned earlier in this section, eliminating the need to machine or countersink protruding rivet heads or weld seams, etc. saves finishing time and costs.

IV. INTERDEPENDENCY OF USER AND SUPPLIER

For purposes of this text, the assumption is made that the user procures adhesives from other manufacturers. The technical expertise, equipment, quality-control techniques, etc., required for the manufacture of adhesives of consistent quality are extremely specialized. The critical factor in establishing a good support and working relationship with an adhesives manufacturer is open, concise, and frequent communications. By and large, adhesives are not purchased as commodity items. Although you may procure adhesives to meet a company or federal specification, there are sufficient subtle differences in handling or other nonstrength properties that distinguish adhesives from sheet metal or bar stock, for example. The very fact that adhesives change-that is, flow, shrink, harden, etc. during processing, identifies them as specialty materials. As such, adhesive response characteristics and behavior during application and cure are as important as their final cured-state properties. The following paragraphs describe areas in which clear communication with the adhesive supplier is particularly important.

A. Acceptance Criteria for Adhesive Performance

Beyond the apparent strength requirement of an adhesive, there are many factors which must be defined. Processibility, durability, appearance, and environmental response are examples. The user must know as exactly as possible what behavior is desired from the adhesive and must share these expectations with the supplier. Some of the more important points which affect joint performance are discussed below.

B. What is the End Product?

The dialogue between user and supplier best starts with a statement of what the end product is and what its functional requirements are. Manufacturers often cloak their product-design projects in undue secrecy, which handcuffs the prospective adhesive supplier. Absolutely mandatory proprietary considerations aside, the start of the adhesive selection process should be as complete a description of the end product as is possible. Given this introduction, the adhesive supplier can review his experience with similar applications and more quickly make well-directed recommendations. Needless to say, an aura of confidentiality regarding the specific applications must be maintained. The point is that the better the definition of both end product and expected part function, the more accurate the initial material-identification will be.

C. Correctness of Design

In an ideal situation, the part designer is aware of the performance capability of adhesives in general. Adhesive technology allows the designer to consider options regarding the use of adhesives. The optimum adhesive joint is designed to handle loads in a mode which is consistent with the major strength feature of any given adhesive. Practicalities-such as geometry of mating members, cost of machining components, placement of attachments on the inside or outside, etc. may influence the designer to use an adhesive in an unfairly demanding fashion. For example, an epoxy adhesive may be specified because of known high lap shear strength. In practice, however, attached members may be of such thinness or low modulus that the applied stresses cause deformation which translates the load into a peel format which, in turn, causes premature bond failure due to the inherently low peel strength of most epoxies. The Knowledgeable designer can offer design options, such as beveled edges on skins, recess cut-fitting of mating members, use of load transfer stringers, etc. to compensate for such situations.

D. Strength Requirements

Requirement, rather than desire, is the law for the strength definition of an adhesive. Anything above the basic-design adhesive strength requirement will usually cost something in price, ease of application, or processing. One must certainly allow for surge loads, etc. but reasonable and accurate prediction of needed strength levels is necessary to allow the supplier to suggest possible materials. If a design calls for 800 psi (5600 kPa) of tensile shear strength, it would be irresponsible to insist upon 2500 psi (175,000 kPs) of adhesive performance. This action might preclude the use of a rapidly setting onecomponent cyanoacrylate and force the use of a higher strength epoxy involving two components, mixing and dispensing equipment, over night cure times, etc. After exercising accurate engineering judgment, a design staff should not arbitrarily impose a safety factor of 100-200% on adhesive strength without understanding the implications.

E. Environmental Survival Requirements

The adhesive user should be able to predict the environmental-exposure requirements of an assembly and relay that information to the supplier. Short-term exposure in a room at constant temperature and 25% relative humidity is a totally different situation from exposure to cycling temperature, fluctuating relative humidity, and ultraviolet (uv) radiation. The same mechanical strength may be required in both cases, and a designer may unwittingly select the same adhesive for both applications based only on that criterion (with one surviving and one failing). Disclosure of the entire expected environment-exposure profile of the bonded structure will permit the supplier to make certain that the adhesive formulation will provide the performance needed. For example, a uv absorber, or pigment, added to an adhesive could extend its exterior-service life 100% or more.

Service Conditions

One of the significant factors contributing to unanticipated early adhesive failure is the rate of load application. Various test procedures specify differing rates and increments of imposed loading. Different test procedures can result in conflicting and misunderstood strength data. Shock loading versus gradual loading, percent of ultimate load, frequency of load application, etc. are among the dynamic variables encountered. Other conditions besides strength which affect adhesive selection are the need for electrical conductivity, radiation resistance, vapor impermeability, etc. These and other service-performance conditions will certainly influence the user/ supplier team in making the best adhesive selection.

C. Reliability

The reliability required of an adhesive bond is a somewhat nebulous property. Of course, a bonded assembly is expected to maintain structural integrity-but for how may use cycles, for how many exposures to intermittent proof loading? Is failure expected to be gradual or catastrophic? Permanence and reliability are not to be interchanged or equated. In adhesive terms, as with any organic or nonmetallic substance, there is no status quo for eternity. The measure of adhesive reliability can best be looked upon as a description of percent strength retention after defined loading, time, and/or conditional exposures.

H. Materials Being Bonded

Metals, plastics, rubber, glass, wood, ceramic, concrete, etc. can all be bonded to themselves or to each other. Material type, condition, porosity, finish, acidity, alkalinity, etc. influence adhesive selection. Certain adhesives have inherent affinities for certain surfaces and conditions. For example, even though epoxies may have higher lap shear strengths in metal-bonding applications, a lower strength structural acrylic might be used because it might be more reliably bonded to the oily surface condition of the metal. In order to use the epoxy to its higher strength advantage, the surfaces must have a higher level of cleanliness which requires more processing cost than the higher strength warrants.

Depending on the particular metal, a metallic surface may be relatively pure or have a top molecular layer of porous or plate-like oxides. Similarly the same plastic can have surfaces which differ in potential reactivity or bondability, depending on whether the item was machined, extruded, molded, etc. The type of surface material, the processing history, and the condition at the time of bonding are important pieces of information in the overall adhesive selection mosaic.

I. Processing Limitations

As discussed earlier, adhesives are normally obtained as an intermediate product-one which must be further processed before attaining its stable use condition. Processing requires equipment, and controls must be available to satisfactorily use the adhesive. Different adhesives require different equipment, which might range from conventional spray guns to sophisticated metering, mixing, and dispensing apparatus or from simple scales and ovens to high-temperature and high-pressure autoclaves. Production rates and the total quantity of bonded assemblies to be produced will influence the choice of adhesives, particularly regarding handling characteristics. The designer must be aware of the impact of adhesive choice on production-facility equipment and processing capability.

J. Cost Considerations

Dollars per pound is the poorest way to compare the cost of adhesives. True material cost is best measured as dollars per application area, at a given thickness. Assuming a constant bondline thickness, the calculations below show that an adhesive with a specific gravity of 1.1 (9.17 lb./gal) costing \$2.00/lb. is less expensive per application than an adhesive with a specific gravity of 1.8 (14.83 lb./gal) costing \$ 1.50/lb.

Adhesive 1 (0.01-in. bondline)

$$\frac{\$2.00}{\text{lb.}} \times \frac{9.17\ \text{lb.}}{\text{gal}} \times \frac{1\ \text{gal}}{23} \times \frac{1\ \text{in.3 of adhesive}}{1\ \text{in. 3 of adhesive}\ \ 100\ \text{in.2 bond area/}\ 0.01\text{-in. thickness}}$$

$$= \frac{\$0.00079/\text{in.2}}{0.01\text{-in. thickness}}$$

Adhesive 2 (0.01-in. bondline)

$$\frac{\$1.50}{\text{lb. gal}} \times \frac{14.83\ \text{lb.}}{231\ \text{in.3 of adhesive}} \times \frac{1\ \text{gal}}{} \times \frac{1\ \text{in.3 of adhesive}}{100\ \text{in.2 bond area/}\ 0.01\text{-in. thickness}}$$

$$= \frac{\$0.00096/\text{in.2}}{0.01\text{-in. thickness}}$$

The actual material cost is usually the least important factor in selecting an adhesive. Among the costs to be included in the expense of using any given adhesive are the labor of measuring, mixing, applying; equipment amortization; quality-assurance procedures; original development and testing; specification control; etc. The fact that some adhesives require minimum handling no weighing, no mixing, no application equipment justifies their higher dollars-per-pound or dollars per job cost, assuming performance is satisfactory.

K. Review Prior to Production

The production arm of the user organization plays a vital role in the selection and application of adhesive. The selection of an adhesive should be coordinated with the production department. This preuse liaison will ensure that the proper equipment is available for both manufacturing and surface preparation, if required. Many factors, such as working life of the adhesive once ready for application versus how much time is required to apply the adhesive and mate the parts, must be reconciled. Work life (pot life) and its relationship to cure times varies according to according to adhesive type. Anaerobic and cyanoacrylate adhesive are one-component systems which can be left on one surface for an almost indefinite time. They cure almost instantly when contained between the two surfaces to be bonded. Solvent- or solution type adhesives begin to cure or harden if left exposed on one surface. Epoxide and polyurethanes have a short pot life compared to cure time in thin-film bonding applications. Some adhesives may have high "grab" and require little or no tooling, whereas slow-curing adhesives may require fixturing during the hardening process. Provision must be made for part storage commensurate with the cleanliness requirements of the adhesive to be used and for proper surface treatment of the parts to be bonded.

Dimension tolerances required for mating parts may very considerably, depending on the adhesive used. For example, some cyanoacrylate may not bond property if the gap between surfaces exceeds 0.001 in. (0.0025 cm), whereas a gap-filling epoxy may be used over almost any distance.

V. DESCRIPTION OF PRIMARY ADHESIVE TYPES

There are two basic categories of polymeric resin materials used in the manufacture of industrial structural adhesives. One group of material is thermoplastic in nature. These materials are capable of being repeatedly softened by heat. They harden upon cooling. Examples of thermoplastic adhesives are not melts, dispersions (synthetic rubber, latex), solutions (acetates, acrylics), and cyanoacrylate.

The second group of materials are thermosetting in nature.

These materials undergo a chemical reaction through the action of a catalyst or other stimulus, becoming, once they have cured, a relatively infusible substance. Phenolics, epoxies, polyurethanes, structural acrylics, silicones, and anaerobics are examples of thermosetting adhesives.

A brief synopsis of major attributes (both positive and negative) of primary adhesive types is presented below to provide a gross overview.

Hot-melt adhesives

Thermoplastic resins-100% solids
Fast application (hot)-fast set (cool)
Rigid to flexible bonds
Bonds permeable or impermeable surfaces
Nonpolar-poor adhesion-poor wetting
Low cost-materials and labor
Requires special dispensing equipment
Moisture insensitive-attacked by solvents
Low heat resistance-degrade
Poor creep resistance-deformation at 5 psi at 125° F (35 kPa at 50° C)

Dispersion or solution adhesives

Thermoplastic resins-20 to 80% solids
Very easy to apply-long shelf life
Set by evaporation-slow or fast
Low material cost
Excellent wetting and penetration
No special equipment required
Moderate clamp pressure needed
Low strength under load-creep
Require permeable surfaces
Heat, solvent, and moisture sensitive

Cyanoacrylate adhesives

Thermoplastic-100% solids-liquid
Easy to apply, cure
Fast cure-from 30 sec to 5 min
Low viscosity-needs well-mated surfaces
Good tensile strength-poor impact
Only simple equipment needed
Will not normally bond permeable materials
High material cost-poor shelf life
Poor solvent and water resistance
Handling hazards-bonds to skin

Phenolics or urea adhesives

Thermoset resins-100% solids or solution
Gas during cure-solvent evaporation
High tensile strength-low impact
Highly polar-excellent adhesion
Long shelf life-easy application
Require high-pressure, oven cure
Low material cost
Excellent wetting and penetration
High shrinkage stresses-brittle

Polyurethane adhesives

Thermoset-100% solids liquid
Flexible sealant/adhesive low creep
Bond permeable or impermeable surfaces
One or two components-room-temperature or over cure
Good flexibility at low temperature
Moisture sensitive components
May undergo reversion with heat or moisture
Moderate material cost
Some toxic formulations
Special equipment to mix, de-air, dispense

Anaerobic adhesives

Thermoset-100% solids-liquid
One component-moderate cost
Easy application-simple cure
Machinery and structural grades
Good cohesive, low adhesive strength
Excellent for bolts, nuts, and static Joints
Require primer for many materials
Not suitable for permeable surfaces
Will not cure where air contacts
Crazes some plastics

Silicone-adhesives

Thermoset-100% solids-liquid
Rubberlike-high impact and peel
Retain properties from-100 to +400° F (from - 70 to + 200° C)
Excellent sealant-low stress

One component-short shelf life
Easy application-1-to 5-day cure
Resist most chemicals and solvents
Simple equipment needed
Some by-products-reversion possible
High material cost

Epoxy adhesives

Thermoset-100% solids-liquid
Variable pot life and cure time
Long shelf life-one or two components
Rigid or flexible bonds-highly polar
Least creep under load-least shrinkage
Resist most chemicals and solvents
Widest variety of formulations available
Some formulations dermatitic
Require careful controls-clean surfaces
Need equipment to weight, mix, dispense, and clamp

Structural acrylic adhesives

Thermoset-100% solids-liquid
Two components-no mixing required
Critical applications-limited to 25-ml gap
Short work life after application
Fast set time
Tough flexible bonds
Minimum surface preparation
Excellent solvent and chemical resistance
Odorous-ventilation required

VI. ADHESIVE SELECTION PHILOSOPHY

There are no absolutely perfect solutions to any adhesive problem. Fortunately, with the variety of industrial adhesives available today, at least one "best compromise" adhesive can usually be identified for most every legitimate application. A flexible and willing-to-compromise attitude is necessary to avoid precluding the use of a system which if farily evaluated can solve your problem an attitude which insists on the use of a specific adhesive regardless of the impact on design or performance or cost is foolhardy. It is understandable that an engineer or design staff may prefer the use of certain adhesives due to past favorable personal or inherited experience. This cannot be totally faulted since familiarity with any technological subject fosters the ability to work closer to performance limits. The optimum strategy is to approach the adhesive selection process by establishing a complete grid of acceptance the adhesive selection process by establishing a complete grid of acceptance criteria. This grid, or screening analysis, will rate the various elements which totally add up a successful adhesive application. The main divisions, or items, of this screening grid would include, but not necessarily be limited to, the following.

Item	Comment
Mechanical strength	The foremost consideration, Must meet real minimum level. Higher performance superfluous unless available at no higher overall cost.
Detail dimension tolerance	What is the cost impact on tolerances of +0.005 in. (0.012 cm) for details needed with adhesive A versus +0.005 in. (0.012 cm) for adhesive B?
Alternate materials to be bonded	Will switching from an acetal to a glass-filled nylon allow a more reliable bond?
Quality assurance	Procurement and process control specifications on one-component versus two-component adhesives. Surface preparation and cleanliness level requirements.
Production quantity	Number of assemblies per unit time versus working time. Storage limitations, warm rooms to accelerate cures, bonding-fixture recycle time, etc.
Personnel training	Workman competency-level requirements vary with the type and form of adhesive. The placement of a stable film adhesive versus the often critical weighing, mixing, and dispensing of a two-or three-component paste adhesive.
Safety	Handling of solvent systems. Some adhesives more dermatitic than others, etc.
Overall costs	Material cost plus the sum of at least all of the preceding items.

The adhesive candidate which gets the highest rating in the above screening analysis and meets all other objectives of handling, etc., becomes the "best compromise" system. This selection is normally of a generic nature. The final adhesive characterization now be comes an optimization within the adhesive-type category itself. Communication between user and supplier cannot be overemphasized at this point. Minor formula variations-such as increasing viscosity by use of a thixotropic agent, color coding by pigment addition, etc.-can be accomplished. In the case of two-component systems, certain ingredients may be switched from the resin side to the harderer side or vice versa to change to a more favorable mixing-ratio. Custom packaging in premeasured kits or disposable cartridges is possible. A given adhesive may be supplied as a two-component package, in premixed fashion as a paste, preimpregnated in a carrier reinforcement, or as as unsupported film. In the case of room-temperature curing or limited life systems, these materials would be stored under refrigeration.

VII. ADHESIVE SELECTION EXAMPLES

The following examples of the adhesive selection process are based on actual industrial applications. These illustrations have been abbreviated to point out the primary factors involved in the adhesive choice.

Example I

Initial description of requirements

Bonding molded plastic to elastomeric material
Assembly will use high temperature [200° F (90° C)]
and humidity- (100% rh).
Severe service conditions

Solution

Not possible with limited information presented.

Further information.

End product is shower spray head
Acetual ring to be bonded to neoprene diaphragm.
1/2-in. square (3.12 cm2) bond area.
5-year service life.

Final recommendation

Many adhesives will meet the strength requirement. Solution or solvent adhesives ruled out because of non-porous substrates. Silicone considered too slow-curing for production rate requirements. Urethane requires unavailable application equipment. Epoxies do not bond well to acetal without surface treatment. Design does not suit anaerobics. Cyanoacrylate would not survive long-term humidity exposure. "Best compromise" candidate is structural acrylic adhesive.

Example 2

Initial description of requirements (same as Example 1)
Bonding molded plastic to elastomeric material
Assembly will see high temperature [200° F (90° C)] and humidity (100% rh).
Severe service conditions.

Solution

Not possible with limited information presented.

Further information

End product is disposable dish scrubber
Polystyrene to be bonded to cellulosic spongs.
Give-away item.

Final recommendation

Most adhesives too expensive relative to total product worth or too time consuming in application or curing requirements. Cyanoacrylate, which would otherwise be suitable crazes the plastic surface causing an appearance problem. Liquid pressure-sensitive adhesives can be used since one surface is porous.

Example 3

Initial description of requirements

Bond aluminum attachment clip to steel curtain panel
Long-term exterior weatherability needed.
Must have field repair capability.

Solution

Strength, weatherability, and cost factors reduce consideration to polyurethane or epoxy. Polyurethane not convenient for field installation. Epoxy has marginal peel-failure resistance. Further analysis required.

Further information

Redesign of attachment clip increased bonding area by 100% and transferred loading to tension, rather than peel, stresses.

Final recommendation

Redesign allows confident use of epoxy for production plus premeasured kit for field installation and repair.

3
HOT-MELT ADHESIVES

1. INTRODUCTION AND DEFINITION OF HOT-MELT ADHESIVES

We can define hot-melt adhesives as thermoplastic materials, solid at room temperature. When heated above their melting point, they become fluid and are able to wet the surfaces to which they are applied. Generally, a quantity of fluid hot melt is applied to one or both of the surfaces to be joined, and the surfaces are brought together. When the adhesive has cooled below its solidification point. The subsirales are bonded. In simple terms adhesive bonding involves the application of a fluid adhesive which can wet the surfaces to be bonded and the subsequent conversion of the adhesive to a solid. As opposed to other types of adhesives, which becomes solid by eliminations of solvents and/or water or through polymerization, hot melts convert from a hot fluid to a solid by cooling.

Such a simplistic definition also applies to asphalt, wax, metallic solder, and even water (ice). However, we will limit this discussion to hot-melt adhesives that contain at least one polymer as a major ingredient. These hot melts may contain the backbone polymer either "neat" (uncompounded) or admixed with waxes, tackifiers, plasticizers, fillers, and/or other modifiers.

The viscosity of a hot melt when measured at various temperatures, that is, as it cools from a liquid to a solid, describes a curve which rises very steeply as the solidification temperature is approached. This curve is characteristic of hot-melt adhesives, but actual values will differ with different systems.

If one plans to use a hot-melt adhesive it is desirable to choose the optimum type. The optimum may not necessarily be the one that is lowest in cost, nor the one that is casiest to apply, nor even the one that is strongest. Often, the best adhesive is a compromise, which has to be judged on a case-by-case basis, with a weighted value given to cost, performance, and production ease.

2. ADVANTAGES AND LIMITATIONS OF HOT-MELT ADHESIVES

An understanding of the viscosity curve (Fig.1) explains many of the properties of hot-melt adhesives, such as fast bonding, low "wicking in", ability to control glueline thickness, and void filling. Rapid setting is simply a matter of losing enough heat to achieve a high viscosity or to solidify. This time can be as short as a small fraction of a second, or it can be delayed by design for several minutes.

A. Advantages

Some reasons hot melts are used:

1. Form bonds rapidly-resulting in high-speed assembly and short clamp time
2. Invisible bonds-no exposed fastener parts
3. Fill "gaps" between surfaces to be joined
4. Bond most materials
5. Clean, easy handling
6. Load distribution through "area bonding"
7. Cost less per unit assembly than many mechanical fasteners
8. Easy recovery and repair of substandard assemblies
9. No problems with solvent or fume flammability
10. Simpler materials inventory and storage
11. Precise bond control through variations of the temperature and the quantity of adhesive.
12. Equipment available for hand or automated assembly
13. Easily maintained equipment
14. Minimal production-line space requirements

B. Limitations

There are several characteristics of hot-melt adhesives, due to their thermoplastic nature, which may limit their use in certain bonding applications. Some of these limitations are

1. Bonds lose strength at elevated temperatures.
2. Some bonds may creep and fail with time.
3. Adhesive may be sensitive to some chemicals and solvents.
4. Some substrates or components may be sensitive to the hot-melt application temperature.
5. Sophisticated application equipment may be required for highly viscous, high-performance hot metals.
6. Some hot melts have a tendency to degrade at application temperature unless protected from the air.

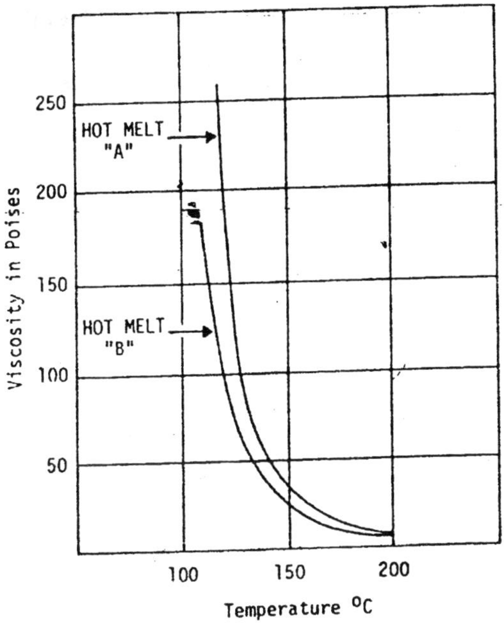

7. Some hot melts become brittle at low temperatures.

TYPES OF HOT MELTS BASED ON THE BACKBONE POLYMER

One way to typify hot-melt adhesives is to distinguish by the backbone polymer. In some instances the polymer is used neat, but often other materials ar incorporated to form the finished adhesive. We obviously cannot discuss all of the available backbone polymers, but Table 1 lists the more commercially significant materials and their generalized chemical structures.

Most of the polymers listed in Table 1 are addition-type polymers. The last three, however, are condensation polymers.

Addition-type polymers are found by combining the base, or repeating units with each other without forming any elimination products; for example, ethylene/vinyl acetate copolymers are formed by the combination of ethylene and vinyl acetate monomers.

Condensation polymers are formed by combining two or more monomers with the elimination of small molecules: for example, polyamides are formed by the reaction of organic acids and amines with the elimination of water.

As a rule the addition-type polymers require compounding to be useful as hot-melt adhesives. Typically, such a formulated hot-melt adhesive would contain the backbone polymer plus one or more of the following: tackifiers, plasticizers, flow modifiers antioxidants, pigments, extenders, etc.

The condensation polymers, by contrast, are often used without compounding.

IV. ELEMENTARY PRINCIPLES OF JOINT DESIGN

Adhesion versus stress-that is what most of adhesive technology is all most.

Adhesion is the force that holds materials together. Stress, on the other hand, is the force that pulls materials apart. The basic types of stress in adhesive technology are illustrated in Fig.2.

A joint primarily designed for mechanical fastening may not prove acceptable for adhesive bonding and may require redesign. Two prime factors should guide the designer. First, the joint should be designed so that the stress is distributed over the entire bonded area. Second, the joint configuration should be designed so that the stress is largely shear or tensile. With peel and cleanage minimized.

Joint design is a critical factor in the success or failure of adhesive bonding.

5. HOT-MELT ADHESIVE USAGE BY INDUSTRY

The most rapid increases are seen in the areas of pressure sensitive tapes, textiles, product assembly, and automotive. The over all growth rate is projected to average about 12%/year.

Approximately 60% of the total hot-melt adhesive use was in packaging. The next largest volume areas ware bookbinding, textiles, and disposables-each with less than 10% of the total.

Over 50% of the total hot melts are based on ethylene-vinyl acetate copolymers. Polyolefins (high-pressure polyethylene and alactic polypropylene) account for over 30% of the balance.

VI. WHERE HOT MELT ADHESIVES ARE USED

The following list shows some of the application areas that use hot melt adhesives. A few examples are illustrated.

Packaging.

Case sealing	Cartons
Bags	Composite cans
Trays	Corrugated boards
Labels	Fiber drums
Tapes	Pouches
	Three-piece beverage cans (Fig 5)

Bookbinding.

Paperbacks	Magazines
Catalogs	Directories
Hardcover books	Calendars

Textiles.

Interliners	Aprons
Hemming	Curtains
Waistbands	Towels
Labels	Patches
Cuffing	Basting
Pillows	

Disposables.

Diapers	Sanitary items
Hospital pads	Hospital garments
	Surgical pads

Furniture.

Edge banding Door panels
Cabinet assembly stereo cabinets
Overlay lamination Window frames

Footwear.

Lasting Counters
Sole attaching Folding
Box toes

Automotive and related industries.

Door panels Trunk and window seals
Hand windshield washer Carpet installation
Tail light assemblies Outboard motor housing
Electronic controls Fire wall insulation
Vinyl roofs Headliners
Seating

Backbone polymers	Chemical structure[a,b]
Ethylene–vinyl-acetate copolymers	$-(CH_2-CH(O-C(=O)-CH_3))_n-(CH_2-CH_2)_m-$
Polyethylene	$-(CH_2-CH_2)_n-$
Polypropylene (atactic)	$-(CH_2-CH(CH_3))_n-$
Styrene-isoprene-styrene block polymers	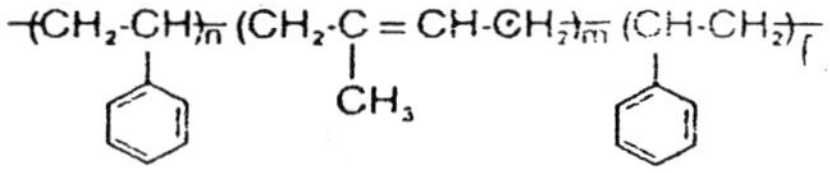
Styrene-butadiene-styrene block polymers	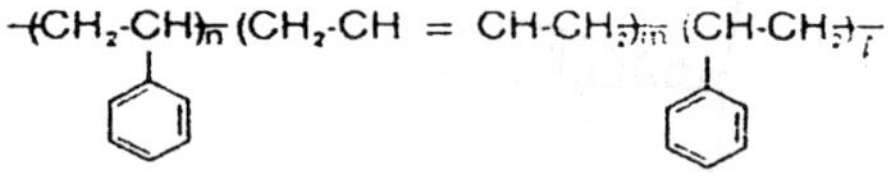
Ethylene-acrylic co-polymers	$-(CH_2-CX(C(=O)-CXH-CH_3))_n-(CH_2-CH_2)_m-$ X = H or CH_3
Polyvinyl acetate and copolymers	$-(CH_2-CH(O-C(=O)-R_1))_n-(CH_2-CH(O-C(=O)-R_2))_m-$
Butyl rubbers	$-(CH_2-CH=CH-CH_2)_n-$
Polyurethanes	$-(R_1-O-C(=O)-NH-R_2-NH-C(=O)-O)_n-$
Polyamides	$-(NH-R_1-NH-C(=O)-R_2-C(=O))_n-$
Polyesters	$-(O-R_1-O-C(=O)-R_2-C(=O))_n-$
Polyesteramides	$-(O-R_1-O-C(=O)-R_2-C(=O)-NH-R_3-NH-C(=O)-R_2-C(=O))_n-$

[a]Generalized structure.
[b]R_1, R_2, and R_3 are organic moieties.
Source: Data from Refs. 2–4.

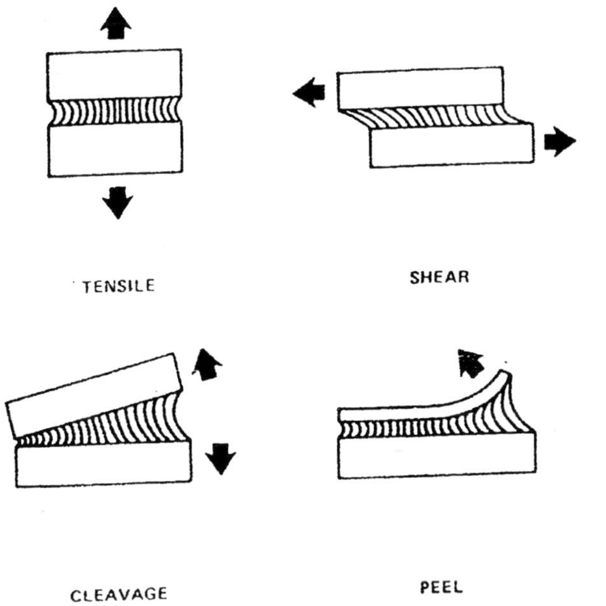

Fig. 2. Tensile stress; shear stress; cleavage stress; peel stress.

Product Assembly.

Vinyl-clad window frames Mirror assembly
Envelope batteries Utensils
Thermal-and noise-insulation pads Flexible ducting
Mobile-home components

Appliances.

Air conditioner components Refrigerator components
Coffee pots Television components
Tape-components

Appliances.

Air conditioner components Refrigerator components
Coffee pots Television components
Tape-cassette holder Calculator display window
Slowcook-pot heaters

Carpets.

Backing Seaming tapes
Tapes [Hot-melt pressure-sensitive adhesives (HMPSA)].

Electrical Sealing
Binding Nylon-or glass-reinforced

Filters.

Oil-automotive Exhaust-gas scrubber
Air-automotive and residential

Table 8 lists problems. possible causes, and suggested solutions associated with hot-melt applications. If these suggest solutions do not correct the situation, contact either the equipment or adhesive supplier or both (1.7).

Table 8. Troubleshooting Guides

Problem	Possible causes	Suggested Solutions
a Bond failure	Inadequate wetout of secondary surfaces.	1. Apply more adhesives.
adhesives on one side only, adhesive surface glossy.	Not enough opne time.	2. Apply adhesives at higher temperature.
		3. Preheat substrate. 4. Shorten time between adhesive application and adhesive. 5. Try a slower setting adhesive. 6. Treat substrate surface.
b Bond failure adhesive on both surfaces with leggy strings.	Movement of the joint while adhesive is solidifying.	1. Apply adhesive at lower temperature 2. Apply ahdesive at lower temperature. 3. Try a faster-setting adhesive.

c. Bond failure adhesive mostly on one side. of substrate.	Condition of the substrate surface or type	1. Treat substrate surface. 2. Apply adhesive at higher temperature. 3. Try another adhesive.
d. Bond failure insufficient adhesivein bond area.	Absorption of adhesive by porous substrate. Adhesive squeeze out.	1. Apply adhesive at 2. Apply more adhesive. 3. Use high viscosity or adhesive.
e. Bond failure bond opening when compression is released.	Adhesive not cooling fast enough. Substrate too hot. Improper adhesive.	1. Cool substrate and or adhesive. 2. Decrease amount of adhesive. 3. Increase compression time. 4. Change to faster setting adhesive.
f. Charring or gelling of adhesive in application equipment	Adhesive temperature too high. Faulty heat control. Adhesive heat stability	1. Lower adhesive 2. Check temperature indicator with inadequate. another thermometer. 3. Try a more heatstable adhesive or clean out applicator more often. 4. Use inert gas blanket.
g. Stringing of adhesive at applicator tip.	Adhesive temperature too low. Adhesive viscosity too high. Substrate too far from application tip.	1. Raise adhesive temperature. Caution: Do not exceed recommended application temperature. 2. Position substrate closer to applicator tip.

h. Adhesive dripping fromapplicator tip.	Worn applicator valve. Dirty applicator tip.	1. Replace valve. 2. Clean applicator tip.
i. Bubbles in adhesive.	Reservoir out of adhesive.	2. Check adhesive for moisture. 3. Try a supply of fresh, dry adhesive. 4. Consult with the adhesive supplier.
j. Excessive adhesive squeeze out	Too much adhesive. .Adhesive too hot.	1. Use less adhesive. 2. Loxer adhesive temperature.
	Compression too high.	3. Decrease compression. 4. Use high viscosity adhesive.

IX. SAFETY SUGGESTIONS FOR USING HOT-MELT ADHESIVES

Working with hot-melt adhesives should not be much more harzardous than cooking the evening meal. However, because of their characteristic rapid solidification at relatively high temperature, they present a potential hazard. Even after solidifying, they are still hot. Therefore, care should be used when working with hot-melt adhesives in the molten state. Severe burns can occur if the molten adhesives in the molten state. Severe burns can occur if the molten adhesive comes in contact with the skin. When handling molten adhesive or working near a machine containing molten adhesive under pressure the use of eye protection and protective clothing is strongly recommended.

Should molten adhesive come in contact with the skin, the following actions are recommended.

1. Do not try to remove the molten adhesive from the skin.
2. Immediately immerse the affected area in water, preferably clean and cold. A supply of water should be readily available at all times near the adhesive equipment. Keep the affected area immersed until the adhesive has cooled.
3. Do not try to remove the cooled adhesive from the skin.
4. Cover the affected area with a clean, wet compress.
5. In cases of severe burns, be alert for signs of shock. If observed, have patient lie down and use blankets to preserve body heat. Call a physician immediately.

X. HOT-MELT ADHESIVES-FORMS AND SHAPES

Since hot melts are applied in a variety of methods from many different types of application equipment, the adhesive suppliers provide a wide variety of forms. These include

1. Powders (various mesh sizes)
2. Pellets (chopped, strand, or beads)
3. Films (various thicknesses)
4. Webs (open mesh "films")
5. Cylinders (tubes, candles, sluge of various sizes)
6. Crushed (irregular chunks of various sizes)
7. Stats (flat pieces of various sizes)
8. Trays (release-coat-lined boxes of various sizes)
9. Metal pails (filled molten, then solidified)
10. Drums (filled molten, then solidified)

XI. HOT-MELT ADHESIVES-ANTICIPATED FUTURE DEVELOPMENTS

We can anticipate at least three areas for future development. Serendipity will probably bring forth others that cannot be anticipated on the basis of today's knowledge.

A. Thermoplastic-Thermoset

A step in the direction of thermoplastic-thermoset, hot-melt adhesives is the radiation crosslinking of HMPSA tapes.

Another route being considered is combining two flows of hot-melt material which can react with each other. This concept may also include melting-fusing of an adhesive rope woven from two or more different polymer strands that have some chemical reactivity with each other.

The expected advantage would be improved resistance to elevated temperatures and chemical attack.

B. Foamable Hot Melts

Putting molten, hot-melt adhesives under pressure and adding an inert gas causes a foaming action as the material is dispensed.

Some of the expected advantages are

1. Control of glueline deposition
2. Extended "open time"

3. Void filling for poorly mated parts
4. Reduced adhesive consumption.

C. Exotic Polymers

Aerospace and related programs are developing exotic, high performance polymers. Some may be adaptable for use as adhesives.

4

PRESSURE-SENSITIVE ADHESIVES

I. INTRODUCTION

The term "pressure-sensitive adhesive" (PSA) refers to that type of adhesive which, when in a dry state, will adhere to a variety of surfaces merely by application of light hand pressure. Such compositions are inherently soft, permanently tacky materials which exhibit a balance of adhesive and cohesive strength depending on the viscoelastic nature of the adhesive and the performance requirements of the particular end use. Pressure-sensitive were first developed in the mid-1800s for use on surgical tapes. Their use has since expanded to include masking tapes for spray painting of automobiles, as well as a myriad of other uses in the consumer-tapes and graphic arts fields. Today PSAS find major applications in tape and labels. Other uses include wall covering, floor tiles, and protective maskings.

II. THEORY

From a performance point of view, the properties most important to the formation of a satisfactory PSA bond are surface tack, peel adhesion, and shear resistance.

A. Surface Tack

Surface tank, commonly known as quick stick, is defined as that property of a PSA which enables it to spontaneously adhere to a surface under very light pressure and to resist removal almost instantly. Softer polymers generally exhibit a higher degree of tack, but at the same time lower cohesive shear strength, then harder polymers. Tack is also a function of the thickness of the adhesive film with higher film thickness contributing to higher levels of tack. Bates, in a study on the nature of adhesive tack, devised a method for measuring tack by determining the energy dissipated during debonding (at constant strain rate) of a substrate from a PSA. Several other techniques have also been developed to measure the tack of PSAs and are widely used in industry today.

B. Peel Adhesion

Peel adhesive is determined by measuring the farce required to remove a pressure-sensitive material (tape or label) by peeling at a constant rate, usually at an angle of 180^0 to the substrate. In addition to the viscoelastic properties of the adhesive, other factors affecting peel adhesion are polarity of the adhesive, thickness of the bond, temperature, the length of time that the adhesive has been in contact with the surface, rate of removal, and the nature of both the substrate and the backing material.

C. Shear Resistance

Shear resistance is the force required to remove a pressure-sensitive item (taps, label, etc.) from a surface in a direction parallel to the surface to which it is affixed. It is a measure of the cohesive strength of the adhesive. Shear resistance can be enhanced by increasing the molecular weight or the crosslink density of the polymer. Either measure will simultaneously result in some sacrifice in tack and peel adhesive. Aubrey maintains that it is necessary to increase the concentration of network or gel so that the adhesive can sustain high shearing forces. Gel concentrations of 30-50% are usually adequate for high-shear PSAs.

D. The Influence of Polymer Structure on Performance Properties

As a first approximation for product design, the tack, adhesive, and cohesive characteristics of a pressure-sensitive polymer can be correlated with three basic properties in addition to the crosslink density, namely, molecular weight, glass transition temperature Tg. and polarity.

1. Molecular weight

Molecular weight and molecular-weight distribution will influence polymer viscosity. The presence of lower molecular weight species in an adhesive contributes to lower viscosity. The neat-polymer viscosity at bonding temperatures is a prime factor in how well the adhesive wets a substrate and forms a bond. When the viscosity is lower, the mobility of the polymer molecular is greater: hence, wetting is improved. However, as the molecular weight is decreased, so is the cohesive strength of the bond. Consequently, polymer viscosity must be balanced with the desired physical and mechanical properties.

The influence of the molecular weight on the performance of a PSA is shown by the idealized representation in Fig. 1. Starting with a low

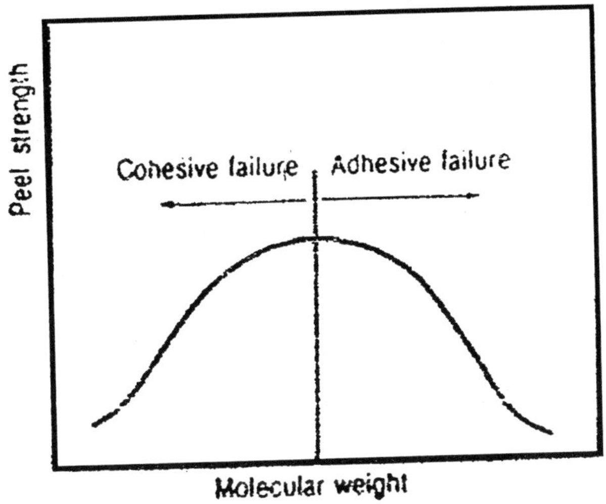

Fig.1. Idealized representation of relationship between average molecular weight and peel strength of a PSA.

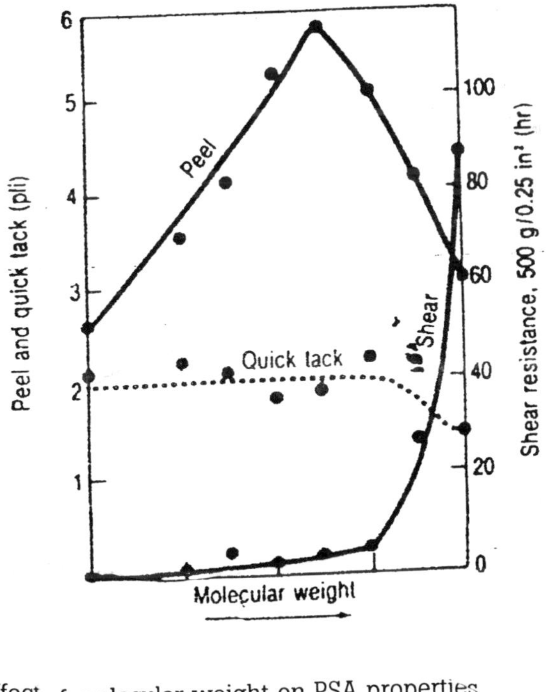

Fig.2. Effect of molecular weight on PSA properties.

molecular weight polymer, an increase in molecular weight results in higher peel values due to an increase in cohesive strength. Wetting of the substrate remains excellent in this range. AS the molecular weight is further increased, a decrease in peel strength is observed, and failure, on a macroscopic scale, takes place at the interface between the adhesive and the substrate.

This relationship is borne out by the results of a series of experiments with an acrylic latex adhesive shown in Fig. 2. The molecular weight of the polymer was varied with a chain transfer agent while keeping the polymer composition constant. Increasing the molecular weight enhanced the cohesive (shear) strength of the polymer but, above a point, adversely affected the adhesive (peel and tack) properties.

To improve the cohesive strength of PSAs without adversely affecting peel, light crosslinking is often advantageously employed. The beneficial effects of incorporating very low levels of multifunctional monomers into a pressure-sensitive polymer system are shown in Fig. 3. In this case, the shear resistance of the polymer increased markedly, while the peel strength was relatively unaffected until higher levels of the multifunctional monomer were employed.

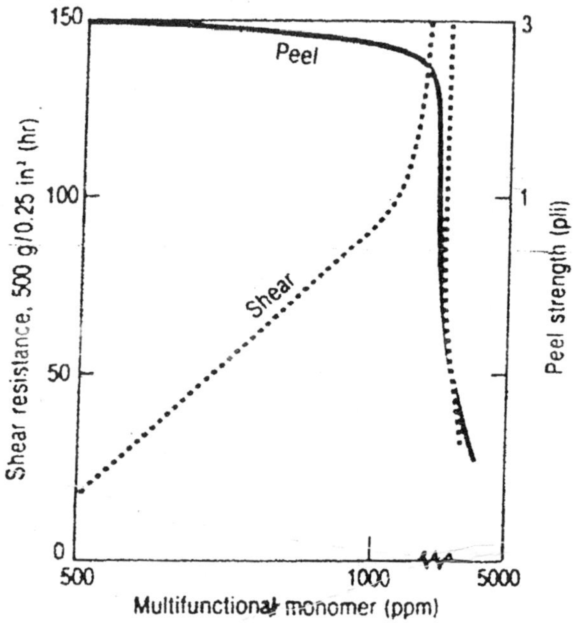

Fig.3. Effect of multifunctional monomer on pressure-sensitive polymer.

2. Glass transition

The effect of Tg on the performance of acrylic PSAs is illustrated in Fig.4. The bonding temperatures of PSAs are above the Tgs for the systems. The greater the difference between the use temperature and the T g, the lower the viscosity and the better the wetting be. However, an optimum Tg must be sought in order to provide a balance between polymer mobility and cohesive properties. Figure 4 displays the divergent influence of acrylic-polymer Tg on adhesive and cohesive characteristics.

In synthesizing a polymer for adhesive applications, special attention must be given to Tg and molecular weight and their interplay with the mobility of the polymer molecules. Glass transition and molecular weight must be considered simultaneously when correlating the adhesive performance of polymers with physicochemical properties.

3. Polar effects

The polarity of an adhesive affects its adhesion be specific substrates. In general, polar adhesives have a tendency to adhere to polar (high-surface energy) substrates by virtue of dipole-dipole interactions and/or hydrogen bonding. Compositions with lower polarity tend to adhere to lower-surface-energy substrates.

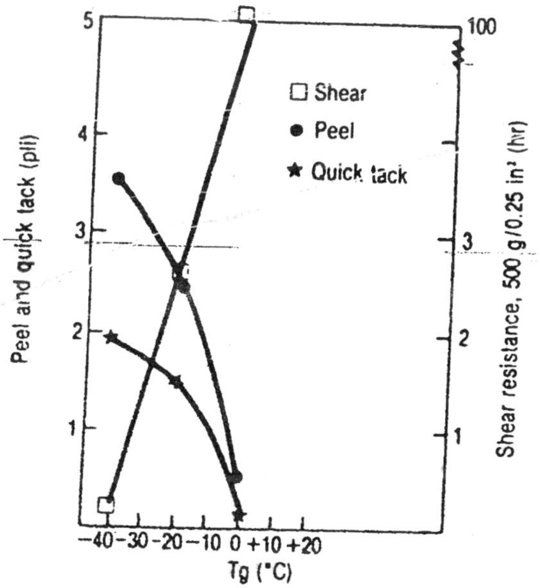

Fig.4. Effect of Tg of polymers on performance of adhesives.

A. Introduction

These adhesives(PSA) consist of a combination of elastomers, tackifying resins, plasticizers, and fillers. Pressure-sensitive adhesives are usually identified by the chemical nature of the elastomer [e.g. natural rubber, styrene-butadiene rubber (SBR), acrylic, etc.]. Natural rubber, was the first elastomer used in PSAs and is the most commonly used today, followed closely by acrylates.

B. End Uses

The two major markets for PSAs are the tape and the label industries. There is also a variety of other products which utilize PSAs. These include

- Wall and shelf covering
- limitation wood grain
- Ceiling and floor tiles
- Disposable diaper tabs
- Medical and sanitary products
- Graphic artwork
- Protective maskings

1. Tapes

Pressure-sensitive tapes, first introduced for surgical applications, are now finding wide use in both consumer and industrial fields. A variety of backing materials are used, including paper, fabric, plastic films (e.g. PVC, cellophane, matte acetate, polyester, Polyolefins), and aluminum foil.

A pressure-sensitive tape consists of backing material to which a PSA has been applied on one side. A thin primer is sometimes required in order to anchor the adhesive to the backing material. The primer is applied to ensure that the adhesive layer will remain in place on the backing when the roll is unwound and later when the tape is removed from the surface to which it has been applied. Nitrile rubber, chlorinated rubber and acrylates are currently used as primers for rubber-based PSAs. Acrylic PSAs do not generally require a primer coat.

In order to facilitate unwinding without splitting the adhesive, a release coating is often applied to the back of the web. The release coat is applied at a very low coat weight (approximately 1-5 g/m2). A controlled degree of release is required, and several release materials are used-including acrylic acid esters of long-chin fatty alcohols; polyurethanes incorporating long aliphatic chains; and cellulose esters. The release layer should be a coating of relatively low surface free energy. Some plastic films, such as biaxially oriented polyperpylene, do not require the use of a primer or a release coat. Adhesion to one side is enhanced by corona treatment to oxidize the Polyolefins surface.

Some pressure-sensitive tapes, such as metal-foil tapes for heating ducts, will utilize a separate release liner, usually silicone coated, which is laminated to the adhesive and removed immediately before use. There are also double-sided tapes which have both sides of the backing material coated with a PSA. The taps is rolled with a separate, silicone-coated release liner. These tapes are useful for mounting and splicing.

Paper-backed pressure-sensitive tapes are used for a variety of applications, the most important being masking tape. Masking tape generally utilizes a crope-paper backing which has been impregnated with a polymeric binder to improve the strength of the paper. Since a major use for masking tape is to protect surfaces during certain painting operations, the adhesive must resist attack by the organic solvents used in paints and be able to withstand the high baking temperatures used in automobile paint bake ovens.

Table 2. Typical Adhesive Performance Requirements

Product	Peel adhesion (pli)	Quick tack (pli)	shear (hr)
General purpose masking tape	2.3	1.1	>167[a]
Glass-reinforced polyester tape	3.2	1.8	>500[a]
Aluminum-foil duct tape	>3.8	1.8	>6[b]
High-performance Polyester strapping tape	2.3	1.1	>200[c]
Polypropylene carton sealing tape	2.2	1.6	>80[a]

a1 in.2/1000 g.
b1 in.2/4540 g.
C1/4 in. 2/500 g.

Plastic films are also widely used in pressure-sensitive tapes for a multitude of applications. Cellophane, one of the original products used in clear pressure-sensitive tapes, is being displaced by cellulose acetate for office and household mending applications. Plasticized PVC has replaced a significant portion of the cloth "friction" tape in electric applications and is used extensively in pipe wrapping and certain medical applications. Recently, biaxially oriented polypropylene film with acrylic latex PSAs has been making significant inroads into the packaging-tape market. It is used for sealing corrugated boxboard containers.

Fiber-reinforced tapes in which Fiberglas, polyester, or nylon filaments have been imbedded in the PSA to increase overall tensile strength and tear resistance are being used for high-performance packaging, palletizing, and reinforcing applications.

The tape industry requires a great deal of versatility in PSAs in order tc satisfy the broad range of properties required for various products. Table 2 shows typical peel, shear, and quick-tack values required for various pressure-sensitive tapes.

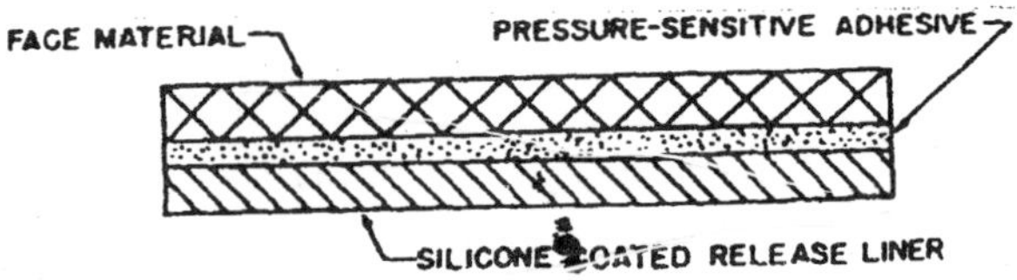

Fig.5. Pressure-sensitive label stock.

2. Labels

Pressure-sensitive adhesives are gaining increasingly wide acceptance by the label industry at the expense of wet adhesives, pregummed remoistenable adhesives, and heat-activated adhesives. Despite their highe cost, pressure-sensitive, or self-adhesive labels offer a number o advantages over conventional labels.

These advantages include cleanliness of operation, speed of labe application, and simplicity of application equipment, as well as versatility and ease of application to irregularly shaped surfaces and containers. The growth rate of PSAs in labels is nearly double that of the overall labe market.

Pressure-sensitive labels and decals are constructed of three component

In the manufacturer of label stock the PSA is generally applied to a silicone coated release liner and dried. In the case of hot-melt adhesives, no dryin is required. The coated release liner is then laminated under light pressur to the face material. This process is commonly referred to as "transfer coating". The adhesive will transfer to the face material when the release liner is removed. The label stock is then either rolled or stacked in sheets for subsequent printing and die cutting into individual labels.

Paper, typically a 60-lb. coated Kraft, is most commonly used as the face material. However, other materials such as plasticized PVC, metal foils, polyestes, and fabric, are also used for specialty labels.

Labels may be classified according to their intended use (i.e. permanent, removable, or repositionable, or low-temperature).Each will require an adhesive with different performance properties. Permanent labels exhibit a sufficiently high degree of adhesion that the label will be damaged upon removal from the surface. A removable or repositionable label requires an adhesive with a balance between adhesive and cohesive strength to allow it to be removed cleanly without destroying the label or leaving a residue of the adhesive on the surface. Low-temperature labels are used primarily for pricing of frozen-food packages and, therefore, require an adhesive that will retain a high degree of tack at extremely low temperatures.

An estimate of the distribution according to the various types is as follows

Type of label	Percent of total label volume
Permanent	80
Low-temperature	10
Removable	5
Miscellaneous	5

At present, the majority of label-stock manufacturers are using solvent-based PSAs. However, ecological and economic considerations have resulted in a trend toward aqueous and hot-melt systems.

3. Other Uses

Pressure-sensitive adhesives find application in a wide variety of other end uses, each with its own specific set of performance criteria. Pressure-sensitive films and papers are used to temporarily protect surfaces from scratches, corrosion, or other forms of damage. For example, Lusite or Plexiglass sheeting is usually covered with a protective masking to prevent scratching until it is used by the consumer. Highly polished or precision-machined metals are often protected with a pressure-sensitive masking during shipping and storage. The adhesive must exhibit a low to moderate degree of adhesion to the surface to allow the masking to be easily removed without leaving a residue or stain on the surface.

Shelf and wall coverings frequently use a PSA on a plasticized PVC backing. The adhesive must have a high degree of adhesion initially and not exhibit a deterioration of the adhesive bond on aging due to migration of the plasticizer form the PVC into the adhesive.
Sanitary and medical products also utilize PSAs. These products include such things as disposable diaper tabs, bandages, and hospital supplies. The adhesives must exhibit a degree of moisture resistance and must not cause skin irritation after long periods of contact.

IV. SOLVENT-BASED PRESSURE-SENSITIVE ADHESIVES

The manufacture of PSA articles by deposition from solvents has a relatively long history. As a result, solvent-based formulations have been developed to such a highly advanced state that their broad range of performance and formulation latitude has generated widespread market acceptance. They represent the largest single market for solvent-based adhesives.

Some general characteristics of solvent-based adhesive systems are summarized in Table 3. Typically, these adhesives consist of various elastomers in conjunction with tackifiers, plasticizers,,fillers, and antioxidants. Common elastomers include natural, reclaimed, and styrene-butadiene rubbers, polyisobutylene or butyl rubber; polyvinyl alkyl ethers; acrylics; or thermoplastic elastomers [styreneisoprene-styrene (S-I-S) block copolymers]. It should be pointed out, however, that acrylics generally to not require the use of tackifiers or antioxidants.

Table 3. Characteristics of Solvent PSAs

Property	Rubber	Acrylic
Adhesive cost	Low	High
Formulating latitude	Excellent	Excellent
Chemical resistance	Good	High
Quick stick	High	Good
Fire hazard	High	High
Aging	Good	Excellent
UV resistance	Poor	Excellent
Clarity	Poor	Excellent
Energy for application	High	High
Space requirement	High	High
Cleanup/changeover	Good	Good

The thermoplastic elastomers appear to have advantages over natural rubber in that they can be used at higher solids levels and tend to be lower in price. These factors, coupled with higher solvent prices, are working to increase the presently small share of solvent-based adhesives held by these elastomers. Acrylic systems tend to require less formulating than the rubber systems and have little need for tackifiers. The bulk of the PSA market (over 3/4) is satisfied by rubbers with most of the remainder using acrylics. Less commonly, products based on polyurethanes, polyesters, and polysilozanes may be used. The siloxanes, in particular, have an exceptional range of high-and low-temperature properties.

In order to provide high-temperature properties, most polymers need to be crosslinked either by thermal or chemical means. It is imperative to control the extent of crosslinking carefully since an insufficient amount may result in shear failure at elevated temperatures, while excessive amounts will lead to a loss of peel and tack. Examples of recipes for both rubber-and acrylic-based PSAs are shown in Tables 4 and 5.

Among the solvents most commonly used in formulating are allphatic hydrocarbons (e.g. hexane, heptane) and toluene, for rubber systems, and esters or ketones for acrylic systems. A thorough discussion of the technical aspects of solvent-polymer interactions in adhesives recently appeared.

Table 4. Rubber Based PSA for High Temperature Masking Tape.

Formulation	Parts
Crude rubber	50
GRS	50
Octyl phenol formaldehyde heat curing resin	20
ZnO	60
Diethylene glycol ester of dihydroabietic acid	110
Antioxidants	2

In recent years, the use of solvents has come under a barrage of legislative pressure concerned with environmental pollution. Other negative pressures bearing on this approach are the high energy costs required for evaporation, concern over flammability and explosion hazards, and the consumption of sometimes scarce and costly solvent. The prices of many solvent have escalated more then fourfold in the past few years. These factors have combined to spur the development of alternate methods of manufacture for PSAs.

Table 5. Solvent Based Acrylic PSA Formulation

Formulation	Parts
Copolymer based on	
Methyl acrylate	100
n-Butyl acrylate	290
2-Ethylhexyl acrylate	590
Glycidyl methacrylate	20
Acetone	300
Benzene	130
p-Toluene sulfonic acid	5
Dried, cured 3 min at 100° C	

The increasing cost of energy will be a strong driving force toward systems which are more efficient - such as lattices, hot melts, and, possibly, radiation curing. Essentially all now capacity is likely to be dedicated to these nonsolvent systems, and in addition, many solvent ovens will be adapted to latex systems. Solvent systems generally require more energy because of the lower solids levels employed and because of the limits on allowable solvent vapour concentrations in drying ovens. Recent equipment innovations may change this outlook, however. Economic analyses of the factors involved in operating a solvent line have been published which compare their cost with the costs of alternative approaches .

Several alternatives exist for those who wish to maintain their present solvent operation, however. These include

Use of "exempt (photochemically nonreactive) solvents. The emission of such solvents is limited, however, and subject to certain requirements.

Solvent incineration with or without heat recovery.
Solvent recovery

An economic comparison and a discussion of incineration versus recovery were presented at a recent symposium. The systems compared were based on flows of 10,000 standard cubic feet per minute (SCFM) of air containing toluene at 25% lower explosive limit (LEL) (Table 6).

V. WATER-BASED SYSTEMS

The deposition of PSA films from a water medium has a number of advantages when compared to deposition from solvents. Many of the troublesome problems apparent with the use of solvents simply do not exist when water is used. To begin with, water is the cheapest possible carrier obtainable and presents no supply problem. Furthermore, it is odorless, nontoxic, nonpolluting, and nonflammable. These combined characteristics make water-based systems a sensible and viable approach when changing from existing solvent-based coating lines.

Table 7. A Comparison of the Oven Energy Consumed in a Label Coating Operation.

Process	% LEL	Oven air flow (thousand SCFM)	Fuel energy required
Solvent	25	34.4	25.9
system	40	21.5	17.5
Latex PSA	-	6.0	13.4
	-	12.0	17.8

a Million Btus/million ft.^{2} substrate.

It is well known that the amount of heat necessary to evaporate water is substantially more than that required to evaporate most organic solvents. However, when account is taken of the nonexplosive nature of the aqueous systems, a net saving in energy cost accrues to the latex coating process over the solvent based line. This occurs because of the vastly reduced need to supply fresh air to the ovens in order to maintain a safe operating level below the LEL. Table 7, taken from recent computer simulation of various PSA coating lines, illustrates these points.

In lattices, the water acts as a carrier, rather than as solvent. Thus, a PSA latex is a suspension of an insoluble liquid polymer in water, prepared so that it is stable for long periods of time. The average diameter of the suspended, spherical polymer particles is in the range of 0.1-0.8 m. In order to obtain this particle size and long-term stability, other components are usually present besides the dispersed resin and water. It is often necessary to have present suitable emulsifying agents (or surfactants). These surfactants function by their surface activity at the interface of the two phases. They are essentially balanced molecules with a "hydrophilic" or "water-loving" part and a "hydrophobic" or "water repellent" portion, such as a long chain hydrocarbon. Another type of emulsifier, or, to use a more general term, stabilizer, is a water-soluble colloid. This class includes high molecular weight, water-soluble compounds for example, natural gums and synthetic or semisynthetic polymers, such as polyvinyl alcohol and hydroxyethylcellulose.

This discussion will focus on lattices resulting from emulsion polymerization. Because of the insolubility of the polymer in water, the viscosities of lattices are not affected by molecular weight and are substantially lower than those of solvent based products. Furthermore, the solids levels of the lattices can be as high as 70%, much higher than it is for solvent products. The polymer produced by emulsion polymerization normally has a much higher molecular weight than that employed with solution PSAs.

Many latex compositions having the requisite characteristics described earlier have been found to have pressure-sensitive properties on drying. A summary of the materials first developed for this application has appeared. Illustrative of the various types are the following.

Copolymers of vinyl acetate or, optionally, a higher vinyl ester an ester of an alpha, beta-unsaturated dicarboxylic acid, such as maleic or fumeric acid.

A homopolymer of the vinyl ester of a carboxylic acid. Also copolymers of mixed vinyl esters provided that

$$\frac{\Sigma\ Mn}{\Sigma\ M}\ 2$$

where M is the total number of molecular units in the polymer and Mn is the total number of carbon atoms in the alkyl groups of the allphatic fatty acid in each ester unit.

Table 8. Recipe for Pressure Sensitive Emulsion a

Ingredient	Parts by weight
Nonylphenol ethylene oxide condensate (97% by weight oxyethylene units)	22.4
Sodium acetate	1.0
Water	465.0
Sodium metabisulfite (in 10 parts water)	0.9
Ammonium persulfate (in 10 parts water)	0.45
Vinyl acetate	83.6
2-Ethylhexyl acrylate	352.0
Acrylic acid	4.4

[a] The polymerization follows a conventional procedure for 3 hr at 60-75° C after which 0.45 parts by weight ammonium persulfite (in 10 parts water) is added and heating continued for 1 hr more. The final emulsion is stable and contains 46% by weight solids.

Compositions in which the main constituent is an acrylic ester to which 5-10% of an acid, such as (meth) acrylic acid or crotonic acid, and 3-25% of a "hardening" monomer, such as methyl methacrylate or acrylonitrile, are added.

Formulations that use up to 5% methylolacrylamide or its nitrogen ethers (e.g. N-butoxymethyl acrylamide) in acrylate ester polymers to improve properties.

Combinations of mixed acrylates with small amounts (about 3%) of (meth) acrylic acid and a glycol ester, such as 2-hydroxypropyl acrylate.

Blends of two acrylic emulsions or a blend of natural-rubber latex containing a noncrosslinked acrylic latex or a styrene polymer.

Terpolymers of vinyl acetate, an acrylate ester which is at least 50% of the monomers, and 1-5% of an unsaturated acid, such as (meth) acrylic acid. A recipe illustrating such a formulation is given in Table 8.

Although refinements have taken place since the aforementioned review, many of the compositions being used commercially today are believed to be comparable to those examples mentioned. The properties of two different types of PSA latex, based on acrylics and SBR, have been described recently and are reproduced in Tables 9 and 10.

Table 9. Rubber Latex PSA Properties

	Properties [a,b]			
Latex [c]	Polyken tack (g)	90° Quick stick (pli)	180° Peel (pli)	Shear (hr)
NR[d]: Foral 85 (30:70)	1420	10	7.3	1.5
SBR latex-K (carboxylated): Foral 85 (50:50)	1320	1.5	4.5	>50
[1:1 (NR:SBR) Latex-K]: Foral 85 (30:70)	2200	4.5	7.5	15.7

[a]Coated on 2-mil Mylar film.
b Tests: Polyken tack (ASTM D-2979-1): 90° Quick stick (PSTC-5); 180° Peel (PSTC-1): 178° Shear [PSTC-7 modified, 1000 g/(1/2 x 1 in.)].

[c]Ratios of dry parts of tackifier resin:rubber latex.
[d]NR, natural rubber.

Natural rubber and SBR have often been used for the manufacture of pressure-sensitive tapes and labels. These materials connot be used as is, however, because the surface tack is extremely low. Furthermore, they require compounding to protect against oxidative and ultraviolet-induced aging. When properly formulated, they do possess good PSA have also been introduced recently.

Acrylic lattices are particularly attractive alternatives to solvent based rubber adhesives because of their excellent stability to heat and ultra-violet (UV) light and resistance to plasticizer migration. Correlations between the adhesive and cohesive characteristics of acrylic polymers have been made with fundamental molecular properties such as Tg, molecular weight distribution, polarity, and polymer branching and crosslinking. Acrylic pressure-sensitive lattices can easily be formulated to modify their properties. Functional acrylic resins can be crosslinked to increase shear resistance. Thus, polymers with carboxylic acid functionally can be crosslinked with urea-formaldehyde at elevated temperature or with zinc acetate at room temperature. Acrylic lattices are believed to offer the most widely applicable, versatile alternative to solvent-based PSAs. Despite the many improvements made recently, some deficiencies need to be corrected for full industry acceptance as outlined in Table 11.

Table 10 Typical Acrylic Latex PSA Properties[a]

Property	Ucar latex 173	Ucar latex 174	Ucar latex 175
Tg (°C)	-35	-45	-60
Peel adhesion[b] (pli)	3	5	6
Quick tack (pli)[c]	1.5	1.7	1.8
Shear (hr)[d]	50-100	2-5	< 0.5
Solvent resistance			
MEK	Poor	Poor	Poor
Toluene	Fair	Fair	Fair
Recommended applications	Industrial tapes General purpose labels Wall coverings	General purpose tapes, labels, floor tiles	Refrig./freezer tapes and labels Other low-temp. applications.

[a]Properties measured on adhesives applied directly to 2-mil Mylar film. The dry adhesive coat weight was approximately 2.4 gm/100 in.2

b 180° Peel adhesion - PSTC 1.
c 90° Quick tack - PSTC 5.
d Vertical shear, 1/4 in. 2/500 g-PSTC 7.

Table 11. Emulsion PSAs: Improvements Needed

Peel strength
Generally not above 3.5 pli.
Solution acrylics available at up to 6 pli, rubber/resin even higher.

Water, high relative-humidity resistance
Plasticizing effect reduces strength and limits exterior use.

Specific adhesion to nonpolar substrates
Share this characteristic with solution acrylics; rubber/resin types better.

Freeze/thaw stability
Possible problems in transit, storage.

Coating quality
Comparable to solution casting possible, but only with more care.

Table 12. Some General Characteristics of HMPSAs

Advantages	Disadvantages
100% solids, no solvent hazard. Simple to ship, handle, and store.	Overall properties not equal to solvent or water based adhesives.
Low energy consumption.	Service temperature is limited.
Faster machine speeds up to 500-1000 fpm.	Limited resistance to attack by solvents or plasticizer migration.
Ability to apply higher coating weights, control penetration into porous stock.	Coating equipment and conditions extremely problem
	Decomposition of the resin in melt a potential problem
	Cannot be applied to heatsensitive substrates.
	Dirt or contaminants cause streaking of coatings.

VI. HOT-MELT PRESSURE-SENSITIVE ADHESIVES

As their name implies, hot-melt adhesives are solid at normal temperature but become molten on heating. When they are applied to a surface in the form of a hot liquid, wetting occurs, heat is lost to the face in the surface, and a bond is formed. The process of forming a bond with a hot-melt adhesive is one of the most rapid of all techniques because neither solvent loss nor chemical reactions is involved. As a direct result of their thermal characteristics, however, hot-melt adhesives have poor resistance to heat. In many instances, solvent resistance is poor as well (see Table 12). Improvements in these properties can be achieved in some cases by post crosslinking with irradiation or by blending with other polymers.

In comparison with other methods of applying PSAS, the HOT-MELT technique is the most energy efficient method availables at present. Furthermore, it offers the highest known production rates, the lowest capital costs for new lines, and because solvents are absent, no pollution problems. Some odor may be apparent during hot-melt operations due to thermal decomposition of the molten polymer. Other advantages inherent in this technique are enumerated in Table 12. The concept of applying an adhesive as a hot melt also has some shortcomings, including the sensitivity of certain substrates to heat and streaking caused by contaminants in the coating. The most serious disadvantages, however, are product deficiencies. To quote a recent industry survey.

It is irrefutable that today's hot melt pressure sensitive adhesive technology is inferior to the wider spectrum of end-use adhesive properties that can be achieved on tapes and label from solvent based and water based pressure sensitive adhesives. Hot melt pressure sensitive adhesives are inferior to the best liquid adhesives in light color, high and low-temperature strength, durability, electrical properties, and outdoor weatherability.

While today's hot melt pressure-sensitive technology cannot possibly duplicate the end use adhesive properties of high-performance PS taps and labels, they can and will duplicate the end use adhesive properties of low and medium performance PS tapes and labels.

A concise review of the history of HMPSA development, with emphasis on the basic polymers and compositions employed, has been published.

For all intents and purposes, commercial HMPSA compositions are limited to block copolymers, such as S-I-S or styrene butadienestyrene (S-B-S), which account for about 90% of usage. These products go primarily into tapes and labels. An excellent review of the characteristics of the thermoplastic A-B-A block copolymers in adhesives has been published .

Table 14. Hot Melt Pressure Sensitive Adhesive Based on S-I-S

Ingredient	Percent
S-I-S (Kraton 1107 rubber)	32.8
Midblock resin (Wingtack 95)	32.8
Plasticizing oil (Shellflex 371)	13.1
Endblock resin (Cumar LX-509)	19.7
Stabilizer (zinc dibutyldithiocarbamate)	1.6

Adhesive characteristic	Value
Shear adhesion failure temperature (^{0}F)	220
Rolling ball tack (PSTC-6) (cm)	1.8
Probe tack (g)	1100
180^0 peel adhesion (PSTC-1) (pli)	3.7
Melt viscosity at 350^0 F (cP)	40,000

One important characteristic of such copolymers is that the polystyrene and polybutadiene (or polyisoprene) segments are in separate physical phases. When other components, such as plasticizers and tackifier resins, are present they may tend to associate preferentially with one phase or the other thereby influencing the adhesive properties. An example of a formulation of an HMPSA based on an S-I-S polymer is given in Table 14. This composition was achieved by balancing the use of components which interact with either the two polystyrene end blocks or the polyisoprene midblock.

Other products which are used to a lesser degree in HMPSAs include ethylene vinyl acetate (EVA), ethylene ethyl acrylate (EEA, and amorphous polypropylene. These material find use in applications which have lower performance requirements, such as floor tiles and will coverings.

Acrylics have long been viewed as superior PSAs, but attempts to develop hot-melt versions of these products have not met with appreciable commercial success thus far. However, newer products are being made available which may overcome some of the earlier deficiencies. Outstanding color, clarity, resistance to degradation by UV light, and an ability to be melt processed in air are claimed to be available in one such product. Further improvements in this area could lead to acrylics capturing a significant share of the HMPSA market. A comparison of the overall properties of acrylics with the widely used rubber resins is given in Table 15.

Table 15. Comparative Properties of HMPSAs

Property	Rubber resin a (unsaturated)	Thermoplastic acrylic b
Peel	High	High
Tack	High	Moderate
Shear	High	Low
O^2 stability	Poor	Excellent
UV stability	Poor	Excellent
Heat resistance	Poor	Poor
Plasticizer resistance	Poor	Excellent
Solvent resistance		
Hydrocarbons	Poor	Good
Oxygenated	Good	Poor
Blead tendency	Moderate-low	None
Melt thermal stability	Good	Good-poor
Cost	Low	Moderate

a Styrene-isoprene styrene block copolymer tackifier with rosin ester and hydrocarbon.
b Low molecular-weight polymer containing a large portion of 2-ethylhexyl acrylate.

VII. RADIATION CURING

Curing by UV or electron beam (EB) radiation is the second of two techniques directed at preparing PSAs without evaporating solvents or carriers. In making a PSA, a properly formulated fluid composition will be applied to an appropriate substrate, such as Mylar, polymerlzed by a few second exposure to a radiation source, and thus converted from a low-strength composition to a tacky, higher-strength adhesive taps with little loss of volatiles. This approach has several potential advantages to offer.

No disposal of solvents into the atmosphere.
Extremely low energy requirements.
High line speeds.
Compact operation.
Heat-sensitive substrates may be used.
Improved adhesive adhesion to substrate due to grafting.

Furthermore, radiation curing has certain advantages over hot-melt technology including greater formulating versatility, inherent thermal stability through chemical crosslinking, and case of coating due to lower viscosities. In fact, radiation is often cited as a means of improving properties of hot melts, as will be discussed later in this section.

Table 16. Comparison of EB and UV Cure

Equipment cost is an order of magnitude larger for EB as compared to UV.
Operating skill requirements higher for EB than UV.
Maintenance costs may be higher for EB.
EB generally utilizes more nitrogen inserting than UV.
Residual monomer tends to be less with EB.
Adhesion to substrates is better with EB.
EB can penetrate pigmented or opaque materials including some laminates.
Fasters line speeds possible with EB.
EB will cure a broader array of functional groups than UV.

In its simplest form, the concept of preparing PSAs by radiation curing is potentially superior to all other methods because the conversion from monomer to polymer can take place directly on the substrate when it is irradiated, whereas solution, emulsion, or hot-melt techniques require the preparation or isolation of the polymer prior to coating. Although example of direct conversion from monomer to PSA polymer have appeared in the literature, in practive neither this nor other variants of radiation curing for PSAs have been much utilized, and only a small percentage of such products is being manufactured this way.

Radiation curing has not captured a larger share of this market for complex reasons that involve the following elements.

Technology less well developed than for alternative techniques a broad array of materials and properties not available.

Raw materials costs tend to be high.

Unreacted monomer residues may remain after cure.

Highly reactive monomers (acrylates) used may be toxic and can lead to sensitization and skin burns.

Inert gas blanketing required in some instances adds to cost,

Yet, the advantages of radiation curing are undeniable, and research is actively continuing on several facets of this technique, including the crosslinking of hot melts.

Both UV light and EB radiation have been widely used for the cure of PSAs. Each of these approaches has its advantages and disadvantages as elucidated in Table 16.

The simplest menas of preparing a PSA, irradiating monomer alone, is rarely employed due to coating problems resulting from the low viscosity of the system, incomplete polymerization, and inadequate properties. Irradiation usually results in a low degee of polymerization due to the simultaneous generation of numerous initiating sites. To overcome these problems, other components are utilized to provide increased molecular weight at the start or sites for grafting or cross linking. Thus, most radiation curable adhesive systems are made up of monofunctional monomers,polymerization monomers, oligomers, and reactive or nonreactive resins which, on irradiation, develop desirable adhesive properties through rapid polymerization. System that are to be photocured also require a photoinitiator or photosensitizer, which absorbs the impinging light and induces polymerization. Electron-beam-cured formulations do not require these initiators, however.

The literature on radiation curable PSA composition was reviewed. The majority of compositions utilized for radiation curable PSAs has contained acrylate components in the form of monomers or polymers.

An example is known in which PSAs were prepared by radiation of monomers alone. In this case, a blend of butyl acrylate containing 9% acrylic acid was applied at a thickness of 50 m to an aluminum foil and subjected to 5 Mradsof EB radiation. The resulting PSA displayed a 180^0 peel strength of .42 lb./in. and a dead load shear time of 10 hr.

The preparation of PSAs by UV cure of solutions comprised of acrylate monomers containing a small amount (5%) of a polyvinyl alkyl ether has been described. More recent work has discussed the advantages of using higher levels of polyvinyl alkyl ethers. Excellent PSA properties have been obtained with compositions based on both monofunctional and multifunctional acrylates with polyvinyl alkyl ethers. Excellent properties were also observed when using other polyalkyl ethers. such as poly (alkylene oxides).

More commonly, acrylic polymers have been utilized as the sole or major components of radiation-curable adhesive systems. These acrylics have include a homopolymer and many example of copolymers. One UV cured acrylic ester copolymer system cited was claimed to have 180^0 peel strengths of 4.8-5.5 lb./in.

Radiation-curable systems based on copolymers of vinyl acetate and 2-ethylhexyl acrylate have been reported more frequently than other composition and have sometimes been applied by hot-melt techniques. These PSAs have shown 180^0 peel strengths ranging from about 1.5 to 3 lb./in, when cured by either UV or EB radiation.

Normally, a small amount of a photoinitiator is required to cure UV systems efficiently. Several patents have described the use of specially prepared monomers or polymers which contain built-in photoinitiator.

Table 17. Hot Melt Pressure Sensitive Adhesives Cross linked by EB Radiation

Composition[a]	Percent
S-I-S (Kraton 1107 rubber)	39.6
Resin	39.6
Plasticizing oil (Shellflex 371)	9.9
Stabilizer (butyl zimate)	0.8
Trimethylolpropane trimethacrylate	9.9

	Radiation dose (Mrads)		
Property	0	5	10
Peel temperature, limit (c)	110	>200	>200
Gel	0	tight	tight
Rolling ball tack (cm)	2	5	15
Polyken probe tack (g)	200	400	400
Holding power to steel (min)	5	50	200

[a]Coated on Kimberly Clark crepe paper at approximately 90 gm/m^2. Cured with Energy Sciences Electrocurtain equipment.

Not surprisingly, solutions of acrylic polymers in acrylic and vinyl monomers have also been used as radiation-curable PSAs.

Although acrylates have received the most attention a number of other polymer types have been reported in radiation-curable PSAs. Several systems have contained polybutadiene and its copolymers, particularly SBR. Other rubber bases utilized have included those derived from natural sources, polyisobutylene, and silicones.

In addition, components such as tackifiers, fillers, and (meth) acrylate monomers have been employed in these rubber based systems.

Ethylene copolymers, specifically EVA ethylene 5-ethylidene-2 norbornene propylene, have been used with tackifiers. Pressure-sensitive adhesives based on an entirely different type of chemistry, namely polythiol-ene adducts, have also been patented. A UV cured system of this type has been reported to exhibit a 180^0 peel strength of 3.5 lb./in.

Radiation curing is also being used increasingly to upgrade the PSA properties of compositions which contain substantial amounts of polymer. This technique is of particular interest for correcting some of the deficiencies of hot melt adhesives based on the thermoplastic A-B-A copolymers. In contrast to other types of PSAs which can be chemically crosslinked by post heating, but-melt products must be largely free of such bonds in order to be melt processable. However, the hot-melt processing of an adhesive which contains a radiation initiated crosslinking component would be a desirable approach to this problem. Because radiation-curable crosslinking agents may also gel when heated, it is necessary to minimize the thermal abuse of such compositions during processing. A successful demonstration of such a process was recently described. On being exposed under nitrogen to a high energy EB, the coated product crosslinked with resultant improvements in both solvent and temperature resistance (Table 17). Without the use of the multifunctional acrylate, relatively little change in properties was observed on irradiation. Rolling ball tack was reduced on radiation, but the resultant properties are claimed to be comparable to the performance of commercial, high-temperature masking tape based on crosslinked natural rubber.

As desirable as the foregoing property improvements may be, they suffer from the disadvantage of requiring the installation of a separate radiation cure device in addition to a hot melt coater. Despite this, however, the use of radiation curing is expected to grow appreciably in the years ahead.

VIII. COATING METHODS

There are a number of coating techniques being used to apply PSAs. The selection of the type of equipment best suited to a specific situation will depend on several factors.

Types and thickness of the web.
Nature of the adhesive: solvent, aqueous, hot-melt
Viscosity of the adhesive
Adhesive thickness and thickness uniformity required

Jacobs, in a discussion of "Fundamentals to Consider in Selecting Coating Metals,"points out that to select the coating method most suitable for a specific application, it is first necessary to know the physical properties of the web and coating to be used and to correlate these with the fundamental characteristics of the coating method.

Grant classifies coating equipment as follows:

Equipment that applies an excess of coating to the web and wipes off the excess leaving a desired amount on the surface.

Equipment that applies a predetermined amount of coating to the surface of the web.

Equipment that saturates the web in a bath and removes the excess coating from the surface by some metering method.

The following are common types of equipment used for the application of PSAs today.

Reverse roll coater. As the name implies, the reverse roll coater apply the coating with a roll rotating in the reverse direction to the travel of the web. They very both as to the number of rolls and the roll configuration. The adhesive is fed either from a pan, via a pickup roll, or from a dam between the metering roll and applicator roll. Reverse roll coater are capable of applying adhesives of low viscosity using a pan fed pickup and adhesives of viscosities >10,000 cP using a damfed arrangement. Reverse roll coater are particularly suited to film thicknesses > 1 mil wet and are not recommended for application of a film < 1 mil thick. The principal limitation of reverse roll coater is the degree of accuracy with which they are built and, in turn, provide a coating thickness with a minimum variation in coat weight.

Gravure coaters. Gravure coaters are built in either a two-roll or three roll vertical design. The bottom roll, which is generally the engraved roll, rotates in the coating pan. An oscillating docter bladeremoves the excess, leaving the coating material only in the recesses of the engraved roll. This premetered quantity of coating is then transferred directly to the web in a two-roll design or first to an intermediate roll in three-roll design. Gravure coating is used where relatively thin coatings (1-3 mils) are required and is best suited to smooth substrates. Gravure coating may be used to apply solvent, aqueous, and hot-melt adhesives at viscosities up to 10,000 cP. The major limitation is in applying heavy coat weights.

Wire-wound rod coating. In the wire-wound rod coating technique, the coating is applied directly to the web from the pickup roll and then metered to the desired film thickness by passing over one or a series of wire wound rods to remove the excess coating. The rods may be rotated in either direction relative to direction of web travel. Wire-wound rod coaters are relatively inexpensive and are used to apply solvent, aqueous, and hot-melt adhesives.

Knife over roll coaters. The knife over roll coater arrangement uses a driven roll to support the web under the knife, which is usually a steel bar with one ocntoured edge that contacts the web. The coating material is held behind the knife blades and contained by dams which are set for the width to be coated. As the web traverses over the roll and under the knife, the amount of coating applied is determined by the gap between the knife edge and the web. Knife over roll coaters are relatively inexpensive and are particularly useful for application of high viscosity adhesives at relatively thick films. Their major disadvantage is the inability to accurately control film thickness, and their use is generally limited to relatively slow line speeds, up to 100 fpm.

Air knife. In the air knife technique, an excess of the coating is applied to a web by an applicator roll, and the excess is removed with an air knife by a uniform jet of air impinping on the surface. The air knife. The air knife is used on all types of webs at speeds exceeding 1200 fp. The major limitation to the air knife is in the solids and viscosities it can handle. Viscosities range from 100 to 1000 cP, and its use is generally restricted to water-based systems.

Hot melt pressure sensitive adhesives are generally applied by either roll coaters, slot die coaters, or extrusion coaters. The adhesive is fed to the coating head in the molten state from either a jacketed melt mix tank or continuously through a single or twin screw extruber.

IX. TEST METHODS

A brief description of the most common tests is as follows.

Peel Adhesion (PSTC-1). The peel adhesion test is a measure of the force required to remove a pressure sensitive tape from a standard stainless steel surface when pulled at a rate of 12 in./min at an angle of 180°. A 1-in. wide tape is applied to a specified stainless steel surface under the weight of a 4.5lb. rubber. The force required to remove the tape is expressed in pli or oz./in, of tape width.

Shear or holding power (PSTC-7). The shear, or holding power, test is a measure of the cohesive strength of a PSA to resist a force applied in a direction parallel to the surface to which it has been applied. It is customarily measured in terms of the time required to pull a standard area of tape from a Test Panel under a standard load, or in terms of a distance the tape has been displaced in a given time on a test panel under a standard load. The procedure involves the application of a tape to a stainless steel surface under the weight of a 4.5 lb. rubber roller. The tape is then cut so that a specified area (usually 1 x 1 in.) remains in contact with the steel panel. The panel is the mounted in a jig at an angle of 2 from vertical to ensure that no peeling forces are acting on the tape when a specified constant load (usually 1 kg) is applied. The amount of time required for the tape to completely separate from the panel or the amount of slippage measured to the nearest 1/16 in. during a prespecified period of time is reported.

Quick stick (PSTC-5). The quick stick test is designed to measure the ability of a pressure-sensitive tape to adhere under minimum pressure. In this test, the tape is placed in contact with a standard stainless steel panel under no pressure other the weight of the tape itself. The panel is then placed in a special jig which allows the panel to move and maintain a constant 90^0 angle with the tape during the test. The force required to remove the tape at a rate of 12 in./ min at a 90^0 angle is reported in pli or oz./in. of width.

Rolling ball tack (PSTC-6). The rolling ball tack test is designed to measure the surface tack of a PSA. It consists of allowing a 7/16-in. diameter steel ball to roll from an inclined plane onto the adhesive surface. The greater the degree of tack, the shorter the distance the will travel.

Probe tack. The probe tack test consists of bringing a metal probe of specified diameter into contact with the adhesive surface under a given load for a specified period of time. The force required to separate the probe from the adhesive is a measure of surface tack. A device for measuring probe tack called the Polyken Probe Tack Tester has been described.

5

WATER BASED ADHESIVES

INTRODUCTION

Continuing environmental and economic pressures on solvent-based adhesives will greatly increase the market potential for water-based adhesives. Quite a variety of water-based adhesives exists today. They range from pressure-sensitive adhesives to high-strength, contact-bond adhesives.

Some of the current uses of water-based adhesives are labels, packaging, wood bonding, fabric bonding, panel lamination, high pressure laminate bonding, construction mastics, bonding of floor and wall tile, and tapes.

There are several types of water-based adhesives. This chapter deals mainly with water-dispersed synthetic rubber adhesives although other types of systems are discussed. Chemistry and formulating are discussed. Information is provided on applying, drying, and bonding of water-based adhesives. Physical and performance properties of water and solvent-based adhesives are compared, and end uses for adhesives based on several types of polymer are given. Characteristics of water-based adhesives are discussed, and techniques for adhesive selection are reviewed.

2. TYPES OF WATER BASED ADHESIVES

In general, the area of water-based adhesives can be divided into two broad categories: water-soluble and water-dispersed products. Water-soluble adhesives include the animal glues, vegetable glues, and other (natural) systems [1]. Water-dispersed adhesives include those based on natural rubber lattices, synthetic-rubber (polymer) lattices, and postformed-rubber (polymer) lattices.

Natural latex refers to material obtained primarily from the rubber tree. Synthetic lattices are aqueous dispersions of polymers obtained by the process of emulsion polymerization. These include polymers of chloroprene, butadiene-styrene butadiene-acrylonitrile, vinyl acetate, acrylate, vinyl chloride, etc. Molecular weights range from 10,000 to 1,000,000, and particle sizes range from 0.001 to 10 m. Artificial lattices are made by dispersing solid polymers. These lattices include dispersions of reclaim rubber, butyl rubber, styrene-butadiene rubber (SBR), rosin, rosin derivatives, asphalt, coal tar, and a large number of synthetic resins derivatives, asphalt, coal tar, and a large number of synthetic resins derived from coal tar and petroleum.

Since the majority of the solution-type adhesives remain water-soluble after drying, their use is restricted to those areas that do not require water resistance in the final bond. Most water dispersed adhesives cannot be redispersed in water after they have once dried and can, therefore, be used in applications that require water resistance. It is expected that of the two types of adhesive, the water-dispersed types are the ones which will replace solvent based adhesives.

3. CHEMISTRY AND FORMULATING OF WATER-DISPERSED ADHESIVES

In addition to the base polymer, all three types of water-dispersed adhesives contain a variety of other materials designed to impart specific properties to the adhesive. These materials, can include emulsifiers, surfactants, tackifiers, antioxidants, fillers, thickeners, antifoams, freeze-thaw stabilizers, corrosion inhibitors, etc.

A. Natural Rubber Lattices

The natural rubbers are combined with tackifying resins and antioxidants to obtain pressure-sensitive adhesives. The tackifiers are anionic or nonionic resin emulsions that cause the rubber particles to swell and soften by virtue of their mutual solubility. These resins include polyterpenes, aliphatics based on petroleum feedstock, esterified-hydrogenated rosins and others.

B. Synthetic-Rubber (Polymer) Lattices

The majority of today's water-dispersed adhesives fall into into the category of synthetic-rubber lattices.

1. *Neoprene lattices.* The polychloroprene materials, produced by E.I. Du Pont and others, are obtained by emulsion-polymerization techniques and have predominantly the trans 1,4, configuration. Solids usually range from 40-60% with molecular weight,chain branching, gel, and crystallinity differing from product to product. Copolymers of 2-chloro-1,3 butadiene and monomers like 2,3 dichloro 1,3, butadiene, acrylonitrite, methacrylic acid, and others

are commercially available able and provide specific property modifications. The neoprenes are generally combined with rosin dodifiers, adhesion promoters, crosslinking agents, antioxidants, and other materials to obtain high-performance adhesives. Resins used to modify neoprene include the terpenes, terpene phenolics, coumarone indenes, t-butylphenolics, rosin esters, pentaerythritol, and resorcinol formaldehyde types. These modifiers can provide adhesion to specific substrates, increase autoadhesion, increase open times, and reduce rawmaterial costs. Adhesion promoters are used commonly and include colloidal silicas for bonding glass, metals, and leather; blocked isocyanates for bonding elastomers, and synthetic fabrics; proteins, and other materials for obtaining specific adhesion. The varied crosslinking agents used include metal oxides, methyl ureas, melamines, epoxy resins, and others.

2. *Styrene-butadiene rubber lattices.* The SBR materials are obtained by emulsion-polymerization techniques finest developed by Bayer in 1912 and improved for large-scale production in later years. Carboxylated SBRs provide an excellent range of polymer properties. Their high tensile and elongation, excellent water resistance, excellent aging stability, and out standing adhesion to fibers make them the materials of choice in many synthetic-fiber adhesive applications. As with the carboxylated neoprenes, the carboxylated SBRs provide a mechanism for self-curing and are, therefore, useful in many high performance adhesive applications.

3. *Acrylic lattices.* The acrylic materials are also obtained by emulsion polymerization techniques and usually consist of copolymers or terpolymers. Many types of properties are possible, depending on the monomers utilized, ranging from pressure sensitive adhesives (PSAs) to high-performance adhesives. Typically, the waterborne acrylic lattices have provided PSAs with unusually varied properties. With the appropriate monomer-to-charge ratios, crosslinking mechanisms may be synthetically incorporated to regulate tack, shear, and cohesive strength. In these systems the molecular weight, glass transition temperature Tg, polarity, and functionally are also very important in providing the final required PSA properties.

Acrylics have fundamental properties in the area of ultraviolet (UV) resistance, thermal stability, and plasticizer resistance. Enhancement of these basic properties may be obtained using a variety of crosslinking or curing mechanisms. Monomers, such as acrylamide, N-methylolacrylamide, glycidylmethacrylate, and dimethylaminoethylacrylate, are commonly used to provide internal curing sites. Zinc acetate, urea-formaldehyde, and sodium carbonate or sodium sesquicarbonate may also be considered for use as external crosslinkers.

More recently acrylic lattices have been considered the basis for higher performance adhesives. Particular acrylic polymers with Tgs in the range of 0-10^0 C have been tackified to give green strength, open time, adhesion to nonporous substrates, and high-temperature resistance.

4. Other lattices. Other synthetic-rubber (polymer) lattices that are used as water based adhesives include the butadiene acrylonitrile copolymers, polyvinyl acetates, vinyl-acetatevinyl-chloride-copolymers, ethylene-vinyl acetate copolymers, ethylene acrylic acid copolymers, polyurethanes, carboxylated butadiene vinylidene chloride copolymers, and many others.

Postformed Rubber (Polymer) Lattices

Reclaim rubber is recovered from fabricated rubber products, such as automobile tires and tubes. These materials are broken down, devulcanized, and dispersed in water to give high-solids, latex or mactic adhesives. Often they are combined with asphalt for use in the automotive and construction markets as sealers as well as adhesives.

Another type of postformed rubber latex is the butyl-rubber system. Here the monomer is solution polymerized and dispersed in water. The organic solvent is removed. The latex is then generally formulated at a manner similar to those lattices derived from emulsion polymerization.

IV. FILM FORMATION OF WATER DISPERSED ADHESIVES

In the wet state, the particles of polymer, resin, and other modifiers in water-dispersed adhesives exist as individual particles. These particles coalesce into a homogeneous film during the drying operation (Fig. 1).

The most consistent theory on film formation of water dispersed adhesives is the one proposed by Vanderholft. Initially, there is a uniform rate of water loss until particles begin to contact each other and coalesce. This phase is followed by a period of decreasing rate of water loss during which particle coalescence becomes irreversible. Finally, an exponentially decreasing rate of water loss occurs through capillary action and/or diffusion. Heat treating ar air-dried film of water-dispersed adhesive will allow the polymer rubber particles to intermix and will provide improved adhesive properties. This is normally accomplished in the usual process of force drying.

Fluid Properties

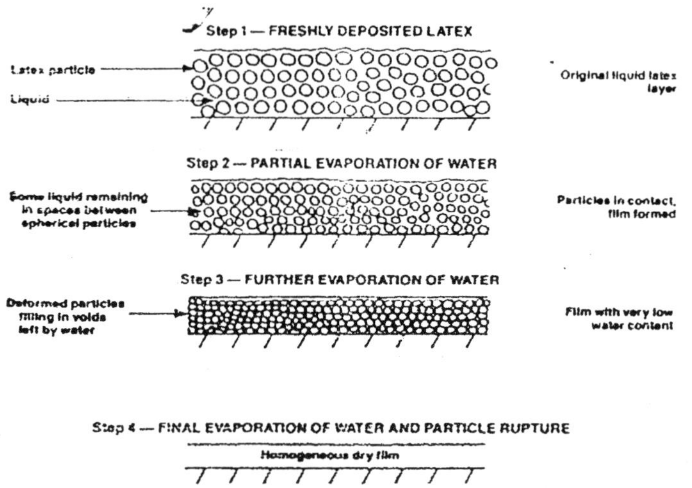

Fig. 1. Film formation of water-dispersed adhesives.

V. APPLICATION OF LATEX ADHESIVES

The normal methods of adhesive application-spray, roll, curtain, flow, brush, and knife coating can be used with latex adhesives. The allowable application methods are governed by certain properties of the adhesives, including viscosity, mechanical shear stability degree of foaming, size and shape of parts to be coated, and the required production rate (Fig. 2).

A. Spraying

Spraying is one of the fastest, most economical methods of applying adhesive to large areas. Three means of application are

1. Air spraying. The most common spray method, air spraying, is usually equated with a paint sprayer. Adhesive is atomized by high air velocity, while relatively low pressure is used to pump adhesive to the spray tip. Air spraying provides a uniform adhesive film of varying texture.

2. Airless spraying. When airless spraying is used, adhesive is atomized by high adhesive velocity and ejected under pressures ranging from 1500 to 3000 psi. No air pressure is directly involved. The high-velocity adhesive is atomized when it strikes the air surrounding the spray tip. Spray pattern depends on the type of spray tip on the gun.

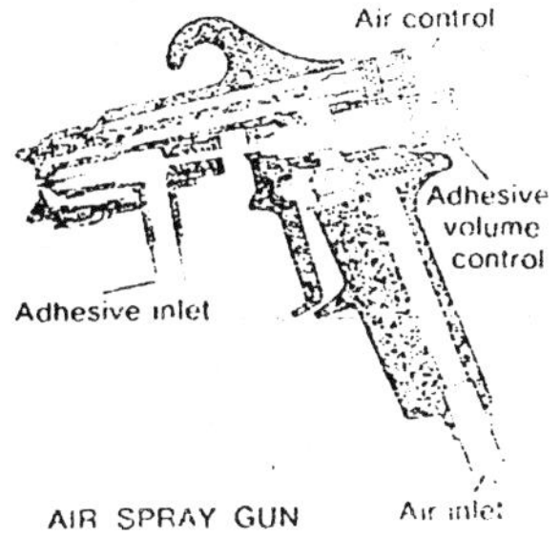

Airless Spray

Automatic

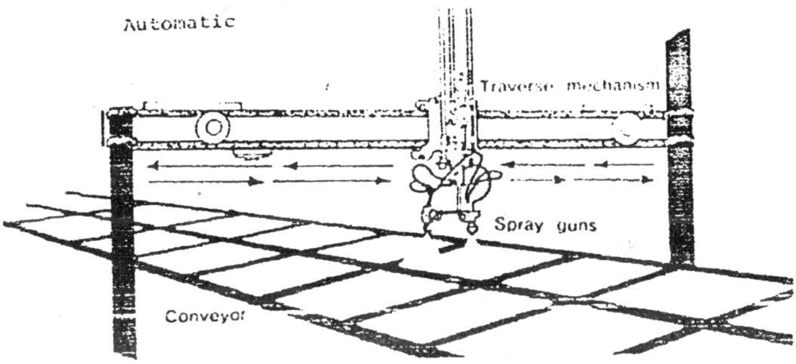

(a)

Fig. 2. Application of latex adhesives. (a) Spraying; (b) Roll coating; (c) Curtain coating; (d) Flow coating; (e) Knife coating.

3. Automatic spray equipment. Large and fast production runs, where the parts are brought to the equipment, can make effective use of automatic spray equipment.

Some latex adhesives can be coagulated by high shear, certain metals, and solvents. Pumps that do not subject the adhesive to a shearing action, such as a diaphragm pump, are normally used. Hoses should be nylon-or polyethylene-lined. Packings and glands in contact with the adhesive should be made of Teflon. All pipe fittings should be plastic, stainless steel, or nickel plated.

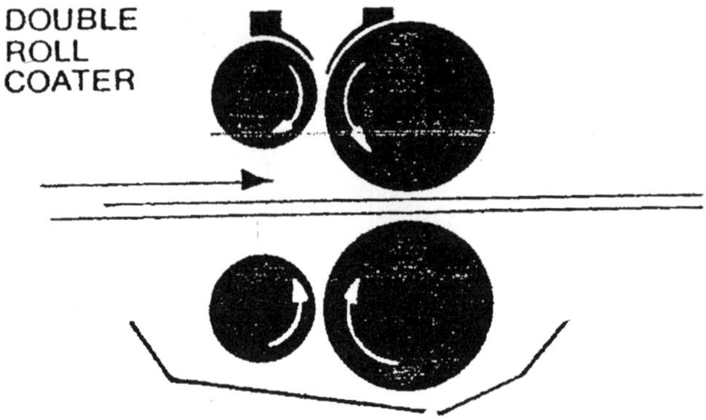

(b)

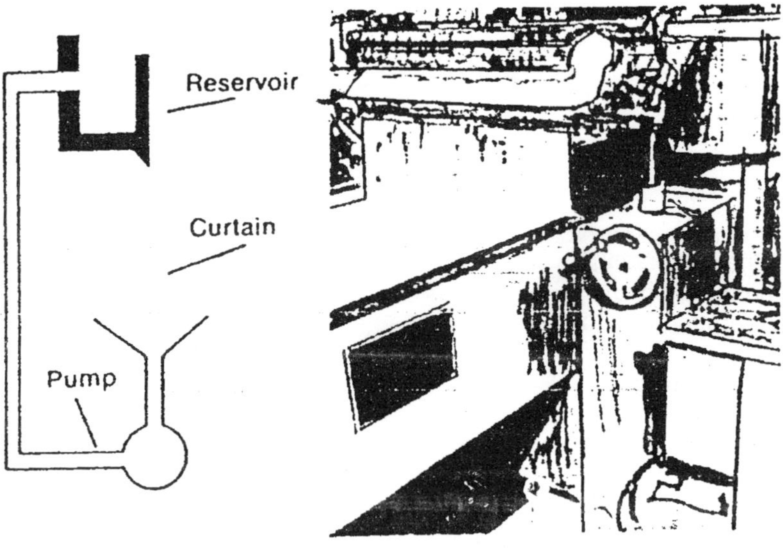

(c)

Fig. 2. (Continued)

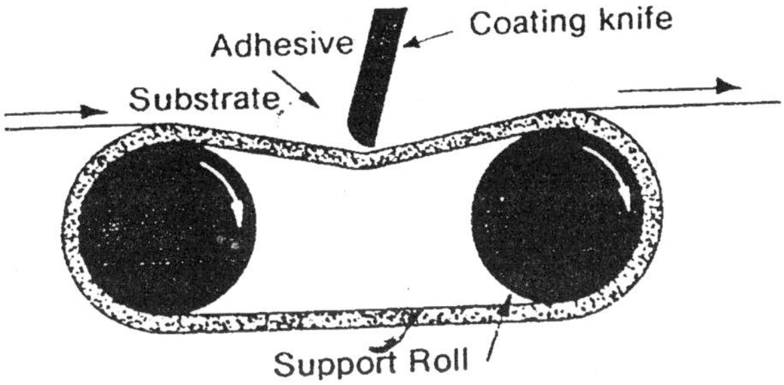

If the equipment was previously used for handling solvent based products, the hoses should be replaced before using a latex adhesive since solvent absorption into the hose could coagulation of the adhesive.

Roll Coating

For low-volume production or small jobs, paint rollers are convenient applicators. For high-volume or multistation production, pressure fed hand rollers are available.

Roll coating is used on large, flat areas when large volume and fast production are required. Line speeds of 50 60 ft./min are common. The adhesive is transferred from the surface of the roll to the substrate. Double roll coaters coat from both sides of the substrate simultaneously.

The quantity of adhesive applied is usually controlled by using an engraved roll. The latex adhesive must be designed to prevent excessive foaming during the coating operation since foaming will prevent the roll from depositing the desired quantity of adhesive. Excessive foaming can also present a housekeeping problem.

C. Curtain Coating

Curtain coating is faster than roll coating, but only one side of the substrate can be coated at a time. A wide and continuous waterfall of specially formulated adhesive coats the substrate as it passes under neath. Film thickness is controlled by the adhesive solids content and the speed of the substrate. This method is most useful with broad surfaces.

D. Flow Coating

Equipment for flow coating varies with production requirements. For high-speed production, a continuous flow gun is used. A remotely operated pump maintains constant pressure and adhesive flow. For intermediate or low volume applications, hand operated caulking-type guns are satisfactory. A collapsible tube filled with adhesive is the simplest piece of flow equipment.

E. Brushing

The use of a paint brush is common for small-area applications. For higher production rate, a flow brush is recommended. A flow brush is pressure-fed and is usually recommended for continuous application. Intermittent application permits the adhesive to dry on the bristles.

F. Knife Coating

Knife coating, with a mechanically driven unit, is used to apply high viscosity adhesives at high production rates. Adhesive is applied to the substrate in excess. The substrate then passes under the knife, and all adhesive, except the required amount, is removed. The knife spreads and meters the adhesive.

The simplest version of knife coating is a patty knife used with a mastic adhesive for small jobs. Trowels are used for larger-area applications, such as floors.

VI. BONDING TECHNIQUES

The bonding techniques used for latex adhesives are about the same as those used for solvent adhesives: wet bonding, open time bonding, contact bonding, and solvent reactivation.

The bonding technique used depends on the parts being joined, the adhesive itself, the immediate bond-strength requirements, and temperature and humidity conditions. All methods cannot be used with all types of latex adhesives.

A. Wet Bonding

When the wet bonding technique is used, at least one of the bonding materials must be porous. Appropriate materials include wood, masonry, fabric, most flexible foams, leather, cardboard, fiberglass, felt, and cork.

It is usually necessary to apply adhesive to only one surface. The surfaces to be bonded are assembled while the adhesive is still wet. Immediate bond strength is usually low. In some cases it may be necessary to keep the parts being joined under pressure until enough strength has developed for subsequent handling.

B. Open-Time Bonding

Open time bonding is a technique in which the adhesive in applied to both surfaces and allowed to stand (open) until suitable tack or stickiness has been achieved. This technique works best when at least one surface material is porous or semiporous. It is probably the most widely used method of making small-or medium-sized bonds. The simplest test to determine the right tack is to touch the adhesive with the knuckle. If the adhesive feels sticky and does not transfer to knuckles, it is ready. This method cannot be used with some types of latex adhesives that go directly from the wet to the dry state without passing through a tacky range.

C. Contact Bonding

Both surfaces are coated for contact bonding, and the adhesive is permitted to become dry to the touch. Within a given time, these surfaces can be pressed together, and nearly ultimate bond strength is immediately achieved. Contact bonding is preferred which bonding two non-poroussur surfaces. Contact-bond-adhesives are usually based on specially compounded neoprene lattices. Drying times prior to bonding are about 30 min under ordinary conditions of temperature and humidity. This time can be reduced to seconds by force drying with heat.

D. Solvent Reactivation

In bonding by solvent reactivation, the adhesive is applied to the surface of the part and let dry. To prepare for bonding, the adhesive is reactivated by wiping with solvent or placing the part on a solvent impregnated pad. The surface of the adhesive tackifies, and the parts to be bonded are pressed together. The tack range is short, so the technique is useful for relatively small-sized applications. It is not generally applicable on large surface areas since the short bonding range gives inconsistent result.

E. Heat Reactivation

Heat reactivation involves the application of a thermoplastic adhesive to one or both surfaces. After the adhesive has dried, coated parts may be stored several weeks or longer before bonding. To prepare a part for bonding, it is heated until the adhesive is soft and tacky. The bond is made under pressure while the adhesive is hot. On cooling, bond strength is as good as the adhesive will provide. This method is used with nonporous, heat-resistant materials when ultimate bond strength is quickly needed.

Heat reactivation can also be a continuous, in-line operation. The adhesive is applied in liquid form to a film or sheet, force dried to remove the water, and then laminated to a second surface while still hot. Temperatures are usually in the range of 250-350 °F.

VII. FORCED DRYING OF LATEX ADHESIVES

The heat of vaporization of water is 540 cal/g. The compares to about 100 cal/g for the common solvents used in adhesives (Table 1)

When bonding high-pressure laminate to plywood, a water-based latex contact adhesive requires about a 30 min drying time at 75° F and 50% rh. Under the same conditions, a solvent-based contact adhesive requires a drying time of about 10 min. Under very high humidity conditions, the latex adhesive will not dry at all. The drying time for the solvent adhesive will be extended, but it will eventually dry.

Table 1. Table of Solvent Properties

Solvent	Heat of vaporization (cal /g)	Evaporation rate (ethyl ether =1)a
Hexane	88	1.9
Toluene	87	4.5
Xylene	82	9.2
1,1,1-Trichloroethane	59	2.6
Acetone	125	1.9
Methyl ehtyl ketone	106	2.7
Ethyl alcohol	204	7.0
Ethyl acetate	102	2.7
Water	540	45.0

a Higher numbers indicate siower drying.

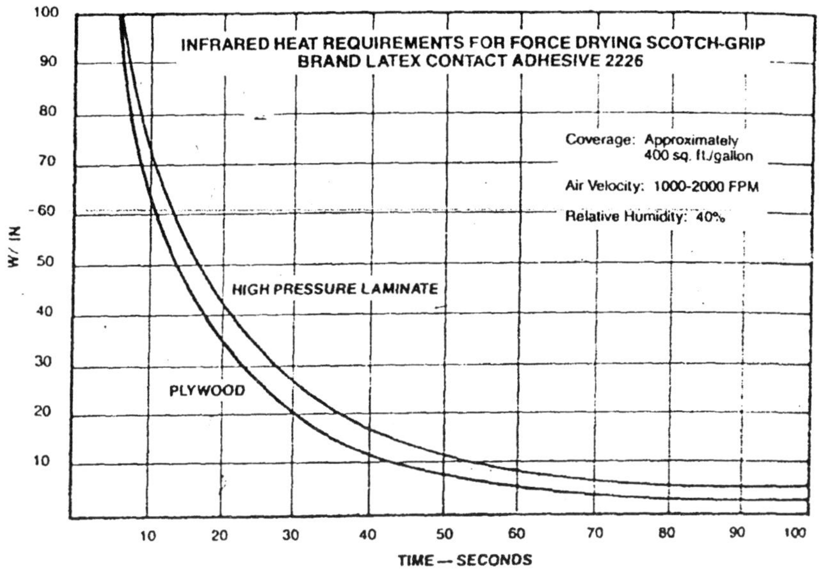

Fig. 3. Infrared heat requirements for force drying Scotch-Grip Brand Latex Contact Adhesive 2226.

When the contact-bonding technique is used and high-humidity conditions exist or a high production rate is required, it is necessary to force dry the adhesive prior to bonding.

One of the most efficient methods of drying latex adhesives is through the use of an infrared heat source in conjunction with air flow over the adhesive. As the water evaporates, air movement reduces the high humidity directly above the adhesive surface and speeds the drying.

Infrarcd heat sources are usually specified by a certain wattage per unit. Total wattage is expressed as KW/ft.^{2} or W/in.^{2}. Unite are commercially available with capacities up to 100 w/in^2. With equipment of this type, neoprene latex contact adhesives can be dried in a few seconds even on heat-sensitive substrates, such as polystyrene foam (Fig .3). The rate of drying enables line speeds for latex adhesives to equal those normally used for solvent adhesives.

VIII. PROPERTIES OF LATEX ADHESIVES VERSUS SOLVENT BASED ADHESIVES

The overall strength properties of a latex adhesive based on a given polymer will be similar to those of a solvent-based adhesive containing a solution polymer of like composition.

The solids content of a latex adhesive is normally in the 40-50% range. This range compares to about 20-30% for solvent-based-adhesives.

Since latex adhesives contain little, if any, organic solvent, they are usually cheaper than a comparable solvent system. The cost differential becomes even greater, in favor of the latex adhesive, if the comparison is made to a nonflammable solvent adhesive that contains expensive chlorinated solvents.

Latex adhesives have good brushability and usually require less pressure for pumping or spraying then solvent-based adhesives. Prior to drying they can be cleaned up with water. They are nonflammable in the wet state, and the vapors are nontoxic.

In most cases, latex adhesives must be protected from freezing during shipment and storage. Some materials will recover after freezing, but most of them will coagulate and become unusable.

Solvent-based adhesives tend to have better overall adhesion to substrates such as oily surfaces, metal, rubber, and certain plastics.

IX. APPLICATIONS FOR VARIOUS TYPES OF LATEX ADHESIVES

Latex adhesives, based on neoprene rubber, are popular as general adhesives because they offer an excellent balance of properties. Products based on neoprenes were the original contact adhesives. Some of their properties are

1. The contact-bond characteristic which allows two nonporous surfaces to be joined without trapping water
2. Very high strength immediately after bond
3. Excellent resistance to continuous load stress
4. Good elevated-temperature strengths
5. Excellent film aging.

Neoprene contact adhesives are used to bond foamed plastic, plastic laminate, wood, plywood, wallboard, wood veneer, plaster, canvas, leather, and many other substrates. They are not normally recommended for use on metal substrates. Neoprene latex adhesives with high elevated temperature strength and with metal adhesion are under development. Typical uses include desk tops, hollow-core wood doors, countertops, etc.

Adhesives based on styrene-butadiene lattices are among the lowest cost rubber-based adhesives, but they are not as strong as neoprene latex adhesives. They are usually used to bond lightweight material. These materials include synthetic and natural fabrics, felt, plastic foams, fiberglass insulation, canvas, linoleum, cardboard, cork, sponge, paper, foam rubber, and metal. Many of the latex PSAs are based on styrene-butadiene lattices. Adhesives based on butadiene-acrylonitrile latex can be formulated to have good resistance to oil, plasticizers, and gasoline. Applications include the bonding of polyvinyl chloride (PVC) film, aluminum foil, leather, wood, and metals.

Polyvinyl-acetate latex adhesives are the "white glue" of the industry. They are very versatile materials and are used extensively in the bonding of wood and paper products.

Quite a variety of latex adhesives based on acrylate polymers are available. the end uses are varied. They include PSAs laminated aluminum foil, paper, fabrics, foams, and PVC film. Other applications include adhesives for flocking and installing various types of floor coverings.

X. CHARACTERIZATION OF LATEX ADHESIVES

Latex adhesives are characterized by measuring quite a variety of physical, applications, and performance properties. Properties that are measured for any particular adhesive depend on the designed end uses for the adhesive. A few examples of some of the many properties that are measured are shown below.

A. Physical Properties

1. Solids content-weight and volume
2. Viscosity
3. Weight per gallon
4. Colour

B. Application Properties

1. Brushability, sprayability, roll coatability, etc.
2. Mechanical stability
3. Chemical stability
4. Ease of cleanup

Performance Properties

1. Wet strength
2. Bonding range
3. Required bonding pressure
4. Rate of strength build-up
5. Adhesion
6. Dynamic and static strength in peel, shear, tensile, and cleavage measured over a temperature range.
7. Freeze thaw stability
8. Bacterial resistance
9. Bond durability tests, resistance to
   a. oxidation
   b. UV light
   c. chemicals
   d. temperature humidity cycling
   e. heat aging
10. Flame spread
11. Smoke emission
12. Self extinguishing properties.

XI. ADHESIVE SELECTION

The object of adhesive selection is to find the most economical adhesive that has the desired application and performance properties.

A good place to start is with the adhesive supplier. If sufficient information about the bonding operation is provided, the supplier can submit several products for evaluation. The quality of the adhesive recommendation will be directly related to the quality of the information provided. This information should include.

1. Problem description
2. Allowable economics
3. Desired application method
4. Desired bonding method
5. Substrates to be bonded
6. Operating temperature range
7. Environmental conditions (humidity, water, fuel, UV, etc.)
8. Strength required (peel, shear, etc.)
9. Special requirements

6

TESTING OF ADHESIVES

Adhesives are tested by manufacturing people to :

1. Assist in selecting an adhesive for a particular use
2. Monitor the quality of an incoming product.
3. Confirm the effectiveness of the bonding process.

The adhesive selection process usually concerntrates on tests of joint strength. The goal is to determine which of several adhesives is the most suitable. The quality of incoming adhesives is primarily assessed by checking adhesvie properties such as viscosity, percent, solids, infrared spectrum, and bond strength. Destructive tests of joint strength are usually used to verify that the bonding process, for example, cleaning, mixing, curing, etc., has been correctly performed.

TYPES OF TESTS

A. General Requirements

Most adhesive tests of interest to manufactures can be considered tests of the adhesive material or tests of adhesive bonds. The vast majority of these tests are based upon procedures approved by the American Society of Testing and Materials (ASTM). An entire volume of their test specifications is devoted to adhesive testing (1). Whether ASTM tests or tests of your own design are used, it is imperative that the test conditions be rigorously specified in order to make comparative judgements based upon test results. Surface cleaning and other preparation, joint geometries, method and extent of mixing, method of application, fixtures utilized, and cure conditions are among the obvious variables that can effect joint strength. Repetitive tests must be carried out under identical conditions if ueful reults are to be obtained.

B. Material Tests

The most commonly used tests for properties of adhesive materials measure viscosity, shelf life, pot life, tack, cure rate, and percent solids.

1. Viscosity

Viscosity is defined as the resistance of a liquid material to flow. Adhesive viscosity is an indication of how easily pumped or spread the product will be. Viscosity may also reflect errors in compounding or excessive age of the material. Adhesives may be Newtonian, thixotropic, or nonflowable liquids. Viscosity measurements for free-flowing Newtonian or near-Newtonian adhesives are usually based on one of the following methods,

a. Volume flow cups. Volume flow cups measure the time required for a given volume of adhesive to flow through an orifice in the bottom of a metal cup containing an accurately known volume of material. Cup size and orifice diameter are chose so that the flow-out time is not more than approximately 60-90 sec. Results are reported as the time in seconds required for various volume flow cups

b. Rotating spindle method. The rotating spindle method, which is used for products which range in viscosity form 50 to 200,000 cP. measure sthe rotational resistance encountered by a metal spindle of a particular size spinning at a predetermined rate (1). The test is accurate and fairly rapid. It can be adapted to prouduction-floor conditions although it is most conveniently performed in a laboratory.

The Viscosity of thixotropic adhesives is usually determined by ASTM Standard D-2556 (1). Thixotropic materials exhibit a viscosity which is shear-rte dependent. the viscosity is determined at several different shear rates., usually with an electrically driven spindle, disk, T-bar, or coaxial cylinder rotated in the adhesive. A plot of apparent viscosity versus rotational speed is prepared, and from this plot the apparent viscosity associated with the particular rotation speed and spindle shape is obtained.

c. Extrusion. The viscosity of nonflowable products is often determined on the production floor by an extrusion test. A test of this type typically utilizes a Semco 440 nozzle attached to standard extrusion cartridge filled with the adhesive to be tested. Air at a pressure of 90-95 psi (630-665 kPa) is used to extrude a bead of the product. Viscosity is reported as the extrusion rate in grams per minute based on the average of three 10-sec extrusion trials.

2. Shelf life

The shelf life of an adhesive is usually determined by noting changes in viscosity or in bond strength which occur after periods of storage. The usual methods of determining viscosity or bond strength are used.

Time and temperature of storage, as well as the size and nature of storage containers should be agreed upon in advance by the adhesive user and supplier. There is no universally accepted change in viscosity or average bond strength which denotes a nonusable product. Any decision relating to this question should be based upon agreement reached by the supplier and user of the adhesive at the time the original adhesive selection is made.

3. Pot life

The pot life of an adhesive is that period of time over which it is actually usable. Pot life may very from minutes to hours and is clearly an important parameter. Methods of determining pot life, which, like the shelf life tests, are based upon changes in either viscosity or bond strength. Any accurate method of determining viscosity or of testing for bond strength may be used. Decisions concerning the rejection of a product because of changes in viscosity or bond strength should be based upon agreement reached between the adhesive supplier and user at the time the adhesive is originally selected. To simply say that a given percent change in viscosity makes the product unusable is not sensible. Considerable prior testing is usually required to make such a determination.

4. Tack

Tack is that characteristic of an adhesive which results in the easy sticking of an adhesive-coated surface to another surface upon contact. High-teck adhesives are those which are "sticky". A number of tack measuring devices have been used. Many of them measure the force required to separate two surfaces, one of which has been coated with the adhesive, after they have been in contact over a specified area at a specified pressure for a specified time.

Another type of tack test measures the distance that a steel ball will roll over an adhesive coated surface after the ball has traveled down an inclined plane . The higher the tack, the shorter the roll will be.

5. Cure rate

It is often desirable to know how the strength of a bond will vary with the rate of cure. A recommended practice for determining the bond strength at intervals of two fifths, three fifths, four fifths, five fifths, and six fifths of the prescribed cure time. The actual bond strength may be determined with a standard ASTM tensile test. Results are commonly reported as a graph of average breaking load versus cure time.

6. Percent solids

The solids content of an adhesive should be checked to ensure that formulation or dilution errors have not been made. Solids are usually determined by weighting a sample of the adhesive and then heating or curing it until a constant weight is obtained. Percent solids is equal to the sample weight before heating or curing multiplied by 100 and divided by the sample weight after heating or curing.

C. Joint Tests

A numbers of tests of finished bonds have proved to be of value in checking the assembly process. If bond strength suddenly decline using good ahesives, it normally indicate that something has gone awry with the surface preparation or the assembly process. Not all of the following tests need to be utilized in every situation. Lap shear and impact tests are probably the most commonly used, but the others might be chosen if they more accurately reflect the most critical stresses to which a particular product might be exposed in service.

1. Lap shear

Lap shear testing is very widely used to determine adhesive bond strength. The test which utilizes specimen is easy to carry out and is, therefore, widely used. Lap shear generates peel or cleavage sources at the ends of the bond and is, thus, a stringent measure of bond strength. Test results are reported in failing load per unit area.

2. Tensile tests

A number of tests, of which the ASTM D-897 standard is the most common, have been devised for determining the tensile strength of an adhesive bond. In all cases the specimen is loaded in nominally pure tension. Test results will be significantly lower if cleavage forces are allowed to develop in the loaded samples.

3. Peel

Peel tests measure the force required to peel a flexible substrate away from rigid or flexible material. The climbing drum peel test, which is widely used in the aircraft industry to determine bond strengths involving honeycomb sandwich structures. In all cases, it is important to specify the peel rate. Peel strength are reported in load per unit bond width.

4. Cleavage

Adhesive bonds are usually tested for resistance to cleavage failure. The bonding surfaces are 1 x 1 in. and the test requires that both adherends be rigid. The specimen is usually loaded at 500-800 lb./min. The results are reported in breaking load per unit area.

5. Impact

Impact testing measures the force required to break an adhesive bond when one adherend is rigidly held and the other is impacted, typically be a pendulum. It is often difficult to achieve reproducible results with impact testing and, as a result, the test is not widely used in production situations.

6. Fatigue

Fatigue testing of adhesive bonds is generally carried out using standard fatigue test machines and lap shear bond. The specimen is subjected to cyclic axial or bending stresses. It is important to specify the frequency, amplitude, temperature, and type of stress as well as its magnitude. Cycles to failure and the corresponding loads are plotted on coordinates of stress versus the logarithm of the cycle. The point at which the smooth curve connecting the points of minimum stress crosses the 10 million-cycle line is known as the fatigue strength.

7. Strength retention

It is often desirable to know the rate at which an adhesive bond will lose strength in service. These data are extremely difficult to obtain with much accuracy. Accelerated aging test are difficult to extrapolate to the service conditions. Nonetheless, strength retention studies are frequently used as a basis for adhesive selection since they will often identify the most durable adhesive from a list of candidate materials.

Strength-retention values may be based upon the effect of applied stresses under ambient conditions or after exposure to a controlled environment.

Stressed aging tests are important because they more accurately simulate service conditions encountered by most bonded products than simple, on-the-shelf static aging tests do. Bonds may be subjected to stress in a number of wasy, the simplest of which is probably simply hanging the specimen from a hook and attaching an object of known mass so that a constant stress is experienced by the bond.

The Alcoa Stress Test Fixture is a much more sophisticated, yet simple-to-use, device for applying stresses of various magnitudes to lap shear bonded samples. Specimens are removed at various intervals and tested in the normal way. A plot of strength versus time can give informative data about the loss of bond strength under stressed conditions.

Environmental exposure is commonly used to simulate accelerated aging of the bond. Exposure typically is to elevated temperature, water, salt spray, or various chemical solutions which will simulate the service conditions of the part. A number of standard chemicals in which bonded specimens are soaked for seven days at room temperature. The concentration of the chemical is important and should be specified. After suitable exposure, bonds may be tested in whatever manner seems appropriate for the use at hand.

7

ADHESIVE MATERIALS, FORMULATIONS & APPLICATIONS

In this chapter various types of adhesives individually have been discussed. Description of their compositions properties, manufacture, formulation and application have been incorporated.

SYNTHETIC RESIN BASED

More then 95% of total adhesive used worldwide are based on synthetic resins. These resins are high polymers prepared at plant synthetically from individual petrochemical based raw materials. Almost every type of high polymers and their derivatives have been used for making adhesives.

Phenolics Resin Adhesives

Phenolic-resins are the reaction products of phenol or substituted phenol with formaldehyde. Almost unlimited variety of resins are possible depending on the choice of phenol, the molar ratio of phenol and formaldehyde, the type and amount of catalyst used and the time and temperature of the reaction.

Resole resin

The active positions on the phenol molecule are the two ortho and one para positions. When more than one mole of phenol in the presence of an alkaline catalyst is used, resole is formed. The temperature of curing determines the final form of product, a low viscosity, water soluble liquid or a grindable solid. If the reaction is carried too far, the resol changes to gel. The reaction is conducted under controlled conditions.

Recoles or alkali catalysed resins are cured to the final or C-stage by heat; hence they are commonly called one-stage resins. The cured resin is termed as Resite. The so-called water soluble Phenolics resins are actually dispersions of resoles in alkaline solutions. Resoles are resistant to weather, boiling water and biodeterioration. Their resistance to elevated temperature is good. Their gapfilling properties are poor and inferior to Novolac resins. Their joints require a conditioning period of up to 2 days. Though durable and resistant to many solvents, bonds are brittle and prone to fracture under vibration and sudden impact. Resols are used as one pack adhesive which are heat cured.

Novolak resins

The reaction of one mole of phenol with less than one mole of formaldehyde, under acid conditions, results in a novolak resin. Novolak resin contains methylene links and are phenol terminated. Methylol and methylene ester groups that are present in resol resins are absent in a novolak. This type of resin is incapable of further reaction without the addition of more formaldehyde. This is accomplished by the addition of hexamethylene tetramine. Hexamine makes the thermoplastic novlak capable of reacting under heat to a cross linked product. In formation of novolak resins no water of reaction is evolved during cure with hexamine. Molecular weight of Phenolics novolaks are in the range of 500-900.

Novolaks are permanently soluble and fusible and curing agent must be mixed with them. Common curing agents are hexmethylene tetramine and paraformaldehyde. They are commonly known as 2-step resins. They are resistant to weather, boiling water and biodeterioration. Their resistance to elevated temperature is good, but inferior to that of heat curing Phenolics and resorcinol resins. Their excess acidity, due to poor control over acid catalyst content, often leads to wood damage on exposure to warm humid air. Durability of joints at high and low temperatures for extended periods is usually good. Their joints require conditioning period from 1-7 days according to end use. Metals require priming with a vinyl-Phenolics or rubber resin adhesive before bonding. They have good gap-filling properties. They are not recommended as structural adhesives unless glue line acidity exceeds pH 2.5.

Manufacture

A typical Phenolics -resin (Novolak) is made by a batch process in a jacketed stainless steel reaction kettle, equipped with agitator and condenser. Molten phenol and formaldehyde (37-40%) is charged to the kettle and agitation is started. For a novolak an acid catalyst is added and the batch is heated by steam with atmospheric reflux. The reaction is continued for 3-6 hours at 100^{0} C. If the resin is to be solid in solution, the solvent is slowly added to the molten resin in the still, cooled by refluxing and discharged to drums. Most of the solid resins discharged to pans are pulverized and blended with hexamine before packaging.

To make resol resin, an alkaline catalyst such as sodium hydroxide is added to the phenol and formaldehyde before heating the batch to 80-100° C. Reaction time is generally 1-3 hr. Since resol resin is capable of gelling in the still dehydration temperatures a kept below 105° C by the application of vacuum. Solid resol is discharged to resin coolers. The low molecular weight, water soluble resin is finished at as low a temperature as possible, usually about 50° C, whereas the less reactive para substituted resole can be finished at temperature as high as 120° C.

An alkali catalysed or resole resin is prepared as follows. About 35 Kg. phenol, 45.1 kg. formalin (37%) and 1.4 kg. sodium hydroxide (50%) is required for making about 53 kg of resin (90% yield). Phenol is charged first to the reactor followed by formalin and caustic solution. A vacuum of about 450 mm of mercury is maintained by means of two water ejectors operated by a 2-stage centrifugal pump. Temperature is raised to 60° C in 1.5 hours by steam heating through the heating coils. Reaction being exothermic is carefully controlled by passing cold water in the reactor coils at 60° C for 4-5 hours. The resin is cooled to 35° C and vacuum is shut off. Now 8.5 kgs of 66° Be sulphuric acid is added to neutralise the resin to a pH of 6.9 to 7.2. The resin is next dehydrated at the boiling point (98° C) by heating steam through the coils, until 27.3 Kg of water is removed. The batch is cooled and filtered or settled to remove the precipitated sodium sulphate. The resin is then pumped to storage tanks.

The method of preparation of Novolak resin is as described 42 kg. of phenol at 60-6°5 C and 37-40% formaldehyde (27 kgs) at about 40° C are charged to the reaction kettle, 0.1 kg of sulphuric acid is then added and the batch tested for pH. The steam is turned no so that temperature rises to such an extent that the exothermic reaction sets in and ten steam supply is stopped. The reaction takes place at about 60-85° C depending upon the acidity. Mild reactions may be allowed to heat up to atmospheric reflux, while the more strongly exothermic reactions (at lower pH) will be held at 85-90° C by vacuum reflux, until the initial reaction has subsided. When the large part of water has been removed and batch temperature has resin to 120-150° C, vacuum is applied to remove the remaining moisture and some unreacted phenol. The final dehydration temperature will range from 140-160° C and final vacuum will be up to 600-650 mm of mercury. The exact point at which the distillation to be stopped is gauged by a control test made on a sample taken from the kettle. When the resin is complete it is pumped to storage.

For making Novolak resins the ratio of formaldehyde to phenol is usually 0.6 to 1.0 and the reaction is catalysed by strong acids like PTS (P-toluene sulphonic acid), oxalic and sulphuric acid. In the case of Resoles, the ratio of formaldehyde to phenol ranges between 1:1 to 3:1. The commonest alkaline catalyst used is sodium hydroxide.

The resin is formulated into glue by intimately mixing together the powdered resin and the other components in finely divided form. The liquid components are then charged into the mixer and the mass is heated to a uniform glue consistency. The equipment used are some time agitated steel vessels with heating and cooling coils or some time mills are also used.

Application & Formulations

Novolaks are used in wood work assemblies, where service temperature do not exceed 40° C. They are also used in furniture construction and to a minor extent in plywood fabrication, metal to wood joining for exterior use. Resoles are used for fabrication of exterior-grade weather and boll proof plywood. They are also used as glass to metal adhesives in electrical bulbs. Phenol-formaldehyde is employed as an additive to other materials to form adhesives for glass and metals; as a modifying agent for thermoplastic elastomer adhesives, or as a component of thermoplastic resin-elastomer adhesives for metal bonding.

Phenolics are used as binders for wood particles in particle board making. They are also used for bonding of glass-fiber mate particularly for insulation work. They are also used for making abrasive wheels. The quantity of resin employed in this case is about 7 to 15% of the wheel. They are used in making decorative laminates after saturating the paper with the resin followed by curing at up to 15° C and 10 to 20 kg/cm^2 pressure. Very porous surfaces cannot be bonded satisfactorily with P-F resin adhesives due to difficulty of wetting or due to excessive absorption of the adhesive. The surface is coated with a primer of the same diluted before glue application. Phenolics resins are used in neoprene and nitrile contact adhesives as tackifiers and adhesion promoter Resin selection defends on compatibility, reactivity, tack time and other requirements to be met. The uses of Phenolics resins as modifiers or tackifiers are exemplified in table 4.1. Phenolics resins are used in structural adhesives not as tackifiers, but for their strength, durability and heat resistance. They are used for bonding aircraft structures, honeycomb, brake lining to brake shoes, shoes, clutch factings, automatic transmission discs and curtain wall construction. Following table shows a typical example.

Table 4.1

Phenolic Resins for Adhesives

Type of Adhesive	*Polymer or Elastomer Base*	*Major Function of Phenolic Resin*	*Types of Phenolic Resins Used*
Contact	Neoprene rubber	Tackifier	Substituted heat reactive
Contact	Nitrile rubber	Tackifier	One-step Two-step
Contact	Neoprene rubber	Tackifier	Terpene-phenolic
General-purpose rubber based	Butyl rubbers Styrene-butadiene rubbers Polybutadiene rubbers Ethylene propylene terpolymer (EPT rubbers)	Tackifier and adhesion promoter	Substituted non-heat-reactive
General-purpose rubber based	Ethylene propylene copolymer (EPR) rubbers	Tackifier and adhesion promoter	Substituted non-heat-reactive
General-purpose rubber based	Butyl rubbers	Crosslinking agent	Substituted heat-reactive
Hot-melt	Ethylene vinyl acetate copolymers	Tackifier	Substituted non-heat-reactive
Hot-melt	Ethylene vinyl acetate copolymers	Tackifier	Terpene-phenolic
Plastisol	Plasticized polyvinyl chloride	Adhesion promoter	Two-step
Pressure-sensitive	Vinyl ethyl ether	Tackifier	Substituted heat-reactive
Pressure-sensitive	Vinyl ethyl ether	Tackifier	Substituted non-heat-reactive
Structural	Epoxy	Crosslinking agent	Novolac
Structural	Epoxy	Crosslinking agent	One-step
Structural	Nitrile rubber	Crosslinking agent	One-step
Structural	Nitrile rubber	Crosslinking agent	Two-step
Structural	Poly vinyl butyral	Crosslinking agent	One-step
Structural	Poly vinyl butyral	Crosslinking agent	Two-step

	1	2	3	
Nitrile rubber	15	15	15	parts
Novolac hexa	15	15	15	"
Acetone	70	70	70	"
A 1000 silane	-	0.3	-	"
A 189 silane	-	-	0.3	"
Lap shear strength (psi)				
30° C	1450	2350	3120	"
60° C	185	420	375	"
125° C	110	250	360	"

Vinyl/Phenolics

Vinyl formal, vinyl acetal and vinyl butyral may be combined with Phenolics resin to produce tough structural adhesives with good impact strength, resistance to oil and aromatic fuels and good salt spray and weathering resistance. The presence of hydroxyl groups on the vinyl chain makes it likely that crosslinking occurs between the Phenolics resole resin and hydroxyl groups during elevated temperature cure. A typical formula is shown below.

Poly vinyl butyral	18	parts
Phenolics resin	30	"
Toluene	16	"
Ethanol	36	"

Epoxy/Phenolics

Combination of epoxy and Phenolics resins provide structural adhesives with superior high temperature resistance to the elastomer modified adhesives. Both novolac resole formulation for this adhesive is as follows.

Phenolics resin	100	parts
Epoxy resin	20	"
Ethyl acetate	20	"
Hexa	4	"
n-propyl gallate	0.8	"

Adhesive bonds prepared with this formulation exhibited good salt spray resistance. One drawback of the above formulation is its poor filleting action when used to prepare honeycomb cores in sandwich constructions. A formula that provided improved flow and filleting action is as follows.

Phenolics resin (solid)	125	parts
Phenolics resin (liquid)	33	"
Epoxy resin	20	"
Ethyl resin	20	"
Ethyl acetate	20	"
1-hydroxy-2-napthoic acid	2.8	"
n-propyl gallate	1.4	"

Hot-melt adhesives

Phenolics resins play a small but significant role in the formulation of hot melt adhesives. Several starting formulations are shown below.

Hot-melt vinyl film to wood laminating adhesives

EVA copolymer	40	parts
Phenolics resin	25	"
Hydrogenated rosin ester	15	"
Wax	20	"
Antioxidant	0.1	"

Heat resistant hot melt adhesives

EVA copolymer	45	parts
Phenolic resin	30	"
Polyterpene resin	10	"
Wax	15	"
Antioxidant	0.1	"

Hot-melt adhesives for polyester

EVA copolymer	40	parts
Phenolic resin	15	"
Hydrogenated rosin ester	25	"
Wax	20	"
Antioxidant	0.1	"

Hot-melt adhesives for polyethylene

EVA copolymer	40	parts
Phenolic resin	15	"
Polyterpene resins	12.5	"
Silica	12.5	"
Additive	20	"
Antioxidant	0.1	"

Pressure sensitive adhesives (PSA)

Phenolic resins are one type among many that are useful as tackifiers for elastomers in the manufacture of PSA. The most familiar use of PSA is in the manufacture of flexible tape that has found innumerable uses in the home and in the industry. High molecular weight polyvinyl ethyl ether import basic cohesive strength where as low molecular weight polyvinyl ethyl ether serves as a plasticizer for improving tack and low temperature flexibility. The type phenolic resin found useful is para tertiary butyl formaldehyde resole. A recommended formulation is shown below.

Clear laminating PSA

Polyvinyl ethyl ether (high mol.wt.)	4.5	parts
Polyvinyl ethyl ether (low mol. wt.)	13.5	"
Phenolic resin	7.2	"
Plasticizer	0.01	"
Hydrogenated methyl este of rosin	4.8	"
Toluenes	27.5	"
MEK	27.5	"
Hexane	18.0	"

Cold pressed coarse abrasive adhesive formulation

	I	II	
Aluminium oxide	840	780	parts
Powdered phenolic resin (two step)	60	120	"
Cryolite		70	97 "
Liquid phenolic resin (one step)	30	-	"
Furfural/cresylic acid	-	25	"
Calcium oxide	-	3	"
Creosote oil	5	5	"
Cold pressed density (g/cc)	2.64	2.93	"

Cold pressed medium abrasive general purpose adhesive

	I	II	
Aluminium oxide	1050	1050	parts
Powdered phenolic resin (two step)	130	150	"
Liquid phenolic resin (one step)	20	-	"
Furfural/cresylic acid	-	18	"
Cold pressed density (g/cc)	2.64	2.64	"

Hot pressed coarse abrasive adhesive

Aluminium oxide	780	parts
Powdered phenolic resin (two step)	120	"
Cryolite	97	"
Calcium oxide	3	"
Creosote oil	12	"
Hot-pressed density	3.03	"

Resorcinol Formaldehyde Adhesives (RF)

The RF adhesives were found to be outstanding not only for their excellent durability but also for their unique property of curing rapidly without heat, giving high strength bonds to such a large variety of adherends.

In order to produce resorcinol-phenol-formaldehyde resins, the phenol is combined with the formaldehyde before the resorcinol is introduced. Phenol is reacted with excess formaldehyde to form resol. Resorcinol is then be added in sufficient quantity to combine with all the methylol groups, thus forming a resinous copolymer.

Alkyl resorcinol resins are made from alkyl substituted resorcinol to confer special solubility or compatibility properties. In such cases the alkylated resorcinol is directly reacted with formaldehyde to obtain a modified polymer. Such resins have been found to be useful because of better ocmpatibility with elastomers such as butyl or ethylene propylene rubber.

These resins are available as red-brown resins with hardening agent in the form of liquid or powder. Resin may be diluted with alcohol or water or extended with fillers. Setting takes place with condensation reaction in which water is eliminated. Their bonds have the durability comparable to that of heat setting phenolic adhesives and is limited by the durability of the adherent material. Resistance to severe weathering, humidity, boiling water, temperature and biodeterioration is excellent. Maximum chemical resistance develops in 6 days. Maximum durability for hardwood assemblies is achieved by curing at moderately high temperatures. Neutral character of resorcinol resins avoids damage to cellulosic fibers. Staining power of resins often precludes bonding light coloured woods and veneers.

Phenol resorcinol adhesive generally contains about 15% phenolic resins, is slow curing, has a higher minimum curing temperature, is a little cheaper, has shorter shelf life in the cure cycle for accelerating the setting. Crazing is not a problem of either type at 25° C cure temperature.

The potlife of resin-hardener mixture varies between 1½ and 4 hrs. depending to a certain extent on the temperature of the batch at the time of mixing and the ambient temperature. Best results are obtained by cooling during mixing in a jacketed kettle and maintaining the mixture during use at about 20-22° C, Long storage life, and non-reactivity until catalyst addition is made are valuable properties. Hot cured assemblies should not be handled or machined for at least 24 hours. Low temperature cured bonds require a 7 days conditioning period. Gap-filling properties are improved by filler additives phenol resorcinol are suitable for glue lines up to 0.4 mm thick.

Manufacture

Resorcinol resins do not exist as resols, but is similar to Novolaks. Resorcinol is more reactive compared to phenol. Initially phenol is combined with excess formaldehyde. The resole thus prepared is further reacted with resorcinol to combine with all the methylol group thus forming a resinous copolymer. In a steam jacked reaction kettle 35 kg. of phenol and 60 kg of formalin solution (37-40%) are charged. About 1.5 kg of 50% sodium hydroxide lye is then added. The temperature is allowed to increase to 60° C by steam heating. The exothermic reaction starts and the same is controlled by passing cooling water through the jacket After the resol is formed 40 kg of resorcinol is charged into the reaction kettle with continuous agitation and cooling if required. The agitation is continued under vacuum of 500 mm mercury till most of the water is driven away. The liquid resin is discharged into a vessel.

Application

Joints made with resorcinolic adhesives are of high structural strength, usually greater than the wood itself. They are resistant to almost any of the condition to which wood may be exposed and will retain their original load bearing strength during exposure to all kinds of climatic changes. They provide excellent endurance when subjected to such conditions as: fatigue, boiling water, extreme temperature humidity cycling, freezing and thawing and most types of solvent except highly caustic solution. They are capable of bearing heavy loads indefinitely without evidence of creep.

Resorcinolic adhesives are useful in the bonding of many materials such as wood, paper, textiles, plastic, rubbers, metals, glass, ceramics and concrete. Textiles like cotton, rayon and nylon are easily bonded. RF glues are thus useful in bonding tyre cord to the rubber body of the tyres. Plastic materials like phenol. melamine and urea-formaldehyde thermosets, the epoxies, polyurethanes, polyamides, rubbers, acrylates and polyesters may be effectively bonded to each other. However, most of the thermoplastics such as polystyrene, polyolefins, polyvinyl chloride, polyfluroethylene, ethyl cellulose and polycarbonates are not easily bonded with these adhesives because of low surface polarity.

Metals are bonded after being primed with epoxies, polyurethanes or with casein elastomeric primers. By means of this, metal facings may be applied to wood at room temperature. This provides a method for eliminating the thermally induced stresses. The resorcinolic adhesives have the disadvantages of dark colour so that the glue lines appear as dark streaks which cause dark, spotchy areas on the surface which are very difficult to remove.

Commercially, the resorcinol based adhesives are available in two part systems. The liquid portion, Part A is the resinous, constituent. It is generally a solution of the performed formaldehyde deficient resin in a mixture of alcohol and water, having a solid content of about 50%. The reactivity of the glue is controlled by the pH at which the liquid is buffered.

The solid portion B part is a solid powdered mixture of para formaldehyde and fillers. The paraformaldehyde for control of glue mix working life and curing efficiency. Fillers are used for providing suitable consistency to the mix, to form a fibrous reinforcement for the adhesive film and to control thixotropic behaviour of the adhesives. Wood flours are often used to obtain better gap filling. Once the liquid and solid portions are mixed the life of the mixture is limited.

Amino Resin Adhesives

Amino resins are the condensation products of amino compound with aldehyde. The common and widely used amino compounds are urea and melamine, where as formaldehyde is almost always the aldehyde.

Urea formaldehyde resins have the following advantages and disadvantages.

Advantages	Disadvantages
Low cost	Poor boiling water resistance
Colour less glue line	Generally two component
Room temperature curing	
Resistant to mold and fungus	
Gap filling and craze resistant	
Adaptable to electronic gluing	

Melamine formaldehyde resins have the following advantages & disadvantage.

Advantages	Disadvantages
Excellent boiling water resistance	High temperature curing
Colourless glue line	High cost
Resistant to mould and fungus	

UF resins have a shelf life of about 3 to 6 months at 20° C while the powders have a shelf life longer then 1 year. The working life depends on composition and setting temperature, between 0-48 hrs at 20° C; working life of room temperature setting types range between 3-10 hrs. at 20° C. The closed assembly time also depends on composition and varies between 0-24 hrs. at 20° C; when resin and catalyst are applied separately to each adherent, it is about 0-30 minutes. Setting takes place due to condensation polymerization with elimination of water. The full bond strength develops gradually over a few days, but assemblies can be handled after 6-12 hrs.

Bond strengths usually exceed the strength of the wood when glue line thickness ranges from 0.05-0.16 mm.

UF adhesives lack the durability of combination with melamine, phenolic or resorcinol resins and are unsuitable for service conditions which are extreme e.g. high humidity, bonding water and temperatures above 60° C. These adhesives are non-staining and light-coloured and are unsuitable for exterior applications. Resistance to biodeterioration and cold water is good, and may be compounded with additives to improve durability.

Melamine resins are available in the form of film, liquid or powder form. Aqueous solutions of melamine resin adhesives are much less stable than those of urea resins; they are therefore normally spray dried soon after manufacture producing a powder glue with a storage life of at least a year. The user redissolves the powder in water to give solutions, that remain stable for a few days depending on temperature and resin concentration. Instability results in the solution becoming cloudy and later semi-solid. In its early stages this state can be reverised by heating the resin to 40-50° C provided no hardener has been added.

Hot pressed melamine resins are especially resistant to boiling water and are generally equivalent to hot pressed phenolics and resorcinol.

Manufacture

Urea-formaldehde adhesives or resins are available in the form of solutions containing 45 to 67% resins solids and also in powder form as 100% of neat resin, resin-filler combinations and resin-filler catalyst combination. Formaldehyde and urea reactions normally proceeds from liquid aqueous reactants to a solid end-product, but the manufacturer stops the reaction at an intermediate stage, while the product is still liquid; the user initiates the final stage of the reaction to convert the liquid to the solid end product. The final stage i.e. the curing is a continuation of the condensation reaction started by the manufacturer. For this purpose a hardener is generally required, an acid or acid-releasing catalyst is suitable for this purpose.

A typical U.F. adhesive for use in plywood manufacture is made in a reaction kettle equipped with an agitator, reflux condenser and jacket and/or coil for heating and cooling purposes. Formalin is fed to the reactor followed by urea-step wise or fully at the start of the reaction. Mode of addition of urea gives the desired variations in polymer distribution and reactivity of the final product. The mole ratios of formaldehyde and urea are 1.5 to 2.1. Urea dissolves readily with some endothermic effect. pH of the solution is adjusted with sodium hydroxide or other alkali to 7.5 to 8 and the mixture is refluxed at 98° C, until the desired polymerization is reached as measured by solution viscosity. It takes about 4 to 8 hrs. In order to increase the rate of polymer growth. without extending the heating period beyond economical limits, the reaction pH is lowered by the addition of formic acid to a level of 5.6 to 6. This adjustment in pH is done at an appropriate time during reflux when all the urea has been added. At the lower pH. the solution viscosity gradually rises to the control value desired for the product. The resin is then adjusted in pH to about 8 to inhibit further reaction and cooled for packing. In this way resin solutions containing 45 to 65% solids are made.

Powdered urea resins are prepared as above followed by spray drying.

The main factor is the molar ratio of formaldehyde and urea. For general purposes such as plywood, veneering and assembly gluing, the molar ratio is usually of the order of 1 (urea); 1.75-1.9 (formaldehyde) and rarely above 1.2. For the manufacture of wood particle board a somewhat lower ratio is often used in order to keep the smell of formaldehyde to a minimum. Increasing the quantity of formaldehyde results in increased stability in solution, increase water stability but higher sensitivity to atmospheric moisture, and the increase in the smell of formaldehyde in the resin and the finished product. The addition of urea to the resin solution just before use, either directly or in a hardener is a good and generally used way of reducing this smell.

Melamine reacts with formaldehyde to yield methylol melamines. Three reactive amine groups can be reacted with as many as 6 moles of formaldehyde. By reacting 1 mole of melamine with 3 moles of warm formalin until solution is obtained and quickly cooling, crystalline trimethylol melamine may be obtained. The reaction can be represented as below.

The methylol melamine condense to form polymers by heating under mild alkaline conditions. The progressive polymerization of the methylol melamines is dependent on the reaction pH. Small changes in acidity or alkalinity have greater effect on the reaction progress than in the case of methylol area. At a pH of 7 water soluble, hydrophillic polymers are first formed. Under continued heating the resin solution has less tolerance for dilution with water but is readily diluted with water alcohol mixtures. With still further heating, some resin may be precipitated from solution by alcohol and the solution will separate into layers on cooling.

Curing of the melamine resins may be accomplished by simple heating. The presence of small amounts of acid will accelerate the heat cure, especially for butylated products. Unlike urea resins, however, melamines do not cure satisfactorily at room temperature even in the presence of an acid catalyst.

45 litre 40 per cent formalin is put into an agitated reactor with reflux & steam jacket. The pH is adjusted sodium hydroxide solution pH 7.0-7.5. 252 kg melamine and 6 litre ammonia solution are then added, and the mass is heated under reflux until the first bubbles of the slightly exothermic reaction appear. The heat is stopped and is applied later as required. The liquor is boiled gently under reflux for 30 minutes from the start of the exothermic reaction. Care is taken to see that the mass is agitated thoroughly whilst the liquor is relfluxing. The liquor is then vacuum distilled at 76-75^0 C at a pressure of about 25 mm mercury to give a thickish syrup. The pH of the resin syrup is adjusted to 7.5-8.5.

The solids content of the resin syrup is determined as described below.

25 g. of acid-washed silver sand of about 50 mesh size is contained in a flat bottom dish about 3 inch in diameter, 1 inch deep, and made of glass. The dish along with the sand, rod and cover glass are weighed to the nearest 0.001 g. Then about 0.5 g of the resin solution is put in the dish, the covered glass put on and the covered dish, with the glass rod on top, is quickly weighed to the nearest 0.001 g. The object of using the cover glass is to prevent the loss of solvent during weighing, 7 c.c. of acetone or other or other solvent are then thoroughly mixed with the weighed sand and resin solution, using the rod which is left in the mixture. The dish is put in a warm place, such as on top of the oven, to allow most of the solvent at 135^0 C for and then without any further mixing the dish is put in an electric oven at 135^0 C for two hours. The dish is removed from the oven, put the dessicator to cool and reweighed with, of course, its cover glass.

Then from the three weights solids content of the solution is calculated.

Application & Formulation

Urea-formaldehyde resin adhesives are used for bonding wood and related materials with moisture content 7-15%. Manufacture of light woods, thin veneers and plywood furniture assembly and joinery also requires urea formaldehyde adhesives. These adhesives may also be used for timber construction, which is subject to only low stresses. For applications requiring greater moisture-resistance, melamine-urea adhesive may be used. Thus ureaformaldehyde containing adhesives may be used for bonding of plywood, furniture flush doors, boats, laminates, fibre boards, bag seam pastes, particles board and general wood work.

A craze resistant modification of a liquid urea-formaldehyde resin is obtained by the addition of furfuryl alcohol to the urea resin solution near the end of the reflux period during manufacture. Catalysts and extenders are added just prior to use, to obtain a cured glue line. Powdered resin is also usually supplied without adding catalysts, but formulations with powdered resin blended with filler, catalyst and cure retarders are also available. Blending is done with additives in a cone or ribbon blender; sometimes anti-caking agents are added to the blender to aid in retaining free flowing properties during storage. Commonly used fillers are wood and walnut shell flours. Catalysts used are ammonium salts, such as chloride or sulphate. Cure retarders such as tricalcium phosphate are employed of buffer the adhesive mixture and extend the working life of the wet glue mix.

Resins cured with ammonium thiocyanate have superior hot water resistance to those hardened with diammonium phosphate. Use of starch extender reduces water resistance to, increases resin viscosity to overcome adhesive absorption into porous materials, e.g. wood, and lowers cost. Use of phenolic or resorcinol additives promotes resistance to water, weather and temperature changes, with increase in cost. As mentioned earlier use of melamine fortifier increases resistance to water and temperature and improves durability. Melamine or resorcinol fortifiers do not enhance durability, beyond that of phenolic resins. Addition of furfuryl alcohol resin reduces the tendency of the thick glue films to craze and weaken. Addition of fillers improves gap-filling properties. Watersoluble UF glues are compatible with apueous dispersions of PVA; the activity of PVA may reduce the pot life of UF glue and if the quantity of PVA is more then 10% the addition of hardener may be omitted. But, if the quantity is lesser, then hardener must be used, otherwise the low water-resistance of the PVA will get further aggravated, USP 25,92,510 described a PVA/UF composition, which can be spray dried, and can be redissolved or redispersed in water.

A dry mix-formulation is given below.

UF dried resin	100	parts
Zinc oxide	0.5	"
Ammonium	2	"

The packed moisture tight packages and before using it is mixed with water.

UF resins find application in the manufacture of corrugated fibre-board. Addition of 5 to 15% of urea resin with the starch results in minimum changes in operating conditions. The product withstands soaking in water for several days without ply separation.

A cold press adhesive formulation is given below.

UF resin powder	100	parts
Shell flour	15	"
Wheat flour	25	"
Water	105	"
Hardener	5	"

UF resin modified with casein is used as a hot-setting adhesive. Equal amounts of both the constituents are mixed, which result in a plywood glue setting at 100° C. Though it is expensive thiourea may be used to improve the transparency of the resin. A transparent adhesive of this type is given below.

Thiourea	52	parts
Urea	200	"
Trioxymethylene	240	"
Sodium acetate	9	"
Formamide	20	"

The ingredients are mixed carefully and heated at 140° C for 20 minutes to give a viscous mass. On cooling it solidifies into a hard and white mass. On cooling it solidifies into a hard and white mass, which may be ground and used as a thermoplastic adhesive. Formamide acts as a catalyst.

Adhesives for corrugated fibre board

UF resin powder	100	parts
Shell flour	75	"
Wheat flour	25	"
Water	110	"
Hardener	15	"

Particle board adhesives

Wood chips	100	parts
UF adhesive (65% solids)	7-10	"
Wax	2	"

Transparent adhesive

Thio urea	52	parts
Urea	200	"
Trioxymethylene	250	"
Sodium acetate	10	"
Formamide	20	"

The ingredients are mixed carefully and heated at 140° C for 20 min to give a viscous mass. On curing it solidifies into a hard and white mass.

The basic difference in the curing of melamine resin and urea resin is that the urea resin can be cured at room temperature of about 60° C the melamine resin can be hardened at much lower temperature by lowering the pH, but the cured product has poor cohesive and adhesive strength.

Unmodified melamine resins used for the production of water proof plywood, as fortifiers of urea adhesives. For this the resin is dispersed in water. Shell flour is added to obtain a spreadable consistency. Catalyst may be added to shorten the cure cycle, but normally the adhesive is hot pressed in the uncatalyset state. The following formula is suitable.

	Catalysed	Uncatalysed	
M-F resin	100	80	parts
Shell flour	12	20	"
Water	50	60	"
Catalyst	1	-	"
Working life 25° C	5 hrs.	15 hrs.	

Water proof melamine adhesive

MF resin	100	parts
Starch	50	"
Dextrin	20	"
Ethyl alcohol	300	-

Waterproof melamine glue is used as a top coat for decorative laminates.

Polyvinyl Acetate Adhesives

Among the polyvinyl esters, polyvinyl acetate is the most important material for adhesives. As an adhesive it is used in solution aqueous dispersion forms and also as hot melts. Vinyl acetate monomer is a flammable liquid, which is polymerized.

As the molecular weight of the polymer increases the polymer turns into a harder solid. Adhesive solutions are usually made in ketones, lower alcohols and esters. As the m. wt. reaches about 1,00,000 the polymer becomes soluble in toluene. In emulsion form the product is a dispersion of swollen solid particles; mostly it is used in this form. The advantages of aqueous dispersion is not only that it uses water as the medium, but also that a high solids viscosity ratio is possible than with a solution. PVA solutions increase in viscosity as the mol. wt. of the polymer increases and since a proportion of high mol. wt. material is desirable, because of its film strength, a solution, that is fluid enough to permit easy application must necessarily be of low concentration. Emulsion polymerization overcomes this disadvantage, because the mol. wt. of the dispersed polymer has little effect on the viscosity of the dispersed with a high ratio of solids to viscosity can be easily produced.

Polyvinyl acetate is a thermoplastic, odourless, tasteless nontoxic, clear and colourless resin. The resin is unaffected by sunlight, UV light and air; it absorbs some amount of water; the various grades have good have good heat stability below 100° C , show slight discoloration at about 150° C. All grades show outstanding ahesion to many surface porous and non-porus. This excellent adhesion is due in part to the highly polar acetate groups in the polymer and partially to the unique combination of viscosity tack, tensile strength and other properties that exist during application of the adhesive and during formation and aging of the bond. Polyvinyl acetate adhesives have a closed assembly time of about 10-15 min. at 20° C;setting takes place by loss of water or solvent by evaporation or absorption into adherent. These adhesives show low resistance to weather and moisture, hence are suitable only for interior application. Solvent solution have slightly better resistance to water than emulsion types. Resistance to most solvents is poor, but the adhesives withstand contact with grease, oils and petroleum fluids and are not subject to biodegradation. Their heat resistance is satisfactory up to 50-60° C, Gap-filling is not usually good, but the addition of thickening agent improves it. Tensile shear strength has been shown with a variety of timbers to be comparable with urea and phenolic glues, while giving, for unknown reasons, consistently less wood failures.

These are also cost glues with high initial tack but quick setting to give almost invisible glue lines, 1-7 days conditioning period is recommended before handling bonded assemblies.

Polymers redispersible in aqueous media was commercialized the 1960s. The advantages of this product approach were to facilitate blending and to reduce storage and transportation costs. Spray drying of vinyl acetate emulsions provides powders which have good redispersion and good pigment binding characteristics. Physical properties of the commercially available resins are shown in Table 4.2.

Stable dispersions can be reconstituted by adding the powders uniformly and slowly to water under good agitation. If other dry ingredients are involved, preblending simplifies dispersion. The unique advantage of these powders is their ability to be used as a binder in dry mix formulations. The ingredients that can be dry-mixed with poly vinyl acetate powder include synthetic resins (polyvinyl alcohol), natural resins (starch, dextrin, gums), and inorganic fillers (gypsum, clay, cement, mica).

Table 4.2
Redispersible Polyvinyl Acetate Powders

	I	II	III
Particle size of powder	20 microns	15 microns	99% through 100 meach
Volatile content	1.5%	3.0%	<2%
Bulk density	32-38 lb./cu ft.	32-38 lb./cu ft.	33 lb./cu ft.
Viscosity (cps)			
At 55% solids in water (50% solids)	1660	200	5000-7000
At 60% solids in water	7800	700	--
At 70% solids in water	--	11,000	--

Polyvinyl acetate is most widely used in the form of a dispersion of solid resin in water. These dispersions are produced by emulsion polymerization and are more commonly termed "emulsions". Most products for adhesives are sold at 55% solids at a sufficiently high viscosity level to facilitate use. These products are manufactured by one of several techniques-batch, continuous or delay feed, dependent on properties desired. The large volume usage depends not only on the outstanding adhesive properties of the resin but also on the excellent compatibility of the emulsions with many modifying agents.

Homopolymer Emulsions

General Purpose. This is a specific designation for those emulsions that can be used in a multitude of adhesive formulations. These emulsions are usually made by a continuous or semicontinuous process. They have a heterogeneous particle size and molecular weight. They are outstandingly stable to storage, handling, and compounding. Polyvinyl alcohol is the usual protective colloid. Dried films from the unmodified emulsions are redispersible in water, however, the emulsions can be modified or the films treated directly to enhance water resistance.

General-purpose adhesive bases are supplied in several emulsion viscosity grades from 500 to 4000 cps. Solids content is generally 55% and pH is 4 to 5. The average particle size is less than 1 micron. Probably the most important characteristic of emulsions in this class is their excellent compatibility with plasticizers, wetting agents, solvents, furthermore they can be transformed readily into a variety of adhesives.

Special-Purpose Homopolymer Emulsions. Emulsions in this class are similar to those in general purpose. They lack the broad range of compatibility with modifying agents which has been sacrificed to obtain other special properties. For example, high molecular weight for higher heat seal temperatures, coarse particle size for better holdout on porous surfaces, or low -molecular weight for quick-tack may be the chief advantage of such an emulsion. These emulsions are made by the batch or semicontinuous process. Polyvinyl alcohol is the usual protective colloid but often is combined with natural gums or synthetic colloids. Many emulsions in this class are sold to adhesives manufacturers already modified with plasticizer, solvents, surfactants, thickeners, or other agents to achieve better filming, tackiness, freeze-thaw stability, special viscosity, or other effects. These special properties combined with the good adhesion of the PVA colloid system characterize this class of materials.

Free Filming Homopolymer Emulsions. Emulsions in this class form free films at room temperature. The films retain integrity in the presence of water without baking or adding coalescing agents to the emulsions. These emulsions have a small and uniform particle size (0.5-2 microns) compared to particle size of 0.5-10 microns for other classes materials.
The gradual monomer addition process is used to control particle size and molecular weight. Protective colloid content is reduced to improve free-filming character.

A differentiation according to type of protective colloid is useful among emulsions in this class. Emulsions containing polyvinyl alcohol have the advantages of the adhesion of general purpose special purpose polymer combined with more water resistant free-filming properties. Emulsions containing a synthetic colloid other than polyvinyl alcohol (such as methyl cellulose, sodium carboxymethyl cellulose, and hydroxyethyl cellulose) are changed in compounding characteristics. These products are stable to large additions of borax and other polyvalent salts that coagulate polyvinyl alcohol/acetate dispersions under normal conditions. Emulsions containing natural products as protective colloids (natural gums, starches, and dextrins) have excellent stability to further additions of natural products and are noted for excellent tolerance for inorganic pigments, fillers, and extenders.

This class of emulsions, because of their finer particle size, lower molecular weight, and protective colloid content, generally have less tolerance for the more polar organic solvents than other emulsions. However, their compounding stability is good.

High-Colloid Content Emulsions. Under the proper conditions, vinyl acetate can be polymerized in the presence of two to five times the amount of protective colloid used in making general-purpose adhesive emulsions. In this case, the colloid functions in a primary way to impart special properties to the emulsion. Important examples are the emulsions offered as remoistenable adhesives for high-speed machine application. These emulsions are extraordinarily stable to compounding with thickening agents with water-soluble resins, gums, starches, and dextrins. This class includes emulsions polymerized in the presence of pigments, fillers, extenders and other modifying agents, but not emulsions modified after polymerization.

Homopolymer Lattices. Products are characterized by a particle size in the range of 0.1 to 0.4 micron. Their clear, glossy, and water-resistant films make them particularly useful as adhesive coatings. These materials are stabilized primarily by surfactants. Gradual monomer addition processes are used. Solids content is in the order of 46%.

Copolymer Emulsions

Vinyl Acetate/Alkyl Acrylate Copolymer Emulsions. Ethyl acrylate, butyl acerytate, and 2-ethylhexyl acrylate are copolymerized with vinyl acetate in emulsion reactions similar to those used for homopolymers. A wide range of models are commercially available with a variety of protective colloids and other modifiers. 2-ethylhexyl acrylate is the preferred comonomer. Choice of product is dependent on the adhesive property desired (tack, heat seal temperature, creep).

In application, the advantage of these copolymers is their specific adhesion to "difficult" or low energy surfaces. A large volume of copolymer emulsions is used in the bonding of plastic surfaces such as polyvinyl chloride to porous surfaces such as cellulosics. An additional advantage is their ability to heat seal at temperatures such that the plastic surface configuration is not destroyed.

Table 4.3

Vinyl Acetate Homopolymer Emulsions for Adhesives

Properties	*A. General purpose*	*B. Special purpose*	*C. Free filming*	*D. High colloid*	*E. Latices*
Solids (%)	55.9	55.9	59.8	60.5	55.3
Viscosity (cps)	920	2600	1900	640	1068
Particle size (microns)	1-4, 4-6	1-4, 4-8	1-2, 2-4	<1, 1-3	0.05-0.3
Surface tension (dynes/cm)	52.7	53.4	52.8	35	41.2
Molecular weight	Low	High	Medium	Low	Low
Polymer insolubles in benzene (%)	24	3	7.5	20.1	0
Borax stability	Coagulates	Coagulates	Stable	Stable	Stable
Alcohol tolerance (ml/100 g)	55	36	<0.5	<1	<0.5
Chlorinated solvent tolerance	Excellent	Good	Good	Excellent	Fair
Mechanical stability	Excellent	Good	Excellent	Good	Fair
Freeze-thaw stability	Good	Fair	Good	Good	Good
Film water resistance	Poor	Poor	Fair	Poor	Excellent
Gardner scrub (cycles to failure)	32	25	86	17	8281

Table 4.4

Vinyl Acetate Copolymer Emulsions for Adhesives

Properties	*A.*	*B.*	*C.*	*D.*	*E.*
Solids (%)	54.5-55.5	55-57	54-56	54.5-55.5	45
Viscosity (cps)	1000-1600	1100-1600	.1000-1400	700-900	130
Particle size (microns)	0.75-1.5	0.2-1.0	<2.0	<1-2	0.2
Surface tension (dynes/cm)	40-45	—	45	43	34
Molecular weight	Low to Medium		High	Medium	Low
High					
Polymer insolubles in benzene (%)	<3	30-40	6.0	5	15[b]
Borax stability	Stable	Coagulates	Coagulates	Coagulates	Stable
Alcohol tolerance (ml/100 g)	100	Good	65	<0.5	Good
Chlorinated solvent tolerance	Excellent	Excellent	Excellent	Excellent	-
Mechanical stability	Good	Excellent	Good	Good	Good
Freeze-thaw stability	Fair	-	Poor	Poor	Good
Film water resistance	Excellent	Poor	Good	Poor	Good
Gardner scrub (cycles to failure)	2000		320	26	

A new development is the use of vinyl acetate 2-ethylhexyl acrylate copolymer in the pressure-sensitive adhesives. These soft, low Tg polymers are high (>50%) in acrylate content. The water based pressure-sensitive emulsions compete with solution products of similar composition where an air pollution problem exists.

Vinyl Acetate/Ethylene Copolymer Emulsions. Emulsion copolymers of vinyl acetate and ethylene have exhibited a remarkably fast growth in the past decade. Ethylene is an efficient and economical monomer to reduce the Tg of the polymer. Commercial emulsions contain 20-12% ethylate on solids, corresponding to polymer Tg of the 0-10° C range. Pressure vessels (up to 1350 kg/cm2 rating) are used for manufacture of these emulsions.

In use, the products are competitive with the vinyl acetate/acrylate copolymer emulsions. Wetting and adhesion to low energy surfaces are good; creep resistance is improved over the acrylate models similar Tg.

Vinyl Acetate/Alkyl Maleate Copolymer Emulsions. Copolymers of vinyl acetate and maleate or fumarate esters are available in emulsion systems that fit most of the preceding classification. These copolymer emulsions are important as adhesive bases. Tack properties, compatibility with solvents and plasticizers, and film and resin properties generally are similar to those of vinyl acetate/acrylate copolymer emulsions. The glass transition temperature (Tg) of the maleate copolymers is slightly higher than that of acrylates at the same comonomer charge level. Comparable adhesive properties are obtained economical with minor additions of plasticizer or coalescing aid.

Vinyl Acetate/Acid Copolymer Emulsions. Polyvinyl acetate emulsion films or adhesives can be redispersed in alkaline media when the resin is a copolymer containing acid groups. The presence of acid groups also confers better adhesion to many surfaces. The degree of adhesion and alkali redispersibility can be controlled by varying the also be controlled by varying the pH of the emulsion. Aqueous solutions of polyvinyl acetate alkali soluble resins can be prepared from some of these emulsions. Properties and applications of emulsions in this class will depend on the similarly of the emulsion system to the other classes listed here.

Curable Copolymer Emulsions. Curable vinyl acetate emulsions are available but most commercial development has centered on the low glass temperature curable copolymers. Incorporation of a comonomer capable of cross linking either during the reaction or during a postdeposition heating step is the technique employed. N methylol acrylamide and hydroxymethylated diacetone acrylamide are typical monomers used as reactive components, usually at low level (<10%) of total charge. On a molecular basis, these monomers crosslink polymer chains : on a functional basis crosslinking develops chemical resistance polymer insolubility, and increased strength characteristics. For example, the creep of an adhesive bond of a curable emulsion is decreased markedly. A major use for curable emulsions is the bonding of nonwoven fabrics where wash and dry clean resistance is achieved via cure.

Manufacture

For adhesive purpose the Vinyl acetate moreover is usually emulsion polymerized. Emulsion polymer is then spray dried to give solid resin if, so desired. Emulsion polymerization results in uniformities and homogeneity of the product with high degree of polymerization and small uniform particle size.

Vinyl acetate polymerizers by the free-radical addition reaction. Free redicals generated by the decomposition of organic peroxides such as benzoyl or hydrogen peroxide or of inorganic per salts such as potassium or ammonium persulphate are commonly used to initiate polymerization. Reactions ordinarily are accomplished at temperatures above room temperature. Other techniques of polymerization have been used to make novel products; low temperature redox polymerization, irradiation, and ionic catalysis.

High molecular weight and essentially linear polymers, controlled particle size in the case of emulsions, and even polymers with spatially regulated structures are available. Vinyl acetate copolymeizes with various vinyl monomers. Acrylate esters, vinyl chloride vinylidene chloride, dibutyl and other dialkyl maleates and itaconic acids, vinyl pyrrolidone, and ethylene are commercially important comonomers. A monomer that does not combine with vinyl acetate alone can be combined by use of a third monomer. Grafting can be used with monomers such as styrene that do not copolymerize with vinyl acetate.

In a direct persulphate initiated system under reflux, it is not normally necessary to employ an inert gas blanket.

Where a reaction is performed under autogenous pressure no degasification of oxygen is normally necessary for monomers which are added under pressure. With other monomers, it is only desirable to deoxygenate when using redox systems, to reduce the inhibition time at the start.

Organic peroxides such as benzoyl peroxide is used in emulsion polymerization. Benzoyl peroxide is first dissolved in monomer, but it is included rather exceptionally in formulations. Azoli isobutyro t butyl hydroperoxide is occasionally used as an alternative initiator. T Butyl hydroperoxide can be a part of the water or monomer phases, depending on solubility and whether it is a part of the redox system.

In the actual process, the emulsified solution of vinyl acetate is prepared first separately and then this is being transferred to a specially designed (for efficient temperature control) reactor for polymerization, automatic temperature control is used. Then all other ingredients (catalysis, chain transfer agents) are added to this reaction vessel.

With this reactor, reflux condensing arrangement is provided so that vapour can be condensed and again passed to the reactor. Thus the temperature of the reaction is maintained at about 72^0 C by efficient temperature control and this reaction mixture is well stirred for the complete period of about 5 hours. In this period the mixture boils and the vapour forms which is condensed in the condenser (reflux) and returned to the kettle.

Thus after about 5 hours, about 88% polymer form is obtained and then the final product is transferred to the still and by fractional distillation, the solvents and unchanged vinyl acetate are separated out by steam distillation process and this will give about 99% polyvinyl acetate which is run into drums.

But in other way only a small portion of monomer and catalyst are charged and the reminder is added during the course of reaction of polymerization. Better control of rate of polymerization may be maintained in this way and this is particularly important on industrial scale operations where large quantities of materials are involved and heat of dissipation is limited. This also leads to the small particles size and a more separable dispersion. On the molecular level delayed monomer feed leads to more branches in the polymer chain. Emulsifier may also be added as an ingredient. Another common practice, after the polymerization had been run at given temperature is to raise the temperature and finish the reaction in that fashion. In order to assure the absence of unreacted monomer. Thus polymerization may be carried out to over 99% conversion and there is no requirement to strip unreacted monomer.

At the end of polymerization usually done in 2 to 5 hours, there should be only small traces of monomer present. Excess monomer is therefore sometimes removed from the final emulsion by blowing air or nitrogen through the heated product, and it has been practiced that vacuum has been applied to a polyvinyl acetate emulsion stabilized with a modified polyvinyl alcohol merely to remove the last traces of monomer along a considerable amount of vats. The problem of removing excess monomer is sometimes difficult as it is often absorbed strongly by the polymer particles. This problem is sometimes avoided by addition of a second less objectionable monomer at the end of polymerization.

Monomer

Vinyl acetate is the most available and widely used member of the vinyl ester family. This colourless flammable liquid was first prepared in 1912.

Liquid phase processes were commercialized early in Germany and Canada, but these have been replaced generally by vapor-phase processes. Earlier commercial processes were based on the catalyzed reaction of acetylene with acetic acid. The more recent technical development is the production of vinyl acetate monomer from ethylene and acetic acid. Palladium catalyst is used for both liquid and vapor phase processes.

Commercial grades contain diphenylamine (DPA), copper acetate, or hydroquinone (HQ) inhibitors. DPA grades contain 200 to 325 ppm of inhibitor and may be stored indefinitely under recommended conditions. The DPA is readily removed before polymerization by simple distillation through a short packed column. The HQ grades contain 5 to 15 ppm of inhibitor and can be used without removing inhibitor in noncritical polymerization.

Applications & Formulation

The property of excellent adhesion of polyvinyl acetate emulsions to cellulosic materials gave rise to a variety of applications. Some examples of the range of products and uses for polyvinyl acetate emulsions follow: bookbinding, paper bags, milk cartons, drinking straws, envelopes, gummed tapes, convolute tubes, folding boxes, multiwall shipping bags, labels, foils, film and paper board decals, cigarette tips, lagging compounds, wood assembly, padding, automobile upholstery, pencil, leather binding, and tile cements.

One way of classifying polyvinyl acetate adhesives is by the type of the formulation: emulsion and aqueous solution, dry-mix, hot-melt, and solution in organic solvent. The tables following present formulations that illustrate a few of the many adhesive uses of polyvinyl acetate. Thousands of actual "working" formulations exist in the laboratories of adhesives manufacturers.

Adhesives for paper of paper-composition substrates is one of the largest uses for polyvinyl acetate emulsions. Often the emulsions can be used with little, if any, modification. Usually, however, it is necessary to alter physical properties such as viscosity, solids and water resistance: to vary application characteristics such as tack and machinability and to reduce cost.

Starches, polyvinyl alcohol solutions, and clays are examples of cost-reducing agents. Starches provide high viscosity and "body". Polyvinyl alcohol builds viscosity, improves machinability, and water resistance. Clays improve setting properties by controlling penetration into porous substrates.

Improved fast-setting and tack characteristics are achieved by addition of plasticized, solvents, and film coalescing agents. Thin boiling starches and clays also facilitate the speed of set by raising the solids content. Examples of formulations of several paper adhesives are in Table 4.5.

Fast-setting packaging or case sealing adhesives require high wet tack, machinability, low cost, and often, water resistance in addition to fast set. The fast set is improved by addition of solvents (aromatic and chlorinated types) and plasticizers and by maintaining a high nonaqueous content in the adhesive. Addition f rosin derivatives in the solvent or plasticizer improves wet tack. Machinability can often be improved by addition of polyvinyl alcohol solutions. Fast-setting packaging and case sealing adhesives are illustrated in Table 4.6.

Polyvinyl acetate emulsions and polyvinyl alcohol, or combinations, are well suited for remoistenable adhesives on envelopes, stamps, sealing tapes, and ribbons. Major requirements of remoistenable adhesives on paper are rapid reactivation with water after aging, glossy film with low coefficient of friction, and resistance to blocking (temperature and humidity) and to curling. "All synthetic" remoistenable adhesives can be obtained by adding polyvinyl alcohol (20 to 40% acetate content) to emulsions. The polyvinyl alcohol improves remositenability, gloss, and block resistance. Addition of humectant-type plasticizers controls curling and improves remoistenability. Addition of special plasticizers such as butyl ricinoleate improves blocking resistance. "Resin-dextrin" remoistenable adhesives have such advantages as lower cost and gloss when a large proportion of dextin is used with the emulsion. However, they present problems such as curling and possible loss of remoistenability with age. All dextin adhesive can be improved by the addition of polyvinyl acetate emulsions. In taps, ribbon and paper applications, high quality remoistenable adhesives can be obtained with polyvinyl alcohol systems. Table 4.7 contains several remoistenable adhesive formulations.

Polyvinyl acetate and polyvinyl alcohol are important raw materials for wood adhesive applications. High bond strength, fast set, controllable open and closed assembly times, colourless glue lines, and ease of application at room temperature are some of the many advantages of polyvinyl acetate emulsion adhesives ove natural and thermosetting resin adhesives.

Polyvinyl acetate emulsions, specifically plasticized or copolymer emulsions, are bases for successful adhesives for difficult-to-adhere surfaces to a variety of porous substrates. Heat-sealing or wet-bond methods are applicable. Homopolymer emulsions are suitable with appropriate plasticizer and solvent depending on the surfaces involved. Copolymer emulsions and certain higher vinyl ester emulsions frequently possess specific adhesion not obtainable with the others. Some of the formations in Table 4.8 are capable of bonding such difficult surfaces are polyvinyl chloride, pyroxylin, aluminium foil, polystyrene film, and cellulose acetate to paper, chipboard, wood, and cloth.

Table 4.5

General Adhesives for Paper Surfaces

	1 *Bag Bottom Paste*	2 *Bag Bottom Paste*	3 *Kraft Surfaces*	4 *Seam Adhesive*	5 *Tube Winding*	6 *"Quilon" Paper*
PVAC + PVA	20-30	10-20	10-20	-	39-41	-
PVAC + PVA	-	-	10-20	-	-	
PVAC + PVA	-	-	-	-	38-40	-
Dibutyl phthalate	-	-	-	7-9	2	-
Pearl Starch	10-20	10-15	1-2	2-4	2	8-10
Fillers	-	-	10-20	5	24-26	3-4
Clay	-	-	-	7-9	1-2	-
Trichloroethylene						4-6
Ethanol						0-2
Preservative	0-2	0-2	0-2	38-28	33-28	80-73
Water	70-50	78-60	77-53	38-28	33-28	80-73
Remarks	Low cost. High viscosity.	Low cost. Water resistant.	Low cost. Fast setting. Water resistant.	Medium cost. Rapid setting.	Low cost. Water resistant.	High viscosity. Water resistant.

Proportions are parts by weight

PVAC - Polyvinyl acetate
PVA - Polyvinyl alcohol

Table 4.6

Fast Tack and Packaging Adhesives - Paper

	1 *General Packaging*	2 *General Packaging*	3 *Carton Sealing*	4 *Cup Adhesive*	5 *Box-Board*	6 *Glassine to Paper*
Material						
PVAC + Resin	-	-	95	-	-	30
PVAC + Resin	90	25	-	75	-	-
PVAC + Resin	-	-	-	-	90	-
Dibutyl phthalate	10	5	1.5	-	5	10
Hexylene glycol	-	-	-	-	3	-
Trichloroethylene	-	3.5	6	-	10	
Benzene	25	-	-	-	-	-
PVAS	25	-	-	-	-	-
Phosphoric acid	-	-	-	1	-	
"Gelvator" ® 1-90 (10% solution)	10	-	19	-	40	
Water	10	-	-	-	1	10
Remarks	Fast tack.	High wet tack, dark color	Fast set, high wet tack	Water and heat resistant	Very fast tack	Low cost, colorless

Table 4.7

Remoistenable Adhesives

	1 *All Synthetic*	2 *Anti-Block*	3 *Resin Dextrin Combination*	4 *Lay-flat Resin Dextrin*	5 *High Dextrin*
Material					
Resin	50a	50	-	-	-
Resin	-	-	35	35	10
Resin	15	10	-	-	-
Resin	-	-	-	3	-
Diutyl phthalate	-	-	3	-	1
Butyl ricinoleate	-	3	-	-	-
Polypropylene glycol	-	3	3	3	8
70% Sorbitol	-	-	-	X	X
Dextrin	-	-	35	30	40
Water	35	34	24	26	41
Remarks	Colorless film, good aging, fair gloss	Fair gloss, good aging	Good gloss, tan color,	Non-curling, good gloss tan color	Low cost, improved aging

Table 4.8

Adhesives for Difficult-to-Bond Surfaces

Material	1 *General Porous to Nonporous Surfaces*	2 *Porous Surfaces to PVCI and Aluminium Foil*	3 *Cloth Backed PVCI to Porous Surfaces*	4 *Porous Surfaces to Polyethylene and "Mylar"*	5 *Porous Surfaces to Polyester Films*	6 *PVCI Film to Walboard*	7 *Aluminum Foil to Paper and Chipboard*	8 *Bookbinding cover stock*	9 *Aluminium Foil to Chipboard*	10 *Poly-ethylene to Porous Surfaces*
Resin- PVAC	80	95	60	76	90	90	65	90	85	65
Dibutyl phthalate			5	19			10	6	10	10
Ethyl acetate	8									
Butyl acetate	12									
Methyl isobutyl ketone		5								
Toluene			10							
Butyl lactate					10					
Cyclohexanone						5				
Xylene										
PVA			25							25
NH_4OH (3% aqueous)							5			
Casein (15% aqueous)							20			
Santomerse ® SX										0.1
Water				6						
Remarks	High tack, high viscosity	Low viscosity,	Low cost, water resistant	Tacky film,	Clear film, low viscosity	Low viscosity, fast setting	Heat setting, water resistant	Fast setting, clear film	Fast setting, water resistant	High viscosity, tacky film

Table 4.9

Dry Mix Adhesives

	1 *Bag Bottom Paste*	2 *Wood Adhesive*	3 *Wood Adhesive*	4 *Wood Adhesive*	5 *Remoistenable*	6 *Wood Laminating*	7 *Kraft, Bag Seams Paperboard*	8 *Bag Side Seams*
Material								
Resin PVAC	6	20	20	39	49	15	4	4.4
Filler		40		13	7	100		
Clay							12	11
Walnut shell flour						10		
Pear starch	9						5	
Amioca starch								8.6
Ammonium sulphate				1.5				
Ammonium chloride				1.5				
Fungicide	1						1	
Reconstitute to	16% solids	60% solids	30% solids	55% solids	56% solids	desired viscosity	22% solids	24% solids
Remarks	High viscosity. Water resistant.	High bond strength. Short pot life. Water resistant	High viscosity. Low cost	Thermo-setting.	Add 3 parts DBP	Heat curable 300°F	Water resistant	Low viscosity, water resistant

8

EVA EMULSION ADHESIVES

Poly vinyl acetate ethylene copolymer adhesives available commercially are divided into three groups.

a) Those with low VAM content.

These are used for hot melt adhesives. These are manufactured by a continuous bulk copolymerisation at high pressure.

b) Those with equal proportion of VAM and ethylene

These are used for speciality rubber application and as a graft base for PVC polymeisation for impact modification. These are made in solution polymerization at medium pressure.

c) Those with high VAM content

These are made by emulsion polymerization at 20-100 kg/cm2. These are thermoplastic resin.

The copolymerisation of vinyl acetate with ethylene provides the opportunity for the manufacturer to produce an emulsion in which the dispersed resin may have any flexibility which a given application requires in the Tg range of 28^0 C to 30^0 C by simply changing the ratio of vinyl acetate to ethylene. For most of the application of resin dispersions in the coating and adhesive industry binder and adhesive properties are related closely to the glass transition temperature (Tg). It is defined as that temperature at which the thermal expansion coefficient undergoes a discontinuity. Thus a plot of specific volume against temperature for a polymer will undergo a change in slope at the Tg. The Tg is also reflected in the measurement such as heat capacity, dialectic consent and index of refraction.

Macroscopically the glass transition is marked by a noticeable increase in the mechanical rigidity as the polymer system changes from a viscous or rubber stage above the Tg to hard and brittle glass below the Tg Blended polymer will generally exhibit a dual Tg one for each of the components.

The VAE emulsions have found their greatest use in the application listed below.

1. PVC and other film laminating.
2. Packaging adhesives
3. Film to film laminations
4. Pencil adhesives

Formulation

A typical EVA (VAE) emulsion adhesive is as below.

EVA	35%
Rosin	7%
Hydrocarbon resin	5%
Water	45%
Plasticizer	7%
Soda ash	1%

EVA Hot Melt Adhesive

Hot melt adhesives are defined as thermoplastic compounds normally solid at room temperature which becomes sufficiently fluid at elevated temperature to wet substrates. Hot melt adhesives form bonds by resolidification upon cooling. They usually contain neither water nor organic solvents.

EVA copolymer based hot melt adhesives are most often composed of two ingredients plus one or more secondary components. Primary ingredients are the EVA copolymers and one or more modifier resins. Secondary compounds are waxes, plasticizers, fillers and antioxidants. Most of the modifiers are relatively low molecular weight solid resins like rosin and its derivatives, hydrocarbon resins, coumarone Indene resin, polyterpene resin, polystyrene resin, phenolic resin. Phenolic resins re used for imparting high strength of the adhesive at elevated temperature..

Plasticizers are used, usually liquid one to modify and improve the flexibility and adhesion of hot melt adhesives. The plasticizers which are used are DBP, DOP, polyester resins and tricresyl phosphate. Inorganic fillers and pigments are occasionally used in hot melt adhesives. Their contributions are lower cost, colour control and improved cohesive strength. Increased melt viscosity, setting in the melt and tack reduction are some of the negative contribution of the fillers and colours.

There are no defailed set of rules for addition of fillers and colours. Obvious consideration is a good thermal stability and fine particle size. Filler content is usually limited to 20% in hot melt adhesives and they are non catalyst for thermal degradation. Abrasive fillers are usually avoided.

Antioxidants improve the thermal stability of the hot melt blends. Butylate hydroxy toluene is a widely accepted antioxidant. These are usually used at a concentration of 0.1 to 0.2%. A general formulation can be written as:

EVA copolymer (s)	20-50
Modifiers	20-50
Wax	0-20
Plasticizer	0-20
Filler	0-20
Antioxidant	0.1-1.0

These adhesives are used for bookbinding, carton and case sealing, shoe making adhesives and pressure sensitive adhesives for tapes, envelopes and also adhesives for furniture making.

Increase in content of VAM improves the adhesive properties with respect to aluminium, steel, flexible and rigid PVC, polypropylene and HDPE, However, increased VAM content does not have any effect on bonding of paper, wood and ABS plastics.

Some of the typical EVA hot melt adhesives formulations are given below.

Formulation (book binding)

EVA	35-45	parts
Staybelite resin	20-30	"
Pentalyin H	20-30	"
Microcrystalline wax	10-20	"
Antioxidant	0.05 to 0.25 pph	

Formulation (carton & case sealing)

EVA	40	parts
CKM 2600	15	"
Piccolyte A 115	12.5	"
Super STA Tac	12.5	"
Polywax	10	"
Castor wax	10	"
Antioxidant	0.1	pph

Formulation (shoe making)

EVA	25-40%
Modifier	30-50%
Microcrystalline wax	10-20%
Antioxidant	0.1 to 0.3 pph

Formulation D (pressure sensitive adhesive)

EVA	35-50	parts
Plasticizer	0-20	"
Tackifier	30-50	"
Filler	0-5	"
Antioxidant	0.1-0.5 pph	

9

RUBBER BASED ADHESIVES

Natural rubber based

Rubber based adhesives offer the greatest variety of properties of any generic class of adhesives. Relatively low strength system such as rubber cement, pressure sensitive tapes and self seal envelopes, all of which are based upon rubber have become household items. Other type of rubber based adhesives have been developed which are used for high strength structural applications required by aircraft, automotive and other industries. The unusually wide range of properties available in an elastomer based adhesives is due to the wide range of properties of natural and synthetic rubber, and the modifying characteristics of the additives such as tackify, filling, plasticizing and curing.

Rubber based adhesives may contain a wide variety of components materials such as elastomers, resins or tackifiers, fillers, plasticizers and softeners, antioxidants, curing agents and sequestering agents. In addition to the components cited above, aqueous adhesives based on latex rubber contains protective colled, emulsifier thickener and emulsion stabilizer. Rubber based adhesives are produced in a number of forms, such as solvent cement, latex cement, pressure sensitive adhesive, sealant, mastic and hot melt.

Molecular scale contact between adhesive and adherend and the wetting characteristics of the adhesives are two important parameters for good adhesion. Tackifier may enhance the adhesion of nonpolar elastomers by improving wetability, increasing polarly and altering the viscoelastic properties of the adhesive mass. By reducing elastic recovery and facilitating plastic deformation, the tackifier may enable the adhesive mass to contact the surface more intimately, thus enhancing bond strength.

Tack is the property of a material which enables it to form a bond of measurable strength immediately upon contact with another surface. Tack is thus instantaneous adhesion and differs from ultimate strength. The time required for development of strength by means of tack is very short. Tack is a function of the rheological properties and tensile strength of cohesion, yield value, modulus of elasticity and rate of elastic recovery of the adhesive. Tack is sensitive to variations in temperature, pressure, rate of application and removal of pressure and the contact time.

Although natural rubber processes tack characteristics, the bond strength developed by rubber alone is inadequate for many uses, tackifiers in the form of resins are added to these systems to increase their tack properties. The choice of tackifier resin influences the quality of the adhesion. Maximum tack is inversely related to softening point or viscosity of tackifying resin. The higher the softening point, the lower is the resin content at which maximum tack is obtained.

Tensile strength, as measured by the yield stress of an adhesive composition, decreases with increasing tackifier concentration. The ultimate elongation of such blends increases very rapidly as the concentration of tackifying resin increases from 50 to 75%.

Emulsion adhesives contain the usual ingredients of an adhesive, in emulsified or latex form. They also contain a surface active agent and a protective colloid to stabilize the emulsion on storage. Latex adhesives are low cost. reasonably viscous at high solid content adhesives and are free of air pollution problems toxicity or fire hazards.

Solvent cements are generally produced by removing the freshly milled elastomer from the mill and dissolving it in solvent. For natural and SBR, solvents such as toluene, n-hexane, naphtha, gasoline or rubber solvent may be used. For nitrile, polychloroprene and other polar rubbers, polar solvents such as MEK, MIK or ethylene dichloride may be used, alone or blended with nonpolar ones. The dissolved rubber is then blended with solution of additives such as resins, to form the finished cements.

Mastics constitute a special type of adhesives which may be either latex solvent based. The unique of mastics is their extremely high viscosity. Most mastics contain natural rubber, SBR, reclaim or blends of these tackifiers and fillers. Mastics are used in large volume, chiefly in industrial application and in the construction industry where low bond strengths are adequate for the purpose. They are employed to fasten floor ceiling and wall tiles, roll floor covering and in the automobile industry for putting insulation, silencer and lining pads. Mastics are usually applied to both surfaces to be bonded.

Latex systems have many advantages over the solvent type. Major applications for latex adhesives are for porous substrates such as textiles, paper and leather. An effective way to improve tack and adhesiveness of an elastomer in latex systems exhibits better hold out on porous surfaces, one coat of such an adhesive often suffices for good bonding. Latex adhesives furnish adequate strength for a large number of application. Shoe making employ latex cements at some steps in the manufacturing process. Latex adhesives are used on paper for labels, laminations, bags and books and on textile for impregnation of seam bindings.

Pressure sensitive adhesives constitute a significant segment of the total rubber based adhesive industry. The best known example of this type of system consists of a flexible tape coated with a permanent tacky mass. These adhesives lack high strength because they must be soft to tacky. They are also temperature sensitive susceptible to creep. Tape is available in rolls which must unwind easily. The adhesive coating must show quick adhesion to substrates. The pressure sensitive tapes today are offered with a wide variety of backing materials such as crepe paper, aluminium foil, fabric, cellophane, celluloseacetate, polyester film, polyethylene, polypropylene, flexible PVC, woven glass fibre cloth etc. The application are in sealing cartons, insulation tape, labeling tape, surgical tape, etc.

Hot melt adhesives are thermoplastic bonding agents composed of 100% nonvolatile materials i.e. They are solid at room temperature, and becomes liquid on heating. On application, adhesives return to the solid state and develop bond on cooling. Hot melt pressure sensitive adhesives are suited where fast production with cheap raw material cost and the elimination of the solvents are necessary conditions for the economy of the process.

Manufacture

The cut rubber is first milled. The rubber is repeated passed through a two roll mill or a bandury mixing. Here the rubber is subjected to compression and strong shear force. This milling given a dough like material. In the same mill, solvent, tackifier, filler, additives etc. are mixed to get an adhesives of desired consistency and properties. During milling the material is heated to 50 C. Alternately the milled rubber can be mixed other ingredients and solvent in a steam heated closed sturdy agitated vessel with reflux condenser. After adhesive is ready it is discharged into storage tanks.

Natural rubber is obtained as latex which is a water dispersed colloid collected as sap from rubber tree. Synthetic rubbers are produced by emulsion polymerization and are, usually available available also in latex form. Those of large commercial interests are the styrene-butadine, acrylonitrile-butadiene and polychloroprene elastomers.

Various compounding ingredients, such as tackifiers, surfactants, stabilizers, fillers, builders etc., are added to the latex in an agitated steam heated vessel. The mixture is then vigorously stirred with heating till the appropriate consistency is obtained.

Mastics are also made in the same manner. The adhesives have high viscosity and can be made from natural, reclaim and synthetic rubbers and their blends. Some asphalt and bitumen are added together with tackifiers, fillers etc. and solvents in small quantity. The product is then kneaked in a bandury mill or two roll mill. Mastic contains less quantity of tackifiers and plasticizers.

Rubber based hot melt adhesives are prepared by melting the rubber and mixing the various ingredients. The melt at elevated temperature are discharged into cooling trays. The solidified mass is then crushed and ground and packed. While using the powder is melted and applied.

Applications and Formulations

Rubber based adhesives are used for fixing vinyl tiles on floor, in self adhesive envelops, as floor tile adhesives, in fixing shoe soles, as leather adhesives, in automobile internal rim, for carpet making etc. It is also used as a binder for non woven fabric, as the adhesive for pressure sensitive tape etc. Rubber adhesives are also used as sealing mastics and caulking compounds. Acrylic resins are sometimes added to rubber adhesives as a graft copolymer to give higher strength to the adhesive.

Recipe for Latex

Natural rubber latex concentrate (high ammonia, 60% total solids)	1000	parts
Ammonia solution (2% by wt.) 738 parts		
Methyl methacrylate monomer (Stabilizer less than 0.02% hydroquinone)	610	parts
T-butyl hydroperoxide	1.8	parts
Oleic acid	3.0	parts
Tetra ethylene pentamine aqeuous solution (10% by wt.)	7.0	parts

Depolymerized rubber adhesives are of minor interest only and this is because of its use as adhesive for fixing bristles in brushes. This material is a liquid rubber prepared by heating low grade natural rubber in air at 250° C. This material is soluble in most organic solvents except alcohols and ketones and is compatible with many drying oils.

All the formulations are based on parts by weight and normally dry weight unless otherwise stated.

Self adhesive envelopes

60% natural latex	100	parts
10% potassium hydroxide	0.2	"
50% aqueous dispersion of zinc ethyl dithiocarbomate	0.5	"

Ceramic tile adhesive-A

60% natural latex (sodium pentachlorophenate preserved)	100	parts
Methyl cellulose (added as 5% solution)	5	"
Gypsum	130-200	"
Bentonite	10	"
Surfactant 10% solution	10	"
Tackifying resin dispersion	20	"

Ceramic tile adhesive-B

60% natural latex (sodium penta chlorophenae preserved)	100	parts
50% polyvinyl acetate emulsion	120	"
Surfactant (10% solution)	10	"
Gypsum	200-250	"
Bentonite	20	"
Tackifying resin dispersion	20	"

Floor tile adhesive

60% natural	100	parts
Methyl cellulose (added as 50% solution)	5	"
Clay	150	"
Black reclaim dispersion	50	"
Tackifying resin dispersion	30-80	"
High boiling point naphtha (as emulsion)	10	"

Leather adhesive

605 natural latex	100	parts
Sodium ethylene diamine tetraceate, 20% solution	2.5	"
Antioxidant (polymerized trimethyl hydroquinone as 50% dispersion)	0.5	"

Automobile internal trim

60% natural latex	100	parts
Methyl cellulose (added as 5% solution)	2	"
Antioxidant (as 50% dispersion)	50	"
Clay (as 50% dispersion)	50	"
Coumarone Indene dispersion	20	"

Food jar sealing compound

60% natural latex (ammonia preserved)	100	parts
Clay (as 50% dispersion stabilized with food grade surfactant)	200	

General purpose pure gum adhesive

60% natural rubber	100
Zinc dibutylthiocarmate (50% dispersion)	2
Ammonium caseinate 10% solution	10

Crown Cork Adhesive

60% natural latex	100	parts
Fungicide	0.2	"
Ethylene glycol	0.8	"
Ammonium caseinate, 20% solution in water	11.2	"
Sodium hydroxide	0.10	"
added with water	0.30	"
Formalin	5.10	"
Ester gum	3.7	"
Mineral oil	0.4	"
Water	6.2	"

Fungicale is disso lved in ethylene glycol. Estergum and minerla oil are mixed and then dispersed in the given quantity of water.

Tufted carpet adhesive and backing

	Primary	Secondary	
Natural latex (high ammonia)	100	100	parts
Stabilizer/wetting agent	1.5	1.0	"
Thio urea(added as 10% solution)	1.0	1.0	"
Antioxidant	1.0	1.0	"
Water	to give 75% solids		
Whiting (added as slurry)	400	250	"
Polyacrylate thickener (5% solution)	0.2	0.3	"

Tufted carpet vulcanizing compositions

Natural latex	25	25	parts
SBR latex	75	75	"
Whiting	200	225	"
Baryres	10	225	"
Clay	10	225	"
Sulphur, zinc oxide & accelerators	10	10	"

Adhesive binder for non woven fabrics

Concentrated natural latex	100	parts
Amionic stabilizer	0.5	"
Sulphur	2.0	"
ZDC	1.5	"
Zinc mercaptabenzthiozole	0.75	"
Antioxidant	1.0	"
Zinc oxide	5.0	"

Surgical tape adhesive

Natural rubber	100	parts
Ester gum	100	"
Lanolin	20	"
Zinc oxide	50	"

Industrial pressure sensitive tapes

Natural rubber (pale crepe)	100	parts
Poly (B-pinene) resin, m.p. 70° C	75	"
Colourless petroleum oil	5	"
Polymerized trimethyldihydro	2	"

Industrial pressure sensitive tape

Natural rubber	100	parts
Coumarone Indene resin (35)	30-150	"
Antioxidant 1.5 "		
Calcium carbonate or zinc oxide	30-150	"

General purpose transparent adhesive

Natural rubber	100	parts
Rosin (ww)	10	"
Antioxidant	1	"

General purpose black adhesive

Natural rubber	100	parts
Whole tyre reclaim	100	"
Coumarone resin	50	"
Whitting	50	"
Antioxidant	1.5	"

General purpose black adhesive, heat resistant

Natural rubber	100	parts
Whole tyre reclaim	100	"
Zinc resinate	50-80	"
Clay	50	"
Antioxidant	1.5	"
Polyisocyanate	10	"

Vulcanizing cement

	Part A	Part B	
Natural rubber	100	100	parts
Sulphur	2.0	-	"
Butyl ziamate	-	7.0	"
Zinc oxide	20	-	"
Antioxidant	5.0	-	"

Fabric combining for coated fabrics

	Part A	Part B	Part C
Robac gamma (ultra accelerator)	15.0	-	-
Waxolene red	0.12	-	-
Coal tar naphtha	84.88	-	-
Natural rubber	-	21.60	7.90
Zinc oxide	-	1.10	-
Antioxidant	-	0.30	-
Rubber petroleum solvent		- 77.0	73.20
Sulphur	-	-	17.40
Waxolin yellow	-	-	1.50

Fabric combining for double texture water proof

	Part A	Part B	
Natural rubber	100	100	parts
Zinc oxide	10	-	
Sulphur	8	-	
zinc isopropyl xanthate	-	4	"

The above parts are mixed by volume in the propertions of 1:20:1

Reclaim rubber dispersion with asphalt

Whole tyre reclaim	100	parts
Surfactant	2-5	"
Caustic potash	1-2	"
Ester gum	20-30	"
Clay	30-40	"
Asphalt emulsion	175-185	"
Water	70-80	"

Road repair compound

Natural rubber (powder)	1	part
Asphalt	60	parts
Sharp sand with fine aggregate broken stone	34	"

Graft copolymer primer for PVC

Copolymer	5	parts
Titanium dioxide	0.1	"
Solvent	100	"

10

BUTYL & POLY ISOBUTYLENE RUBBER ADHESIVES

Butyl and poly isobutylene rubbers are elastomeric polymers which are used quite widely in the adhesive and sealants, are used both as primary binders and also as tackifier and modifiers. Butyl rubber is a co polymer of isobutylene and isoprene, and poly-isobutylene is a homopolymer. The carbon hydrogen structure of the butyl-rubber is relatively long and straight, containing between 47000 to 60000 units. This regular structure, with few double bonds or reactive sites, make butyl rubber stable and inert to the corrosion agents and temperature. It is resistant to vegetable and animal fats and also to attack by many chemicals. The butyl elastomers have a low water absorption and they do not interfere with the orientation of the rubber molecule.

Polymers of isobutylene are not crystalline. The completely amorphous nature of these polymers gives them internal mobilities which imparts flexibility, permanent tack and resistance to shock. These polymers are non polar hydrocarbon with good tack property. Their attraction to many surfaces is weak and therefore, they are often mixed with resins which impart some polar character to the blend. The poly-isobutylenes have the same chemical backbone as butyl rubber, but they are essentially free of double bonds in the polymer chain.

Chlorobutyl rubber is prepared by chlorinating the regular butyl polymer under controlled conditions. Chlorine substitutes hydrogen atoms and also reacts with the unsaturation. Chlorobutyl rubber can be readily blended and cured with other unsaturated elastomers.

Butyl rubber latex is an emulsion of the elastomer. It has a solid content of 63% and shows pH of 5.5. Butyl rubber latex has excellent mechanical, chemical and freeze thaw stability which make them widely compatible in compounding and blending with other ingredients. A number of partially crosslinked butyl rubber and other modified forms are available. These products are used in adhesives and sealants where equipment limitations prohibit the use of normal forms of butyl rubber.

Manufacture

Butyl latex is normally compounded to make adhesives in an agitated tank with heating device. Ball milling is done for dispersion of filler in the adhesive. Butyl and PIB are often shredded before adding to the mixing vessel.

Compounding of adhesives by blending various compatible polymers result in high strength with high tack and other characteristics. Fine pigment addition increase cohesive strength and stiffness, reduce cold flow and tack. Coarse pigment addition increases tack. Platy inert pigments such as mica, graphite and talc are preferred for imparting acid and chemical resistance and-also the cohesive strength. A wide range of tackifiers and plasticizers are used to extend the viscosity range. The most common plasticizer is polybutene. Resins like polyterpenes modified rosins, blocked phenolics are added to develop the desired level of tack. Butyl rubber and poly-isobutylene are soluble in hydrocarbon solvents and chlorinated hydrogen solvents which give solutions of much higher viscosity on all equal weight percentage basis. There are four curing systems used (a) the quinoil cure. (b) cure with sulphur, (c) resin cure and (d) zinc oxide cure.

A heavy duty kneader is used to make a butyl rubber solution in mineral spirit. This solution is transferred to a low duty mixer for further compounding with pigments, resins, plasticizers and other ingredients.

A master batch of the polymers and elastomers and filler is made in a ball mill and the master batch is mixed with solvent a mixer.

Paper cement

Isobutylene polymer	100	parts
Hydrocarbon solvents	900	"

Laminating cement for polyethylene film

Butyl rubber	100	parts
Terpene phenolic resin	5	"
Hydrocarbon solvent to give appropriate viscosity		

Flocking adhesive

Isobutylene Polymer	200	parts
Terpene phenolic resin	20	"
Butyl zimate	0.5	"

Hydrocarbon solvent give appropriate viscosity

Butyl self curing cement

	Part A	Part B	
Butyl oxide	50	50	parts
Zinc oxide	2.5	2.5	"
Stearic acid	1.5	1.5	"
SRF black	-	40	"
Hydrogenated rosin	20	-	"
Sulphur	0.7	0.7	"
p-quinone dioxime	2	-	"
PbO2	-	4	"
Solvent heptane	400	400	"
92% isopropanol	5	5	"

Chlorobutyl high strength cement

Chlorobutyl	100	parts
Ditridecyl phathalate	5	"
Diethyl thiourea	5	"
Toluene	360	"
Isopropyl alcohol	40	"

PIB based Pressure Sensitive Adhesive

Polyisobutylene	100	parts
Hydrogenated methyl ester	35	"
Hydrocarbon resin	45	"
Polybutene	70	"
Antioxidant	0.5	"
Solvent to coatable viscosity		

Chlorobutyl blend PSA for general purpose tape

Chlorobutyl	50	parts
Styrene butadiene rubber	50	"
Polymerised rosin	30	"
Poly isobutylene	30	"
Ethyl antioxidant	0.5	"
Solvent to coatable viscosity		

Simple butyl PSA for transparent tape

Butyl rubber	100	parts
Poly isobutylene	75	"
Solvent to coatable viscosity		

PSA for vinyl floor tile

Butyl rubber	100	parts
Poly isobutylene	20	"
Terpene phenolic resin	70	"
Solvent to coatable viscosity		

Solvent adhesive for surgical tape

Poly isobutylene	100	parts
Zinc oxide	50	"
Hydrated alumina	50	"
White oil	50	"
Phenolic resin	70	"
Hydrocarbon solvent to coatable viscosity		

Pipe wrap

Butyl rubber	100	parts
Carbon black	90	"
Whiting	20	"
Polymerized rosin	3	"
Phenolic rosin	7	"
Copper oxide	2	"
Process oil	5	"

Architectural sealing tapes

Butyl rubber	100	parts
Silica	50	"
TiO2	50	"
Whiting	300	"
Talc	150	"
Polybutene	200	"
White antioxidant	2	"

Electrical insulation tape

Butyl rubber	100	parts
Poly isobutylene	10	"
Resin D	1	"
Zinc oxide	5	"
Vapour talc	60	"
Clay	60	"
Carbon black	10	"
Polyethylene	5	"
Hydrocarbon resin	5	"
Polyac	0.5	"
P-quinoue dioxime	0.2	"

Solvent release sealing compound

Butyl rubber, 50% mineral spirit	500	Parts
Poly isobutylene	20	"
Isostearic acid	5	"
Fibre talc	300	"
Whiting	200	"
TiO2	25	"
Phenolic resin	35	"
Polybutene	100	"
Blown soya oil	15	"
Cobalt naphthenate 6%	0.5	"
Silica	20	"
Mineral spirit	55	"

Automotive sealants

	Type A	Type B	
Butyl rubber	100	60	parts
Chlorobutyl	-	40	"
Silica	50	-	"
CaCO3	-	50	"
Carbon black	140	100	"
Polybutenes	140	115	"
Hydrogenated rosin	30	-	"
Zinc oxide	-	0.4	"
Stearic acid	-	0.4	"

Chemically curing insulated window sealant

	Part A	Part B	
Butyl rubber	60 40		parts
CaCO3	75	-	"
Epoxy silane	4	-	"
Polybutene	10	-	"
White antioxidant	1.5	-	"
P-quinone dioxime	3.5	-	"
Thixseal	6	-	"
PbO2	-	7.5	"
Fumed silica	-	10	"
Toluene	46	30.5	"

Insulated window sealant

Poly-isobutylene	100	parts
Talc	48	"
Carbon black	2	"

Wax blends & hot melt adhesives

Ethylene vinyl acetate copolymer	25	parts
Microcrystalline wax	30	"
Petroleum hydrocarbon resin	35	"
Poly isobutylene	10	"
Antioxidant	0.5	"

Rope form of hot melt adhesives

Butyl rubber	20	parts
Beta-pinene resin (m.p) 15° C	20	"
EVA copolymer	20	"
Low mol. wt. polyethylene (12000)	20	"
Low mol. wt polyethylene (20,000)	19	"
Antioxidant	1	"

Latex adhesives

Butyl latex	100	parts
Piccovar	65	"
CaCO3	90	"
Polybutene		40 "
Piccopale	45	"
Dispersant	1.0	"
Thickener	0.9	"

Latex general purpose adhesives

Butyl latex	100	parts
Casein (ammoninated)	25	"
Piccopale	50	"
Silica	25	"

11

NITRILE RUBBER ADHESIVES

Nitrile rubbers are elastomer copolymer of unsaturated nitriles with dienes. The commercial nitrile rubber are prefominantly copolymer of butadiene and acrylonitrile. The oil resistance and adhesive properties of these copolymers increase with an increase in the nitrile content. The nitrile rubbers are compatible with phenol formaldehyde resins, resorcinol formaldehyde resin, hydrogenated rosins, epoxies and coaltar resins. The nitrile rubber adhesives are applied in the form of emulsion, mastics and film on tapes. They have out standing shelf life and elevated temperature resistance. They have been used for coating fabrics to provide oil resistance and wear resistance. They have been used for coating fabrics to provide oil resistance and wear resistance. Blended with phenolic resins they have been used to (a) laminate aluminium to stainless steel, (b) fabricate many airplane structures, (c) bond abrasives to metal, (d) bond break lining to brake shoes, (e) fabricate panels for curtain-wall construction, (f) bond metal to nitrile rubber stocks, (g) laminate leather, (h) attach soles in shoe manufacturing, (i) and bond cork, card board, leather board, paper, nitrocellulose, nylon and other polymeric films.

The nitrile rubbers are compatible to polar adherends such as protein fibre, cotton fabric, paper and wood.

For spraying applications

	Type A	Type B	
Nitrile rubber	10.0	10.0	parts
Methyl ethyl ketone	79.0	79.0	"
Water	11.0	11.0	"
Carboxylic vinyl polymer	-	0.5	"
Di(2-ethyl hexyl)amine	-	0.5	"

Black curing cement

Nitrile rubber	100	parts
Zinc oxide	5	"
Sulphur	3	"
EPC black	50	"
Resin D	5	"
Coumarone Indene resin	25	"
Refined coal tar	25	"

Non-black curing cement

Nitrile rubber	100	parts
Stearic acid	0.5	"
Zinc oxide	10	"
Sulphur	2	"
Calcium silicate	100	"
TiO2	25	"
Coumarone indene resin	10	"
Dibutyl phthalate	10	"
Accelerator	1.5	"

Laminating adhesive

	1	2	3	4	
Nitrile	20	10	20	10	parts
VMCH	-	10	-	5	"
Phenolic resin	10	5	10	5	"
Triphenyl phosphate	-	-	-	2	"
Monochloro benzene	-	-	90	40	"
Methyl ethyl ketone	100	75	30	40	"

Adhesives for leather to vinyl

	1	2	3	4	
Nitrile rubber	9	9	9	9	parts
VMCH	18	18	18	18	"
Triphenyl phosphate	2	2	2	-	"
Phenolic resin	-	-	-	2	"
Tetrahydrofuran	-	5	8	-	"
Methyl ethyl ketone	73	-	20	73	"
Toluene	-	-	48	-	"
Cyclohexanol	-	25	25	-	"

Low temperature curing adhesives

Nitrile rubber	10-50
Epoxy resin	90-50
Methyl ethyl ketone	80
Triethylenetetramine	2-20

These adhesives cure at 60° C in 30 minutes and at room temperature in 4 to 34 hours.

Adhesive for polymeric film metal bonding

PVC polyvinyl acetate and other polymeric films are laminated with aluminium, brass and other metals foils or sheets by coating the polymeric film and the metal with an adhesive of following formulation :

Nitrile rubber	150	parts
Vinyl chloride vinylidene	50	"
Chloride copolymer	20	"
Plasticizer	10	"
A barium stabilizer	6	"
Sulphur	1	"
Benzothiazolyl disulphide	1	"

Adhesive for textile pile surface

Cellulose acetate flocks are adhered to textile material to make a pile surfuce using following cement.

Nitrile rubber	100	parts
Sulphur	3	"
Mercoptobenzothiazole	2.4	"
Phenyl guanidine	0.6	"
Zinc oxide	7.5	"
Coumarone resin	37.5	"
Dimethyl phthalate	300	"
Bix (2-ethyl hexyl) phthalate)	45	"
Methyl ethyl ketone	378	"
Methyl isobutyl ketone	256	"

General purpose cements

Heat activated

Nitrile rubber	100	parts
Phenolic resin	50	"
Methyl ethyl ketone	100	"

Self curing cements

Master batch

Nitrile rubber	100	parts
Zinc oxide	5	"
Carbon black	100	"

Component A

Base master batch	205	205	parts
DBA	4	-	"
MBT	-	4	"
Sulphur	4	4	"
MEK	40	40	"

Component B

Base Master batch205 205 parts			
ZBX	4	-	"
Ethazate	4	-	"
Butene	-	4	"
CPB	-	4	"
MEK	40	40	"

Low temperature curing cements

Nitrile rubber	100	100	parts
Zinc oxide	5	5	"
Sulphur	6	-	"
Channel black	50	50	"
Coumarone indene resin	25	25	"
Aldol-l-naphthyl amine	5	5	"
Aromatic oil	25	25	"
Mercaptobenzothizaole	-	6	"

Splice adhesive

An adhesive designed for splicing cured or uncured nitrile compound to themselves with heat is shown in the next formulation.

Nitrile rubber	100	parts
Zinc oxide	15	"
Aminox	2	"
Carbon black	50	"
Coumarone indene resin	25	"
Phenolic resin	20	"
MBT	2	"
Sulphur	2	"

Adhesive of high tack

	Part A	Part B	
Nitrile rubber	100	100	parts
Carbon black	10	10	"
Zinc oxide	150	150	"
Resin D	5	5	"
Refined coal tar	35	35	"
Benzyl alcohol	18	18	"
Dibutyl metacresol	35	35	"
Sulphur	5	-	"
Sulphur	-	8	"
Butyraoldehyde aniline	-	8	"

An extra tacky adhesive is be prepared by dissolving 1.4 kg. of A in 500 ml of chlorotoluene and making up to 1 litre with chlorobenzen. 1.4 kg of B is dissolved 500 ml of chlorotoluene and made up to 1 litre with chlorobenzene. Mix equal propertion by volume by volume just before using.

Spreading compounds

The following spreading compounds are recommended for maximum resistance to petrol and mineral oils and for low temperature flexibility.

Nitrile rubber	100	100	parts
Zinc oxide	5	5	"
Sulphur	2	2	"
Carbon black	75	60	"
Triacetin	35	–	"
Benzotiazyl disulphide	1.5	-	"
Litharge	-	10	"
Resin D	-	2	"
Dioctyl phthalate	-	25	"

General purpose spreading compound

Nitrile rubber	100	parts
Zinc oxide	5	"
Sulphur	2.5	"
Carbon black	75	"
Castor oil	10	"
Synthetic resin extender	20	"
Benzothiazyl disulphide	1.5	"
Stearic acid	1.0	"

The above spreading compounds are dissolve in nitroethane before use.

Coating adhesive for paper, resistant to oils

The recipe below is for fast curing adhesives for paper coating that is retained after hot oil ageing at 70° C .

Nitrile rubber	100	parts
Zinc oxide	5	"
Sulphur	1.5	"
Carbon black	20	"
Clay	75	"
Whiting	75	"
Phenolic resin	40	"
Plasticizer	10	"
Resin D	1	"
Benzothiazyl disulphide	1	"

3% hexamethylene tetramine, 5% isopropyl alcohol and 95% methyl ethyl ketone are added to make up as a 35% solids adhesives before use. The adhesive can be cured at 70° C and can be refrigerated to prolong working life.

Vinyl to fabric adhesive

Nitrile rubber	100	parts
Calcium silicate	40	"
TiO2	10	"
Refined coal tar	25	"
Coumarone indene resin	25	"
Chlorinated rubber	100	"

Methyl ethyl ketone is used to make 15% total solids

Non black cement formulation

A similar non black cement suggested for the adhesion of cotton, wood paper, leather nuclear shoe soling is given below.

Nitrile rubber	100	parts
Stearic acid	1	"
Zinc oxide	5	"
Calcium silicate	10	"
Sulphur	2	"
Dibenzylamine	2	"
Methyl ethyl ketone	600	"

Pressure sensitive adhesive

This adhesives especially useful as a gum coating for plastic, paper, fabric tapes and labels.

Nitrile rubber	100
Coumarone indene resin (M.P. 45-55^{0} C)	100

Solvent methyl ethyl ketone and toluene
Solid concentration 20% by wt.

The rubber and the resin are a blended in an agitated vessel and solvent is added until a smooth, free flowing cement is obtained.

Nitrile rubber phenolic resin tape formulation

Nitrile rubber	100	parts
Phenolic resin	75	"
Zinc oxide	5	"
Sulphur	3	"
Accelerator	1	"
Stearic acid	1	"
Carbon black	20	"
Filler	100	"
Plasticizer	10	"

Leather adhesives from nitrile rubber

Leather adhesives have been formulated from nitrile rubber using the following composition.

Nitrile rubber	100	parts
Vinyl chloride vinyl acetate	100	"
Zinc oxide	5	"
Stearic acid	1.5	"
Calcium silicate	2	"
Solvent	600:800	"

Structural adhesives

Nitrile rubbers blended with phenolic resin may be used to bond a wide variety of construction materials including iron, wood glass, masonite, fibre board, card board, cork, phenolic resin, vinyl chloride and many porous materials.

Part A

Phenolic resin	45	parts
MEK/M chlorobenzene (70/30 by vol.)	90	"

Part B

Nitrile rubber	100	"
Carbon black	50	"
Zinc oxide	5	"
Stearic acid	0.5	"
Sulphur	3	"
Benzothiazyl disulphide	1.5	"
MEK/M-chlorobenzene	165	"

12

SBR ADHESIVES

Styrene butadiene rubber which found limited applications as adhesives earlier, has now surpassed natural rubber in consumption for making adhesive. The limitation of SBR as adhesive component in developing tack and cohesive strength, have been eliminated through blending of resin. SBR based adhesives offer good heat ageing and water resistance properties. SBR dissolves easily in hydrocarbon solvents to form an excellent base for adhesives. The adhesive compounder is no longer dependent upon SBR designed for dry rubber compounding. The SBR rubber manufacturers now supply the solution to the compounder. Styrene and butadiene are also emulsion copolymerized and a SBR latex is produced. The latex is used to make water based adhesives.

Properties : SBR is less polar compared to other synthetic rubbers and unlike natural rubber SBR does not develop surface peroxidal activity upon mastication. Poor tack of SBR can be overcome by reducing its molecular weight, decreasing its viscosity and adding tackifiers. SBR is rarely used alone as an adhesives.

Pressure sensitive adhesives

SBR is mainly blended with tackifying resins such as hydrogenated rosin esters, terpene phenolic resin and alpha pinene polymers.

(a)	SBR (54 money viscosity, 23.5% styrene)	100	parts
	Hydrogenated rosin ester	75	"
	Antioxidant	2	"
	Toluene	1003	"

(b)	SBR (77 mooney viscosity, 25% styrene)	100	parts
	Terpene phenolic resin	100	"
	Solvent	1000	"

formulation to obtain improved heat and UV light resistance.

(c)	SBR (54 mooney viscosity, 25% styrene)	100	parts
	Thermoplastic polyolefin rubber	150	"
	Phenolic resin	15	"
	Sp 1056	5	"
	Zinc resinate	5	"
	Antioxidant	2	"
	Toluene	50	"

Other elevated PSAs can be prepared using sulphur and butyl eight as the curing agent as shown in the following formulation.

(d)	SBR (77 mooney viscosity, 23.5% styrene)	100	parts
	Zinc oxide	40	"
	Hydrogenated rosin ester	100	"
	Mineral oil	10	"
	Sulphur	3	"
	Butyl eight	8	"
	Antioxidant	2	"
	Solvent	100	"

(e)	SBR (54 mooney viscosity, 23.5% styrene)	100	parts
	Polyterpene resin	70	"
	Polybutene	15	"
	Toluene	815	"

PVC adhesive tape

SBR (50 mooney viscosity, 23.5% styrene)	50	parts
Natural rubber (crude smoked sheet)	50	"
Polyterpene resin	45	"
Phenol terpene resin	45	"
Phenolic resin	12	"
Alumina	10	"
Di-tert-amyl hydroquinone	2	"
Carbon black	10	"
Calcium carbonte	50	"
Heptane	640	"
Ethanol	10	"

Box board adhesive

SBR (54 mooney viscosity, 25% styrene)	100	parts
Polyolefin rubber	150	"
SP-1056	15	"
Zinc resinate	2	"
Superlite	5	"
Toluene	50	"

Sprayable adhesives

The application of adhesives to substrate such as paper, cardboard, wood, plastic and cloth can be conveniently done using a sprayable adhesives. A typical formulation shows a blend of two SBR containing 27.3% styrene and 0.7% divinyl benzene and 20 parts of cross linked SBR containing 27.6% styrene and 0.4% divinyl benzene. The two rubber are milled together for about 2.5 min at 30-75^0 C.

Crosslinked SBR	100	parts
Dimerized rosin	100	"
Hydrogenated rosin ester	40	"
Stalite	2	"
Morpholine	1	"
Hexane	450-500	"
Methylene chloride	50	"

Tyre tread adhesives

SBR polymer are useful in making tyre tread adhesive particularly when used with oil extended SBR tyres. The following recipe is an example.

High mooney SBR	100	parts
Kerosine	40	"
Petroleum softener	10	"
Carbon black	60	"
Zinc oxide	5	"
Sulphur	2.2	"
BLE	1	"
Santocure	1.2	"
DPGO.	3	"

One hundred parts of the milled compound is dissolved in 900 parts petroleum naphtha to form an adhesive solution.

Panel & flooring adhesives

SBR (23.5% styrene, divinyl benzene cross linked)	40	parts
SBR (45 mooney viscosity, 43% styrene)	60	"
Clay	130	"
Calcium carbonate	130	"
Hydrogenated rosin ester	75	"
Terpene phenolic resin	52	"
Antioxidant	2	"

Sealants

SBR (25% styrene)	12	parts
Polymerized rosin	19	"
Methyl ester of hydrogenated rosin	2	"
Aromatic plasticizer	2	"
Soft clay	17	"
Fibrous talc	10	"
Toluene	26	"
Xylene	12	"

Automotive putty

Unsupported tapes of putty like consistency based on oil extended SBR have been found to give good bonds to oily metal surfaces.

Oil extender SBR	70	parts
Phenolic resin & hexamine	75	"
Petroleum distillate	50	"
Zinc dust	100	"
Tetramethyl thiuram monosulphide	1.2	"
Diorthotolyl guanidine	1.2	"
Sulphur	2.0	"
Caloxal	10.2	"

Heat resistant adhesives

SBR (23.5% styrene, 0.5% divinyl benzene)	35	part
SBR (45 mooney viscosity, 43% styrene)	35	"
Polychloroprene	9.5	"
Zinc oxide	3.5	"
Accelerator	0.3	"
Antioxidant	1.5	"
Magnesium silicate	13.0	"
Stabilized rosin	6.0	"

The above mixture is blended for 35 minutes at 110° C. On cooling 65 more parts of stabilized rosin plus 30 parts of a hydrogenated methyl ester of rosin are added. On dissolving the mass in 250 parts of rubber solvent, a permanently tacky adhesive is obtained.

Heat resistant adhesives can be formulated from SBR using the alfin catalyst system with SBR as the sole elastomer. The formulation is shown below.

SBR (15% styrene)	30	parts
SBR (50% styrene)	70	"
Magnesium oxide	4	"
N-phenol-1-naphthylamine	2	"
Alkyl phenol polymer	50	"
Hexane	200	"
Toluene	200	"

Spreading and laminating adhesives

SBR	100	parts
Sulphur and accelerator	1-20	"
Wood rosin	150-200	"
Solvent	200	"
Mill at 125-200° C		

The milling gives a partial cure. After cooling, solvent is added to give the desired consistency.

Tyre cord adhesives

Good tyre cord adhesives can be prepared using a rubbery SBR copolymer which has been polymerized in the presence of a nitrogen containing hetetrocyclic modifying agent of the vinyl pyridine class, which greatly increase the ozone and heat resistance of the latex adhesive. Other tire and cord adhesive can be prepared base on the use of phenol formaldehyde rosin as the example below.

Resorcinol	10.93	parts
Distilled water (20% solids)	5.23	"
37% formaldehyde	1.35	"
10% sod hydroxide		
Rubber latex (41.4% solids) (vinyl pyridine diene styrene)	50	"
Rubber latex (41% solids) (SBR)	6	"
Rubber latex (70% solids) SBR	24	"
Rubber latex (63% solids) ester modified SBR	20	

Tufted carpet adhesives

Natural	25	parts
SBR	75	"
Whiting	200	"
Barium sulphate	10	"
Clay	10	"
Sulphur	10	"
Zinc oxide/ Accelerator	10	"
Dispersing agent as required (karaya gum)		

Packaging adhesives

SBR latexes find application as packaging adhesives. They do not have particularly good wet tack properties and must be compounded with tackifying resins like estergum. They offer good stability and oxidation resistance. A folding carton sideseam adhesive is shown below.

SBR latex	40	parts
Vinsol emulsion	10	"
Resin emulsion	30	"
Arrco EO	19.5	"
Lanolubric	0.4	"
Penta chloro phenol	0.1	"

Fabric adhesives

SBR latex compound can be used for bonding sheet materials together such as two as more fabrice, fabrics to paper and fabrics to leather. Typical combining cement formulation are shown below.

Curing type

SBR latex	100	parts
10% potassium caseinate	2	"
Dispersion	4	"
Diothiocarbonate	3	"
Water	6	"
Thickener as required		

Non-curing type

SBR latex	250	parts
10% potassium caseinate	20	"
50% butyl zimate dispersion	4	"
Thickener as required		

Both the above formulations are applied by wet combining process.

13

THERMOPLASTIC RUBBER BASED ADHESIVES

Thermoplastic rubber is a new class of polymer. It has the solubility and flexibility of polystyrene, together the toughness and resilience of vulcanized natural rubber or polybutadiene at ambient temperature. These characteristics result from its structure in which the rubber molecules terminate with hard, glass like end blocks which are different from the rubbery middle blocks. All such polymers consequently consists of two phases in the solid state, a continuous rubber phase and a basically discontinuous plastic phase which locks the rubber molecules building blocks in place.

Resins are added to improve the adhesion of the end block phase, to adjust its melt viscosity and to control the modulus of elasticity of resultant adhesive formulation. Resins with low solubility such as rosin esters, terpenes phenolic resins, are used to impart pressure sensitive tack quality and to improve the adhesion characteristics of the mid block phase with the polar substrates. Plasticizers are added to decrease the hardness and modulus of elasticity and enhance pressure sensitive tack quality and to the improve low temperature flexibility. Plasticizers also reduce melt and solution viscosity decrease cohesive strength and substantially lower the raw materials cost. Fillers such as clay, talcs, whitings etc. are used to increase the hardness, modulus of elasticity, abrasion resistance and density of the product.

Adhesive formulations are prepared from thermoplastic rubber by solution hot melt techniques. Formulations can also be prepared as emulsions or in powder form if desired.

The dissolution process is carried out an mixer with paddle type agitator providing adequate shearing action to the mix. Agglomeration of the swollen sticky crumbs with large lumps is prevented by vigorous mechanical agitation. Charging of rubber crumbs from containers to the processing vessel generates static electricity producing sparks causing fire hazards. This is to be avoided by appropriate safely measures. For commercial SBS and SIS rubber 80–115° C is the usual temperature for range mixing and application. Temperature about 115 C to thermal degradation. At temperature below 80° C, the viscosity becomes so high mechanical disintegration of the rubber may occur. The preferred mixing temperature is at 90–110° C.

Depending upon melt viscosity and on the nature of adhesive application various types of equipments are available. These include pressure nozzle, print wheel, doctor blades calender, die coater, fountain coater and extrusion coater.

Hot melt pressure sensitive adhesive

	1	2	3	
S-I-S rubber	100	100	100	parts
Mid block resin	100	100	100	"
Plasticizing oil	-	40	40	"
End block resin	-	-	60	"
Stabilizer	5	5	5	"

Characteristics

Shear adhesion failure, C	60	45	75
Rolling ball tack, cm	5.9	0.6	1.8
Probe tack, gm	1300	700	1100
Melt viscosity	200000	30000	40000
Thermoplastic rubber content % w	49	36	33

Pressure sensitive adhesive based on SBS

SBS rubber	100	parts
Mid block resin	200	"
Stabilizer	1	"
Properties		
Rolling ball tack, in	10	
Probe tack, gm	1700	
180 degree, peel adhesion, psi	7.6	
Shear adhesion failure temperature, C	180	
Thermoplastic rubber content % w	33	
End block/mid block ratio	10/30	

Hot melt applied assembly adhesives

SBS rubber	100	parts
End block resins	150	"
Plasticizing oil	50	"
Middle block resins	50	"
Stabilizer	2-5	"

Properties

Melt viscosity at 120° C	16000 cp.
Tensile strength, TB	600 psi
Elongation, EB	700%
Hardness	90
Lap sheat (plywood/plywood)	214 psi
Flexibility at °C	good
Shear adhesion failure temp. °C	72 C
End block/middle block ratio	51/49

Heat activated adhesive

This is a solution adhesive which can be coated on two substrates dried and bonded by pressing at 60° C.

SBS rubber	100	parts
End block resins	75	"
Low mold wt. end block resins	25	"
Stabilizer/antioxidant	0.6	"
Solvents		
Toluene	120	"
Cyclohexane	120	"
Methyl ethyl ketone	60	"
Properties		
Peel adhesives psi		50
Creep (180° degree peel at 40° C)		0.2
End block/middle block ration	65/	35

Contact type assembly adhesives

SBS rubber	100	parts
End block resin	37.5	"
Middle block resin	37.5	"
Stabilizer/antioxidant	0.6	"
Properties (30 min. open time, no heat) 180 peel strength		
Canvas/plywood	14	
Canvas/stainless steel	14	
Canvas/vinyl asbestos	9	
Lab shear strength	137	
End block/middle block ratio	39/61	

Contact adhesives

	Type A	Type B	
SBS rubber A	100	-	parts
SBS rubber B	-	100	"
End block resin	40	40	"
Mid block resin	10	10	"
Solvents			
Hexane	150	150	"
Acetone	150	150	"
Toluene	150	150	"

Contact adhesive-effect of heat reactive resin

	Non reactive resin	Reactive resin	
SBS rubber	100	100	parts
Reactive resin	-	45	"
End block resin	40	-	"
Mid block resin	10	-	"
Magnesium oxide	-	8.6	"
Zinc oxide	-	5.0	"
Stabilizer	1	1	"
Solvents:			
Hexane	150	127	"
Acetone	150	127	"
Toluene	150	127	"
Properties			
Peel strength, psi (canves/canvas)	48	25	
Peel adhesion failure temp ^{0}C	176	230	

High viscosity construction mastic

SBS rubber	100	parts
End block resin	75	"
Soft clay	200	"
Stabilizer: zinc dibutyldithiocarbamate	2	"
Properties		
Lab shear strength, psi (wood/wood)	590	"

Hot melt assembly adhesive

SBS rubber	100	parts
Mid block resin	100	"
Paraffin wax	85	"
Stabilizer	1	"
Peel strength pli (canvas/canvas)	45	

Sealant for concrete joints

SBS rubber	100	parts
Asphalt	180	"
Plasticizing oil	60	"
Mid block resin	60	"
Stabilizers	1	"
Properties		
Penetration at 25° C dmin	86	
Resilience at 25° C %	83	
flow at 40° C, in	0	
Viscosity at 125° C, cps	2060	
Softening points R&B, °C	85	

Binder for carpet backing

SBS rubber	100	parts
Plasticizing oil	150	"
Whiting	700	"
Stabilizer	1	"
Properties		
Hardness	55	
Specific gravity	1.8	

14

POLYCHLOROPRENE ADHESIVES

Poly chloroprene, is the basis for one of the largest and most important groups of rubber adhesives. Polymer structure of commercial polychloroprene is determined by the manner in which the chloroprene monomer, 2-chloro-1, 3-butadiene grows as polymer chain. On polymerization the chloroprene molecule may take any of four isomeric forms possible. Rapid bond strength development of contact adhesive is associated with crystallization resulting from a very high level of trans configuration in which there is no side groups bulker than the chlorine atom.

Four important applications for polychloroprene contact adhesives are the bonding of high pressure plastic laminates, automotive adhesives, shoe adhesives and adhesives for the construction industry.

Shoes consume the adhesive for the permanent attaching shoe soles. Automotive industry uses this adhesives for bonding sponge insulation strips to doors and trunk hood lids and tops to roofs.

High pressure plastic laminates are bonded to substrates such as wood, metal, stone etc. with polychloroprene contact adhesives.

Polychloroprene adhesives enjoy an important position as an elastomeric binder at the expense of other less costly materials, e.g. natural rubber and SBR, primarily because of early bond strength development, bonding range, high, ultimate strength and creep resistance on bond to variety of surfaces durability, flexibility, chemical resistance and resistance to burning.

Some typical contact adhesive formulations are shown below.

Polychloroprene contact adhesive

	A	B	C	D	E	F	G	
Polychloroprene	100	100	100	100	100	100	100	parts
Phenolic resin	46	39	50	-	-	-	-	"
Pentaestergum	-	-	-	8	50	39	25	"
Hydrocarbon resin	-	-	-	-	-	7	25	"
Rosin	-	-	-	42	-	-	-	"
Chlorinated rubber	-	-	17	-	-	-	-	"
Dicotyl phthalate	-	-	-	-	-	-	2	"
Antioxidant	2	2	2	2	2	2	2	"
Toluene	417	417	-	542	542	466	606	"
Benzene	-	-	374	-	-	-	-	"
Hexane	-	57	217	-	-	-	-	"
Methyl ethyl ketone	57	-	-	-	-	-	-	"

The major uses of the fast crystallizing adhesives are for bonding decorative laminates and laminated panel for curtain walls and partitions automotive trim and a host of industrial applications. Example of a typical fast crystallizing formulations as well general purpose industrial adhesive follows.

Fast crystallising & general purpose industrial adhesive

	Decorative	Laminates General purpose	
Polychloroprene	100	100	parts
Magnesium oxide	5	5	"
Zinc oxide	2	2	"
Antioxidant	1	1	"
Phenolic resins	45	45	"
Terpene phenolic resin	-	20	"
Hexane	275	277	"
Acetone	215	138	"
Methyl ethyl ketone	-	138	"
Toluene	122	138	"
& solids	20	20	"

Mastic compounds

Polychloroprene	100	parts
Antioxidant	2	"
Magnesium oxide	4	"
C_aCO^3	100	"
Zinc oxide	5	"
Ethylene glycol	20	"
T-butyl phenolic resin	15	"
Hexane, Toluene, MEX by weight to 65% solids		

Sprayable formulation

To achieve maximum sprayability characteristics, a high speed paddle mixer is used for formulation mixing.

Polychloroprene	100	100	parts
Antioxidant	2	2	"
Magnesium oxide	8	8	"
Zinc oxide	5	5	"
Milled stock	115	115	"
T-butyl phenolic resin	45	45	"
Hexane, Toluene, MEK	by weight to 65% solids		

Sprayable formulation

To achieve maximum sprayability characteristics, a high speed paddle mixer is used for formulation mixing.

Polychloroprene	100	100	parts
Antioxidant	2	2	"
Magnesium oxide	8	8	"
Zinc oxide	5	5	"
Milled stock	115	115	"
Water	2	2	"
Ethyl acetate	-	300	"
N-propyl acetate	115	340	"
Di-isobutyl ketone	620	-	"

Sprayable contact adhesive

Polychloroprene	100	parts
Heptane	150	"
Thiuram	0.5	"
Accelerator	0.5	"

To above dispersion the following chemicals are added during compounding.

T-butyl phenolic resin	40	parts
Tackifier	0.20	"
MgO	2	"
ZnO	4	"
Antioxidant	2	"
Water	1	"

Tertiary butyl phenolic resins act as optimisers of adhesive properties, solution viscosity and stability. Increased resin levels are particularly effective in compounds containing high level of magnesium oxide and formulated for maximum heat resistance.

Increasing magnesium oxide content markedly increases cohesive strength. Polar solvents are required to stringiness of adhesive and to improve its viscosity stability. Metal oxide serves as that of an acid acceptor and with phenolic resin it forms resinous products which do not melt and give better heat resistance. Antioxidants helps in order to achieve the excellent long term ageing properties. Fillers are used primarily to reduce cost. The heat resistance of polychloroprene cements can be increased by compounding with a variety of curing agents. Solvents influence the rate of strength development, open time, cost, adhesion, application properties, solution viscosity and to some extent ultimate strength.

Latex based contact adhesives : foam to wood

Latex I	100	-	-	parts
Latex II	-	100	-	"
Latex III	-	-	100	"
Zinc oxide	5	5	5	"
Antioxidant	2	2	2	"
Phenolic resin	87.5	87.5	-	"
Cumarone indene resin	50	50	-	"

Polychloroprene latex adhesive formulation

	Contact	Mastic	Foil	
Latex I	100	-	-	parts
Latex II	-	100	-	"
Latex III	-	-	100	"
Zinc oxide	10	15	15	"
Antioxidant	2	2	2	"
Terpene phenolic resin	85	-	-	"
Liquid terpene resin	50	-	-	"
Estergum	-	75	-	"
Casein	-	-	60	"
Methyl cellulose	-	4	-	"
Defoaming agent	-	-	2	"
Stabilizer/surfactant	2	2	2	"

15

POLYSULPHIDE SEALANTS & ADHESIVE

Sealants based on polysulphide liquid polymers have found wide acceptance in a number of applications requiring a flexible, adhering chemically resistant film.

Polysulphide liquid polymers preparation involving reaction of bischloro ethyl formal with sodium polysulphide solution containing specific emulsifying and nucleating agents.

The sulphur is present in the polymer as a mixture of disulpide and trisulphide. High molecular weight polymer is then split and terminated by merscaptan groups.

The mercaptan terminated liquid polymers are readly polymerised to elastomeric solids by the use of active oxidizing agents. Lead dioxide has been the most widely used in sealant applications.

A polysulphide sealant is specifically formulated to get the desired properties. Lead dioxids is the most widely used curing agent for sealants due to its high reactivity, availability and relatively less price. Formulation for lead oxide pastes is shown in the following.

Lead dioxide accelerator pasts

Lead dioxide	55	parts
Stearic acid	7	"
Accelerator	20	"
Toluene	20	"

The oxidation and reaction of thiol groups is accelerated in an alkaline environment and retarded in an acidic environment; consequently pH plays a major part in cure rate. A number of acidic retarder has been evaluated for lead peroxides, the two most effective being stearic acid and lead stearate.

Most used for liquid polymers require reinforcing fillers which both improve the physical properties and reduce the cost of the compound; furthermore fillers are used to impart thixotopy and colour to the sealant compound.

A number of adhesion additives have been evaluated for the adhesion to glass, aluminium and steel in the pressure of water, cold and heat. They are mainly phenolic resin and liquid epoxy resin.

The use of primers may be necessary if the curing agent is too sensitive. Few primer formulations are shown below.

Silicone tetrahydrate	3.85	parts
Tetrabutyl titanate	1.15	"
Isopropanol	45	"

Chlorinated rubber	20	parts
Toluene	30	"
Silicone tetrahydrate	2.5	"

Manganese oxide, ammonium dichromate and formulations based on cumene hydroperoxide give cured sealants with improved heat resistance property. The resultant by products of the oxidizing agents used also have a considerable effect on heat aging properties. Typical formulations, which exhibit improved heat resistance are given in the following.

Heat resistant polysulphide sealant

Polysulphide polymer	100	100	100	parts
TiO_2	-	50	-	"
Sulphur	0.1	-	-	"
$(NH^4)_2\ Cr_2\ O_7$	6	-	-	"
DMF	14	-	-	"
Carbon	40	-	-	"
Stearic acid	1	-	-	"
Phenolic resin	5	-	-	"
Manganese dioxide	-	2	-	"
Dinitrobenzene	-	0.5	-	"
Silica	-	-	20	"
Ethyl hydroxy ethyl cellulose	-	-	1.2	"
MgO	-	-	4	"
Cumene hydroperoxide	-	-	6.5	"
Maleic anhydride	-	-	0.5	"

The use of non black reinforcing agents gives composition having very satisfactory electrical resistant properties.

Polysulphide sealants are used for sealing and repairing of internal fuel tanks and fuel cell cavities of aircraft. The sealant are further required to prevent leakage in spite of temperature variation from from -20 to 60° C.

This sealant is used in sealing acrylic sheets to aluminium window assemblies. The requirements are adhesion of sealant to the acrylate sheet and aluminium frame under exposure to various environments. The sealant must be flexible over a wide temperature range and short optimum performance over a pressure gradient. It also finds its use for repairing large oil suction and discharge loose covers. Poly sulphide resins are used as a modifier to epoxy adhesives. One very practical application for this modified polysulphide adhesive is bonding old concrete to old concrete and new concrete to old concrete. These adhesives have definite application in the construction and maintenance of concrete structures such as highways, bridges, buildings, dams, airport, runways, sidewalks, driveways, commercial and industrial floors for patching overlaying, surface sealing and skid proofing.

In the following table a comparison table a comparison is made between these modified adhesive with pure epoxy adhesive.

	Straight Poly epoxy control	sulphide/ epoxy adhesive	
Polysulphide	-	100	parts
Liquid epoxy	100	100	"
Calcium carbonate	179	71	"
Ethyl hydroxy	30	15	"
Tensile shear bond strength (psi)			
Room temp.	1700	4500	
Tested at 75° C	2000	1500	
Tested at 25° C	1400	2500	
Peel strength	8	18	"
Bond strength	100	140	
Shear bond strength after 30 days drop immersion (psi)			
Water	1000	1700	
Sea water	0	1100	
Isopropyl alcohol	2000	3200	
Ethylene glycol	1600	3700	
Methyl ethyl ketone	1600	500	
Dibutyl phthalate	1800	3400	

Modification of epoxy resin with polysulphide liquid polymers gives compositions which in many cases have uniqe physical and chemical properties. This reaction between polysulphide liquid polymers and epoxy resin is catalysed or promoted by organic amine compounds.

Polysulphide construction sealants

	A	B	C	D	E	
Part A						
Polysulphide polymer	100	100	100	100	100	parts
Stearic acid	1	1	1	1	1	"
Phenolic acid	5	-	-	-	-	"
Calcium carbonate	-	25	-	-	-	"
TiO2	-	10	10	-	-	"
Lithopone	-	30	90	50	-	"
Kenflex	-	-	-	-	15	"
Sterling	-	-	-	-	10	"
Sulphur	-	-	-	-	0.15	"
Butylphthyl butyl glycolate	-	25	40	-	-	"
Part B						
Accelerator	15	15	15	15	15	"
PbO2	-	-	-	-	13.8	"
Dibutyl phthalate	-	-	-	-	-	"
Recommended use	aircraft sealans	building sealants	casting sealants	potting sealants	deck sealants	

16

EPOXY RESIN ADHESIVES

Epoxy adhesives consist of a liquid or a fusible solid containing epoxide groups, and a curing agent containing functional groups with which the epoxide groups combine to form a crosslinked polymer. Curing agent is also known as hardener. Epoxy resin, in its unhardened state, contains epoxide groups.

The adhesives are available as one or two component systems. The reaction between resin and hardener is capable of taking place at room temperature. The two components are mixed immediately before use, i.e. the adhesive is supplied as two component system. If the mixture of resin & hardener is relatively inactive under ordinary storage conditions the components may be mixed together and supplied as single passage system. Two component systems are available as liquids, puttees, or liquid and hardener powder. The one component systems are available as liquids, puttees, or liquid and hardener powder. The component systems are available as solvent free liquid resins, solutions in solvents, liquid resin pastes, fusible powders, sticks, pellets and paste, supported and unsupported films, performed shapes cut to fit a particular joint.

Depending on the particular system i.e. the modifying or the curing agent used, the epoxy adhesive bonds show differing properties. Epoxy bonds maintain excellent strength and durability under many environments. Bond is usually not affected for several years in contact with oils, greases, hydrocarbon fuels, alkalies, aromatic solvents, acids, alcohols, water, hot or cold weather. They show poor resistance to ketones and esters. Some formulations are less resistant to greases, oils and prolonged immersion in hot water. Polyamide cured adhesives show poor resistance to hot water and alkalies. Polyamine and anhydride systems have poor cold resistance whereas polyamide types are satisfactory even up to 200° C. Anhydride and polyamine systems show best heat resistance while the polyamide types can be used up to 70° C only.

The epoxy adhesives show following properties and advantages, which make them special adhesives.

1. These adhesives have high surface activity and good wetting properties for materials suc as metals, glues and ceramics etc. They can be formulated to give mixes of low viscosity with improved wetting, spreading and penetrating action. They show good adhesion to even copper and phenolic laminates for making printed circuits.

2. High cohesive strength for cure polymers, which exceeds th adherent strength.

3. These adhesives systems are 100% solids type i.e. they do no form any water on condersation and do not contain any solvent hence they are convenient for even bonding of impervious surface such as metals and glass.

4. They give stronger bonds with less strain in the glue line due to very low shrinkage during setting. Addition of fillers such as silica aluminium and other inorganic fillers reduces the shrinkage to even less than 1%.

5. Epoxy adhesives show low creep with better retention of strength under sustained loading than thermoplastic.

6. The epoxy adhesives can be modified easily by proper selection of the resin and hardner and addition of another polymer and filler

7. Unlike various other adhesives, the epoxies are not affected by moisture they have very good resistance to solvents. They are effective barriers to heat and electricity.

Epoxy adhesives are almost universal in their applications, only a few materials are there which cannot be bonded with them. Such materials are crystalline and less polar plastics, untreated polyethylene, silicones, untreated fluorocarbons, plasticized vinyl and butyl rubber.

As described above, cured epoxy resins are fairly brittle. Although flexibility can be achieved by incorporating plasticizers of ester type, but they result in loss of shear strength. So epoxy resins are modified for increased toughness by addition of other polymeric materials. The line between resinous modifiers and curing agents, in this context, is not sharp, since the modifying agents often have functional groups capable of reacting with the epoxy. Polyamides, phenolics, acrylates are modifiers.

The polyamide modifiers used are based on dimer acids, for example, dimerized linoleic acid and ethylenediamide. They give adhesives which are characterized by unusual flexibility and toughness. Another class of polyamides used as modifiers are "soluble nylons". They are either copolymers or alkoxy methylated derivatives of nylon 6 or 66. In either case the products are clear, amorphous and soluble in aqueous alcohol, chlorinated aliphatic hydrocarbons and other common solvents. Adhesive from epoxynylon combinations-have toughness, high lap shear strength and high peel strength at ambient and slightly elevated temperatures. These modifiers are room temperature adhesives.

Phenolic resins, preferably resols react with bisphenol. A epoxy resins to give adhesives that are widely used today in moderately high temperature applications. In practive the amount of resol used is considerably greater than required to cross-linked the epoxy, so that the overall effect is principally one of using the epoxy resin to toughen the phenolic and improve adhesion to metal. Epichlorohydrin reacts with Novolak to give modified epoxies.

Fillers are often incorporated in epoxy adhesives to reduce cost and import other beneficial characteristics Lower cost, Less shrinkage Lower coefficient of thermal expansion.

Titanium dioxide, lead oxide, ferric oxide alumine etc. are the common fillers that impart superior strength 750^0 C. At room temperature, however, the unfilled system is stronger than the filled compositions.

Manufacture

Epoxy resins are produced commercially by a batch process; regardless of whether a one-stage or a two-stage process is used.

A batch process of resin preparation on the basis of 300 kg resin is described below. The raw materials required are :

Epichlorohydrin	495 kg
Bisphenol A	307 kg
Caustic soda	110 kg

Epichlorohydrin is charged to a stainless steel kettle equipped with an agitator and reflux condenser. Bisphenol A is then added and contents are mixed. The temperature is raised to 50^0 C. Caustic soda is then added. Exothermic reaction starts by addition of caustic soda. External steam heating s stopped at this stage. Reaction temperature is maintained in between 55-65^0 C. If necessary, cooling water is circulated in the jacket to maintain this temperature. The contents of the reactor are constantly stirred during caustic soda addition which should take 2-3 minutes. The reaction mixture is then held at 60-65^0 C for a further 30 minutes. The caustic soda is added as a 30 per cent solution. The total reaction time is 3 to 4 hours and the yield is 66 per cent of theory. At the end of the reaction, the mixture is allowed to separate into an aqueous and an organic phase.

The organic layer is then charged to a distillation still to recover excess epichlorohydrin. The distillate forms two layers, the bottom being principally epichlorohydrin and the top a mixture of epichlorohydrin and water. The resin remains in the still and is discharged to storage tanks.

Hardeners: The uncured epoxy adhesives are usually honey-coloured viscous liquids, and sometimes brittle light yellow-brown, the latter becoming liquid when heated. On curing the material becomes insoluble and infusible i.e. thermosets. Additions of catalysts or reactive hardener produces heat of reaction, which is good for fast reaction in thick sections; but in the case of thin gluelines, the heat is conducted away into the adherents, hence, when heat is not to be applied from one side, fastest hardeners are to be preferred. Some of the more common materials used as hardeners with epoxy resins are given below.

Aliphatic Amines: Aliphatic amines give adhesives with good strength with adherents including metals, glass, wood and many plastics. The following amines are commonly used.

Triethylene telramine	i.e. TETA
Tetraethylene-pentamine	i.e. TEPA
Diethylene-triamine	i.e. DETA
Dimethylamino methylphenol	i.e. DMP 30

They give cold curing systems, which may be warmed or hot set to reduce the curing time and to improve hot strength. A proportion of 10 parts catalyst to 100 parts resin is common, but not rigid. DMP 30 does not require any external heat for curing but for optimum performance a post cure is preferred.

Aromatic Amines: Aromatic polyamines, used as epoxy hardeners are usually solids. They are hot setting types, require heat for curing and cannot be cured at room temperature. Some of the more important aromatic polyamine hardeners are given below.

m-Phenylene diamine	i.e. MPDA
Diaminodiphnyl methane	i.e DDM
Methylene dianiline	i.e. MDA

DDM may give curing at a much lower temperature, even at room temperature, if a plasticizer, e.g. dibutyl phthalate is also incorporated at about 20% quantity. This addition reduces hot strength but other properties are retained. Addition of a small amount of a monocarboxylic acid, e.g. acetic acid also accelerates the curing action of aromatic amines.

Aromatic amines systems have not lives of several hours at room temperature. The selected curing agent can have a marked effect on shear strength. They give improved adhesive strength as compared to that with aliphatic amine hardeners.

Polyamides. Polyamides made by reacting a dimerised drying oil acid and a ployaminde e.g. dilinoleic acid and ethylenediamine give versatile adhesives with epoxy resins. Polyamides derived from DETA (amine) and dicarboxylic acids are quite good. Liquid type polyamides are preferred. These polyamides are slow curing at room temperature and are heated to reduce viscosity for easy blending with the epoxy resins. DMP is substituted for part of the polyamide where faster curing is required.

Acid Anhydrides. Aromatic and cyclic acid-anhydrides such as phthalic anhydride (PA), pyromellittic anhydride (PMDA) and chlorendic anhydride (HET) etc. are used for special purpose. In their case thermal stability up to 150° C continuously or up to 260° C intermittently is better than that for amine cured systems. They are usually solids or viscous liquids which require heat to disperse them effectively within the epoxy resins. Thus the pot-life is rather low. High curing temperatures are required to achieve high temperature properties. PA gives slightly lower adhesive strength to metal. PMDA (mp. 102° C) is inconvenient to use due to high melting point but gives outstandingly high hot strength.

Boron Trifluoride: Monoethylamine: It is a curing agent for one component adhesive systems and is present as a latent catalyst which is activated when heated, BF_3MEA is activated at 95° C. It is not usually recommended for adhesive formulation although widely used in electrical applications. Shear strengths have poor reproducibility and also the water sensitivity is a problem. Pot life for 1-2% catalyst is about 1 year and curing at 110° C for 4-6 hrs is required.

Aliphatic amines and polyamides are effective flexibilising agents and cured epoxies have excellent mechanical, physical and chemical properties. Cure shrinkage is small. Heat resistance is infertor is inferior to other systems and usually limited to 80° C. Aromatic amine cured systems have better heat stability and these systems perform well up to 120-175° C. For some systems there is a rapid loss of adhesion at 105° C.

Commercial Curing Agents

Materials	Amount used in parts per 100 parts of resin	Pot life	Uses
Diethylene 5-triamine Triethylene	11 -do-	45 min. at 20^0 C	General purpose room temp. curing agent
Piperidine	6	90 hr. at 40^0 C	Castings
Triethylene	10	7 hr. at 20^0 C.	Adhesives
m-phenylene diamine	14	2.5 hr. at 50^0 C	Chemical and heat resistant laminates
p-p-diamino diphenoyl sulphone	30	2 hr. at 200^0 C	
Phthalic anhydride	30-45	14.hrs. at 100^0 C	Coatings
Hexa hydrophthalic anhydride	80	-do-	Castings

Two types of additives are used in epoxy resin adhesives. On type after the processing characteristics of the resin system and the other modify the cured resins. Acculirates and diluents are of first category and plasticizers, pigments and fillers are of second category.

Some additive influence both processing characteristics are end properties.

Accelerators used are commonly tertiary amines, phenols or amino phenols, the preferred being benzyl dimethyl-amine tris (dimethylaminomethyl) phenol.

Reactive diluents are usually mono-epoxy compounds like butyl glycidyl ether, cresyl glycidyl either or phenyl glycidyl ether, but di epoxides like 1:4 butane-diol diglycidyl ether and vinyl cyclohexane dioxide are also employed.

Plasticizers are of two types: external and internal. External plasticizers are phthalate and phosphate esters. Internal plasticizers are longchain dloils or in some case the hardener may itself be a long chain dianhydride or a polyaminde.

17

APPLICATIONS FORMULATION

The use of epoxy adhesives in aircraft industry is most spectacular. Due to creep resistance, excellent bonding of matels with wide variations in temperatures, they are excellent for use in aircraft and missile industry. In aircraft industry epoxies are used for bonding of aluminium to itself or other metals, foam panels and honeycomb sandwich materials, fibre-glass polyester fuel tanks, cyclised rubber to metals and as substitute for rivets. In automobile industry they are used for attachment of reinforcements to light metals for greater rigidity, where welding would casue distortion and painting problems, as a substitute for body solder, and for assembly of fibre- glass body and, in car battery cases. Epoxy resins are used in building industry for bonding old concrete to new concrete, ceramic tiles, walls, floors & concrete repair.

Because of their strength, versatility and excellent adhesion to a variety of surfaces, epoxy resin adhesives have gained wide acceptance by diverse users. Epoxies have high specific adhesion to metals, glass and ceramics. They can be formulated to give mixes of low viscosity with improved wetting, spreading and penetration action. The cohesive strength within the glue line is large and adhesion of the epoxy to other materials is good. The failure under stress often occurs in one of the adherends rather than in the epoxy or at the interface.

The epoxies cure without releasing water or other condensation by products. This makes it possible to bond the epoxies at only contact pressure. The epoxies cure with only very little shrinkage. Less strain is built up in the glue line. the shrinkage can still be reduced by incorporation of silica, aluminium and other inorganic fillers. The cured epoxies like other thermoset resins, maintain their shape under prolonged stress better than thermoplastics such as polyvinyl acetate, nitro cellulose and polyvinyl butyral. The epoxies are insensitive to moisture. Their resistance to solvent is outstanding and they are effective barriers to heat and electric current.

General purpose adhesives

Epoxy resins	100	parts
Polyamide resin	70	"
Filler or reinforcement	as desired	
Epoxy resin	100	parts
Polyamide resin	35	"
Tertiary resin	5	"
Filler or reinforcement as desired		
Epoxy resin	100	parts
Amido amine hardener	70	"
Filler or reinforcement	as desired	

Flexible adhesive

Component I.	Epoxy resin	100	parts
Component II.	Polysulphide resin	175	"
	Fumed silica	8	"
	Tertiary amine	10	"

Cures overnight at room temperature or 2 hour at 71.1.C.

One component adhesive

Epoxy resin	100	parts
Gellan	25	"
Alumina	25	"
Dicy andiamide	6	"

Quick cure adhesive

Component I.	Epoxy resin	100	parts
	Silica flour	60	"
	Carbon black	0.1	"
	Asbestos	3	"
Component II.	Polymercaptan resin	75	parts
	Polyamide resin	12	"
	Tertiary amine	8	"
	Silica flour	50	"
	Titanium dioxide	10	"
	Asbestos	4	"

Gel time 8 min at 24^0 C .

Metal metal sealant

Epoxy novolac resin (ENR)	12	parts
Ethylene glycol esters of ENR	88	"
Phthalic anhydride	43	"
Pyromellitic dianhydride	2.5	"
Silca	55	"
Aluminium powder	35	"
Asbestos	350	"
Pyridine	0.3	"

Cures 15 min at 205° C

Room temperature curing

Component I	Epoxy novolac resin	40	parts
	Epoxy novolac ester	40	"
	Asbesios	20	"
Component II	Trithylene Tetramine	12	"

Phenolic-epoxy tape adhesive

Phenolic resin (80% solids)	125	parts
Phenolic resin (60% solids)	33	"
Epoxy resin	20	"
Ethyl acetate	20	"
1-hydroxy-2-naphthoic	2.8	"
n-propyl gallate	1.4	"

Tape adhesive is prepared by impregnating the above liquid adhesive into a glass mat and precuring at 132° C for 30 min.

Tape adhesive

Polyglycidal ether of disproportionated rosin	80	parts
Tetrahydrofuran	55	"
Epoxy resin	20	"
Polyvinyl formal	20	"
Aluminium dust	100	"
Diaminodi phenyl sulphone	24.5	"

The adhesive is deposited on a glass cloth and dried at 93.3° C for 15 min. It takes 30 min to cure at 240° C.

High peel strength nylon epoxy adhesive

Epoxy resin	25	parts
Nylon resin	75	"
Dicyandiamide	10	"

This is cured in 60 min at 162° C.

Powder adhesives

Epoxy resin	100	parts
Polymeric aromatic amine	11.5	"
Fumed silica	3	"
Red iron oxide	3	"

It takes 3 min to cure at 204° C .

Concrete adhesive

Component I.	Epoxy resin (solid)	90	parts
	Epoxy resin (liquid)	60	"
	Urea resin	20	"
	Methyl ethyl ketone	95	"
Component II	Polysulphide resin	100	"
	Titanium dioxide	100	"
	Carbon black	5	"
	Methyl ethyl ketone	45	"
	Tertiary amine	15	"

Glass adhesive

Epoxy resin	100	parts
u-aminopropyl triethoxy silane	2.4	"
Modified aliphatic amine	20	"

Metal glass adhesive

Epoxy resin	40	parts
Polyamide	30	"
Titanium dioxide	22	"
Powdered quariz	8	"

Putty for sealing

Component I	Epoxy resin	100	parts
	Fumed silica	12	"
	Alumina	200	"
	Furfuryl alcohol	5	"
	Polyethylene glycol	1	"
Component II	Polyamide resin	100	"
	Modified aliphatic amine	12	"
	Fumed silica	15	"
	China clay	250	"

This is used together with an open weave fabric which is wrapped is around flame, treated polyethylene that has been primed with epoxy polyamide.

18

POLYURETHANE ADHESIVES

Polyfunctional isocyanates are reacted with polyhydroxy componends, such as unsaturated polyestor or phenols to form polyurethanes containing free isocyanate groups, which are available for reaction with the adherent. These adhesives are thermoplastic or thermosetting in nature. They are used as one component thermoplastic systems in ketones, hydrocarbons etc. often containing catalysts in small amounts to introduce some thermosetting properties. Two-part thermosetting products are used in liquid form with or without solvents; the second part is a catalyst. One component type set with solvent release at room temperature; to reduce curing time catalysts may be incorporated Two component systems set by polymerization aided by catalysts.

The most important polyurethane adhesive component are TDI (Toluene di isocyanate), MDI (Diphenylmethane 44 di isocyanate), PAPI (Polymethylene polyphenyl isocyanate) and Triphenyl methane di isocyanate together with various polyesters and polyether glycols. Polyester based poly urethanes are emerging as the forerunner over polyether systems because of their inherent high cohesive and adhesive properties.

They have good resistance to water and most chemicals, solvents, oils, greases, salt spray, ozone, radiation and weatheing. Thermosetting compositions can be used up to 70° C while the maximum service temperature for thermosetting types is 175° C. They exhibit excellent shear strength down to 200° C with retention of elasticity and shock resistance. They have good electrical properties and have low combustibility and excellent resistance to biodeterioration. They are relatively expensive compared to other rubber adhesives and have the disadvantage of that isocyanates are toxic and unpleasant to handle. They exhibit high tack, often giving instant strength on contact bonding. Their outstanding property is the toughness and abrasion resistance.

Polyurethane adhesives are used for non-structural applications which are subject to moderate loads. They are used for bonding of metals, rubbers, most plastics, wood, cork, paper, textiles, glass and ceramics. They are particularly suitable for flexible and rigid PVC, where compatibility with plasticizers is good. Their specific uses include bonding of urethane rubber to itself and other substrates, leather to itself and plastic, flock attachment to rubber and textiles, and lamination of vinyl plastics to synthetic fabrics. They are modifying agents for rubber-based adhesives to promote adhesion. Their use is restricted to applications, where they have definite advantages for specific purposes mentioned above, althought forming strong flexible bonds with a wide variety of materials.

In the case of solvent type adhesives, the still tacky surfaces, after drying or solvent heat reactivation, are contact bonded. The 2-part products are mixed and fully cured in 6 days at 20^0 C and may be heat cured in 3 hrs. at 90^0 C to 1 hr. at 180^0 C.

Two component reaction adhesives are of particular interest in the formulation of low solvent and solvent free adhesives. They utilise either a polyol/polyisocyanate combination or an isocyanate terminated terminated prepolymer with a polyol or polyamine curing agent. The most widely used polyols are of the ester or ether type in a molecular weight rang between 500-3000. Best adhesive properties are imported by polyesters whereas polyethers offer, aside from low cost, hydrolysis resistance, excellent low temperature properties and lower viscosity, which provides more latitude in compounding. Branched polyols are empolyed for rigid high strength bonds while linear polyols offer good flexibility and can be used to adjust any intermediate hardness by blending.

All the compounding ingredients are dry otherwise foaming occurs as a result of reaction with moisture after the polyisocyanate addition. Polyols are inherently hygroscopic. It is a good practice, therefore, to add substances that either react with water such as triethyl orthoformate or absorb moisture such as molecular sieves as additives.

Hydroxyl polyurethane solvents. This is used as solvent adhesives, either as one or two component system. Hydroxyl polyurethane are produced by addition of di-iscoyanates, usually TDI or MDI and polyester diols. The molecular weight is controlled over the isocyanate hydroxyl ratio and are in the neighbourhood of 100,000 for useful polymer properties. The various grades of hydroxyl polyurethane differs widely in viscosity, thermoplasticity, crystallization and solubility. The most common solvent used is the methyl ethyl ketone. The largest single user of this type adhesive is the shoe industry for attaching soles and binding linking in to flush moulded PVC boots.

Polyurethane dispersions exhibit properties superior to hydroxyl solvent adhesives. The components that currently yields the higher quality products are isocyanate terminated pre-polymer in a water miscible solvent, such as acetone, with a diamine carboxylate of sulphone. The resultant polyurethane monomer solution is mixed with water, which forms the dispersion and further extends the polymer over the remaining isocyanate groups. Finally, the organic solvent is removed by distillation. Just as with hydroxyl polyurethane, dispersions can also be manufactured to offer different degrees of crystallinity and exhibit excellent stability and yield water resistant films since they do not contain protective colloids or emulsifiers.

Polyurethylanes are blended with polyvinyl acetate, ethylene vinyl acetate copolymers, polyacrylics and nitrile rubber in the form of dispersions. Suitable fillers are whitting, barytes, hydrated alumine and clays are added as a pre-slurry in water. Viscosities can be adjusted with acrylic thickener or partially hydrolized polyvinyl alcohol and high viscosity levels with alginates or cellulosic thickeners.

Applications include wash and dry clean resistant textile lamination, plastic film laminations, flocking, sole attaching and additives to other aqueous system to improve their adhesion performance.

In practice, the high molecular weight polyurethane gum is dissolved in a suitable dry, isocyanate-inert solvent. Such elements are applied to adherend and allowed to dry to the desired tackiness. A solution of polyurethane resin (11.25 parts) geon resin (3.75 parts) and tetrahydro furan (85 parts) is prepared and brushed on to vinyl shoe sole and leather upper. After 1 min air drying under pressure it also shows adhesion to other substrates including rubber, fabrics, metal, wood etc.

A viscous 45% solution in MEK of stable polyurethane elastomer containing no unreacted isocyanate (100 parts) is mixed with 20 parts of a 70% solution in ethyl acetate of orangic polyisocylane, 4.5 parts of liquid polyester and 25 parts of MEK silvent to provide a basic adhesive formulation.

A polyurethane elastomer dissolved in 20% by weight in a mixture of dry ethyl acetate and acetone and 8.3 parts of triphenyl methane trisocyanae in 20% methylene chloride (for natural and synthetic rubber adhesion) or 5 parts of TDI trimethylol propane adduct in 75% ethyl acetate (for non rubber adhesion) is added. These combinations are versatile adhesives for bonding vulcanised rubber to it self, scather, urethane, PVC, cork wood etc. Cure occurs at room temperature and faster at elevated temperature.

Cyanabond textile adhesives

Aliphatic polyester urethane resin	100	parts
MEK (40%)	5	"
Acrylic dispersion	45	"
Vinyl copolymer	15	"

Water based polyurethane adhesives are easier to work with than 100% solid system and are environmentally attractive. The water based adhesives are easy to use, adhesives properties developed at room temperature, low temperature flexible and high cohesive strength. Thermoset versions of polyurethane dispersion exhibit superior heat resistance. As a result of these benefits, water based polyurethane adhesives are used for many speciality application, including bonding PVC to polyurethane foam, ABS, PVC and metallized mylar, paper to aluminium foil, PE film, LDPE films, metal, PE to PP, PU films to rubber and fabric; PVC plastisol to glass and metal and fabric.

19

ACRYLIC ADHESIVES

Acrylics for adhesives and sealants are polymers and copolymers copolymers which re mainly based on acrylic and methacrylic acids and their derivatives, especially the acrylic acid esters:

Other acrylic compounds, e.g. acrylic acid and methyl methacrylate, are normally used only as auxiliaxy monomers for adhesive raw materials. By judicious selection of the monomers and polymerization conditions it was possible to develop a great variety of acrylics eminently suitable for ahesives. They are available in the form of solutions, dispersions, and liquid containing 100% polymer.

At room temperature the homopolymers of methacrylic and acrylic acid and those of lower methacrylic acid estes are hard non tacky products which are suitable only for special applications in the adhesive field. Homopolymer of acrylic acid esters from alcohols with at least two carbon atoms are elastic soft and partially highly tacky products. These are used for a much large range of adhesive application. Acrylic copolymers are of great significance in the production of adhesives. Acrylic monomers can be copolymerized with most conventional monomers. Methacrylate polymers and acrylate polymers are soluble in chloroform, ethylene dichloride, toluene and mixture of toluene and acetone.

Resistance of acrylic cements to weathering and moisture varies from poor (solvent types) to excellent (polymer mixtures). Colour may change from transparent to yellow over a time, e.g. one year or more. They are not affected by alkalies, non-oxidizing acids, salt spray, petroleum fuels etc. but are attacked by alcohols, strong solvents and aromatic and chlorinated hydrocarbons. They are highly resistant to UV exposure. The service temperature of range of acrylic resin adhesives is 60° C to 80° C.

There adhesives are available as emulsions solvents solutions, and monomer polymer mixtures (one or two components) with catalysts (liquid or powder). One component liquids which polymerize under UV radiation, are available. Emulsion solvent type formulations set by evaporation and absorption of solvent polymer mixtures set through polymerization by heat, UV radiation and or chemical catalysts. Solvent types set over a period of 20 days at 20° C or 6 hours at 80° C. Polymer mixture setting times depend on polymerizing method used and chemical action; examples are: 14 days 20° C for 4 hr. at 80° C; UV action 5 hour exposure; heat action 2 hr. at 55° C followed by 8 hr. at 80° C. Bonding pressures range from contact to 17 N/ cm^2.

Manufacture

A number of processes for producing acrylic acid and acrylic acid esters are of commercial importance. The most important one is the BASE Rappe process in which acetylene, water or alcohol and carbon monoxide react under pressure.

Moreover, the synthesis of acrylic esters by esterification of acrylic acid deserves mention. The acid hydrolysis of acrylonitrile in the presence of water or alcohols should also be emphasized in this connection. The synthesis from inexpensive petrochemicals, i.e. the oxidation of propylene, is the most promising process.

The conventional older industrial synthesis of methacrylic acid and its esters starts from acetone cyanohydrin, which is made from acetone and hydrogen cyanide. The oxidation of isobutylene is a modern process.

The most important acrylic acid esters for producing adhesives are methyl acrylate, ethyl acrylate, and 2 ethylhexyl acrylate. At room temperature, these monomers are clear, colourless liquids. Apart from these acrylic acid esters, numerous other monomers of this product class are used as well for obtaining special effects in adhesives. Because of the highly activated double bond, all acrylic compounds are very reactive and capable of undergoing polymerization or other reactions under relatively mild conditions. To prevent spontaneous polymerization during transport and storage e.g.due to the presence of foreign matter, the acrylic compounds are normally stabilized by hydroquinone or hydroquinone monomethyl ether.

Because of the high reactivity of the vinyl groups, acrylic compounds are capable of forming linear polymers of high molecular weight by reacting with themselves or with other types of vinyl compounds.

All industrial polymerization processes are carried out at an elevated temperature in the presence of an initiator. Polymerization can be be carried out in bulk, solution, suspension, or emulsion.

In addition to other factors, the softening point of the polymer and its solubility characteristics are of decisive importance in selecting the polymerization process for a certain system. The processes can be carried out discontinuously or continuously.

In solution polymerization, the monomer or monomer mixture is dissolved in a solvent which is relatively inert to free radicals, e.g. ethyl or butyl acetate, benzene, toluene, petroleum solvent or ketones, then polymerization is effected at elevated temperatures in the presence of an initiator such as an organic peroxide or an azo compound which is soluble in the solvent.

A typical solution polymerization formulation for producing a pressure sensitive adhesive is given below.

n-Butyl acrylate	500	parts
Ethyl acetate	500	"
Benzoylperoxide	0.55	"

The destabilized acrylate is dissolved in ethyl acetate in a mixing vessel and 150 parts of the solution is heated with stirring to 75-80^0 C. After moderate reaction has set in, the residual solution is gradually added within 2 hr at reflux temperature. After the incorporation has been completed, the compound is further polymerized for 1-2 hr.

Properties of the product

K value	50-60
Solids content	50%
Film properties	very tacky

The type of solvent used has a great influence on the reaction speed and the molecular weight of the resulting polymer in solution, because of the different chain transfer activities of the various solvents. Thus, the viscosity of a polymethyl acrylate solution, and the molecular weight of the polymer, decreases in the following order benzene, ethyl acetate, ethylate dichloride, butyl acetate, methyl isobutyl ketone and toluene. The solvent with the highest chain transfer activity gives polymers of lowest molecular weight. The molecular weights of solution polymers are normally lower than those of emulsion polymers. In selecting the solvent to be used, consideration must also be given to the economic and safety aspects.

The emulsion polymerization process for homo and copolymerisation of acrylic compounds is of greater significance than solution polymerization process. It is effected in the presence of emulsifiers and initiators (e.g. alkali persulphate), normally in water as the external phase. Suitable emulsifiers are, for example, alkali salts of long-chain aliphatic carboxylic or sulphonic acids, or sulphated ethylene oxide adducts.

n-Butyl acrylate	1375	parts
Vinyl acetate	1375	"
Acrylic acid	50	"
Surfactant	25	"
Octadecyl alcohol + ethylene oxide adduct	25	"
Water	2500	"
Potassium peroxide disulphate	0.05%	"

To an enamelled vessel with water cooling jacket and stirrer water, emulsifier and acrylic acid are added. The product is neutralized with aqueous caustic to pH 7-8. The other monomers and the catalyst are added the mixture is kept cool, 15-20% of the mixture from the mixing vessel is introduced by pressure and heated to 70-80° C. When the reaction has set in after 1/2-3/4 hr, (this can be seen from the reflux), the residual amount from the mixing vessel is gradually incorporated within 2-3 hr. The reaction is usually not yet completed after this procedure. The mix must be kept at 80-90° C for another 1-1/2 hr. The conclusion of the reaction can be recognized from the viscosity or solids content. Residual monomers are removed by passing a stream of nitrogen over the surface for 30 min at 80-90° C. The compound is then cooled down to 35° C. This yields a dispersion having the following properties.

Properties of the dispersion:

Solids content	ca. 50%
Average particle size	0.2 μ
Viscosity (Epprecht STV. 25° C A III).	ca. 20 cps

Application and formulations

These adhesives are useful for light structural assembly work based on acrylic plastic bonded ot themselves, wood, glass, metals, rubber, leather and fabrics. They are also suitable for colourless joining of decorative plastic laminates, production line assembly of components (cured by UV), outdoor applications such as plastic name plates, aluminium foil work, windshields, instrument panels, lenses and optical components in aircraft, marine and automotive industries. One type n-butylmethacrylate (alone or modified with canade balsam) is used as an optical cement.

Acrylic cements are compatible with pigments where coloured glue lines are required. Gap filling properties vary from 0.025 to 6.3 mm. according to grade used. Bonding of acrylic plastic e.g. Perspex, to other materials of lower expansion co-efficient e.g. steel with acrylics, interlayer of rubber. The rubber is bonded ot other materials with an epoxy resin adhesive.

Because of their high specific adhesion to a great variety of surfaces, polyacrylics acid esters in the form of aqueous dispersions and organic solutions were found suitable for the production of adhesives for surfaces which are difficult to bond. The products in question are either copolymers of acrylic acid esters with one another, or especially in the case of packaging adhesives, copolymers of acrylic acid esters with vinyl propionate or vinyl acetate, i.e. copolymers of vinyl acetate with acrylic acid esters, and vinyl acetate have increased adhesion to metal foils and various plastics and are therefore used for producing adhesives for this field of application. Terpolymers of this type are also very resistant to plasticizer migration, e.g. from plasticized PVC film.

The following formulation serves as a guide for compounding an adhesive for laminating aluminium foil-to-paper.

Acrylic emulsion	95.5 parts
Hydroxy ethyl cellulose 5% in water	4.5 "
Viscosity: 1900 cps 950 cps and 500 cps.	

The adhesive is applied onto the aluminium foil by means of rolls. Lamination can be effected either while the adhesive is still wet or by sealing at 130-150 C after drying.

Acrylic emulsion can also be used for compounding an adhesive for laminating rigid or soft PVC film to paper. Following is a typical formulation.

Acrylic emulsion	100	parts
Ammonia 25%	2	"
Water	15	"
Viscosity: 670 cps 370 cps and 250 cps.		

The required viscosity for application is obtained by thickening with ammonia and, if necessary, by adding water. The adhesive is applied onto the film. Lamination can be effected either while the adhesive is still wet or by pressing between rolls at 60-70^{0} C after drying. The adhesive is usually applied at a rate of 10-12 g/m^2.

Typical applications include lamination of pocket books, maps, posters, etc. with rigid or soft PVC film.

For laminating polyester film to paper, it is necessary to increase the adhesion to the film. A starting formulation is given below.

Acrylic emulsion	90	parts
Acrylic emulsion of large particle size	10	"
Ammonia 25%	2	"
Water	10	"

Acrylic solutions are used on a large scale for laminating high gloss films, e.g. acetate films or cellophane, to pocket books, record covers, etc. A typical formulation is as follows.

Acrylic solution 40% in ethyl acetate	100	parts
Rosin 40% solution in toluene	60	"
Toluene	55	"

Coat weight on acetate film approximately 12 g/m^2 solids
Laminating temperature 40-50° C
Laminating pressure 8-10 kg/cm^2

In laminating acetate film it is advisable to use toluene as a solvent. In this case, too, the adhesive is applied onto the film. The coated film is laminated to the paper web or board sheets after the bulk of the solvent has evaporated. This is carried out with the aid of laminating rolls at moderate temperature in order to prevent the laminate from warping.

Laminates of aluminium foil and paper with good resistance to heat and water can be produced with acrylic solutions according to the following typical formulation.

Acrylic Solution 40% in ethyl acetate	70	parts
Vinyl chloride+Vinyl propionate copolymer 50% in ethyl acetate	30	"

Laminating temperature : approximately 60° C.

The heat resistance of the bond can be increased to above 100° C by adding an isocyanate, e.g. 5 parts by weight 75% in ethyl acetate, (polyfunctional aromatic isocyanate) to the above mentioned formulation. A compound of this type has a pot life of approximately 8 hr at room temperature.

An adhesive coating for heat sealable protective polymer films can be produced according to the following typical formulation.

Acrylic emulsion	99	parts
Vinyl pyrolidone thickening agent	1	"

Type of film rigid PVC film, unstretched
Coat weight 6-10 g/m^2 (solids)
Sealing temperature approximately 100^0 C
Blocking temperature approximately 40^0 C

Films coated in this way can be wound up without blocking.

In the packaging field. acrylics are often used for delayed tack adhesive coatings for labels. Copolymer dispersions of acrylic ester with vinyl acetate, vinyl chloride, or styrene are usually also employed for this application. The backing material, usually paper, is coated after the dispersions have been modified accordingly. The coated papers are tack-free under normal conditions so that the sheets and cuttings can be rolled up or stacked. These types of delayed-tack adhesives consist primarily of one or a mixture of polymer film formers in dispersion form and one or several crystalline plasticizers. The plasticizer is usually employed in the form of a dispersion with very small particle size.

Resin solutions or resin dispersions are used as additives for obtaining certain adhesive effects. The adhesive coating must be dried at a temperature below the melting point of the plasticizer in order to obtain a tack-free surface.

A typical formulation for a delayed tack adhesive based on acrylic copolymers is given below.

Acrylic emulsion	25	parts
Additives	3	"
Plasticizer dispersion	75	"
Resin solution	20	"

Viscosity : 1300 cps and 100 cps.

20

CYANOACRYLATE ADHESIVES

Most of these adhesives are based on methyl 2-cyano acrylate, ethyl-2-cyanoacrylate or a combination of these two. Along with the cyanoacrylate a modifiers is used to regulate the physical properties of the adhesive. These modifiers are polyvinyl acetate, polymethyl methacrylate, cellulose organic esters and polyactic acid. The best bonding action is obtained when the surfaces are thoroughly clean before the adhesive is applied. Surfaces are cleaned usually with a tissue paper soaked in low boiling solvent. A typical adhesive has the following properties.

Refractive index	1.4501
Viscosity at 25° C (cp)	60-300
Specific gravity	1.097
Heat of polymerization	12.5 /Kcal/mole
Boiling point	48-49° C at 2.5-2.7 mm Hg
Vapour pressure at 25° C	$<$2 mm Hg

A very small adhesive is required for making the bond generally 1 drop per square inch for a smooth surface. Rough surface require a little more.

The properties which make the alkyl 2 cyanoacrylate unique are its abilities to polymerize rapidly at room temperature without addition of a catalyst and its abilities to give high bond strength between a wide variety of adherends.

The nature of various bonds between various substrates for cyanoacrylate adhesives is given below.

Substrate	*Bonding action*	*Bond strength*
Glass-glass	rapid	strong
Glass-rubber	rapid	strong
Polyester polyester	rapid	intermediate
Metal-cork	rapid	strong
Metal-leather	intermediate	strong
Nylon-nylon	rapid	strong

Manufacture

An alkyl cyano acetate is condensed with formaldehyde to give a poly (alkyl 2 cyano acrylate). This is depolymerised at high temperature to yield cyano acrylate ester. The condensation is carried out in an nonaqueous medium (toluene or xylene) which helps in removal of water from the reaction medium. The pH of the reaction mass is kept controlled at the acidic range and cyanoacetate formaldehyde ratio is regulated. The alkyl 2 cyanoacrylate are inhibited from polymerizing by a stabilizing agent such as maleic anhydride, alkyl sulphates, alkyl sulphones, mercaptans etc. Properties of cyanoacrylate can be modified by addition of polymethacrylate, polyvinyl acetates, polyacrylates, cellulose organic acid esters. The impact resistance of the bond of cyanoacrylate adhesives can be improved by addition of plasticizers such as aliphatic monocarboxylic acids, trialkyl/aryl phosphates, alkyl phthalates etc.

Applications and Formulation

The rapid set time of these adhesives is used to speed the assembly of items such as trophtes, fountain pen, rubber imprinting plates, optical lenses, tools and Hifi phonographic cartridges. The abilities of the adhesives to bond dissimilar materials is an advantage.

Typical formulation is given below.

2 cyanoacrylate	30	%
VAM	20	%
Emulsifier	3	%
Plasticizer	3	%
Colour	0.1	%
Water	43.9	%

21
ANAEROBIC ADHESIVES

Anaerobic materials are single component liquids those can be stored at ordinary temperatures in presence of oxygen and then polymerize rapidly to solids on being confined between two surfaces that exclude air. Anaerobic products are used as machinery adhesives where their ability to lock threaded parts against vibration loosening, seal a variety of tubular and flat objects and retain collars, gears and pulleys to shafts, offers simple chemical solutions to problems those were solved previously by mechanical means only with difficulties and often not in a wholly satisfactory manner. Several billions of parts now-a-days are assembled every year with anaerobic adhesives.

There are four major application areas for anaerobic adhesives sealants. These are locking threaded assemblies, strengthening cylindrical assemblies, sealing threads porous and flanged assemblies and structrical bonding. The benefits are: (a) the ability of the adhesive to fill inner spaces in metal assemblies and cure with minimal shrinking and in the cured state, the capability of reducing degradative forces on the assembly. Anaerobics find use both as a design tool and in the maintenance and repair. They are used to improve mechanical methods of assembly making equipment more reliable. Numerous parts like lock ashers, keys and pins can be eliminated. Anaerobics simplify assembly procedures and increase assembly rates by lowering the scraps and rework which normally occur with mechanical methods.

The anaerobic adhesives can be cured without heat or mixing. Surface activators provide refined cures and high strength. The single component adhesives are stable during storage and use. Automatic application equipment can be run easily and efficiently. No adhesive is wasted due to pot life restriction. Adhesive remains uncured outside the boarderline. Cleanup is easy with organic solvent.

Major application are glass bonding and magnet bonding. A typical anaerobic has the following properties.

Refractive index	1.54 + 0.002
Coeff. thermal expansion	5-8x10^5 in/inch ^{0}F
Elasticity	2%
Light transmittance	95%
Tensile shear strength (st/st)	2500-2850 psi
Tensile shear strength (st/gl)	550-850 psi

A typical formulation of anaerobic adhesives follows.

Polyethylene glycol dimetha acrylate	50%
Cumene hydroperoxide	20%
Trimethyl amine	10%
Polystyrene	10%
Plasticizer	10%

22

POLYAMIDE ADHESIVES

Polyamide resins used in adhesives can be divided into four classes. These are (1) the liquid thermoset adhesives; (2) nylon-epoxy adhesives; (3) thermoplastic hot melt adhesives and (4) thermoplastic resins which interact in molten stage of form thermoset adhesives.

Class 1: adhesives are usually blended of epoxy resin and polyamide resins which chemically combine or crosslink at room temperature to form an infusible salt.

Class 2: are based on nylon-epoxy resin blends with improved creep resistance. The latent catalyst generally used requires heat for activation.

Class 3: are based on polyamide resins.

Class 4: are combination of solid/liquid epoxy resin with polyamide resins.

These resins adhesives are useful for bonding various metals, plastics, masonry, wood, glass and ceramics. They are not recommended at temperature of more than 110° C. These resins are used in areas of aircraft, automobiles, construction, electrical & electronics, household repair, packaging, product assembly, show and wood working.

A typical formulation follows.

Component A		
Epoxy resin	100	parts
Silica flour	60	"
Carbon black	1	"
Component B		
Polymercaptan	60	parts
Dicyandiamide	10	"
Silica flour	10	"
Triethylene tetra amine	20	"

Solid epoxy acid solid reactive polyamide when brought together by various methods and method give an adhesive of hot melt type plus the strength and resistance of a thermoset resin. This adhesive is very useful in shoe making and wood working.

23
SILICONE ADHESIVES

Silicone is a semi inorganic polymer or poly-organosiloxane, which may be fluid, elastomeric or resinous according to the type of organic groups on the silicon atoms and the extent of cross-linkage between polymer chains. Dimethyl silicone elastomers are useful because they remain rubberlike over a wide range of temperature; however, they are attacked by solvents; hence a new class of silicone elastomers has been developed (cyanoalkyl silicones) that shows excellent resistance to many solvents. They also have temperature flexibility; and stability up to 250^0 C. Totally condensed cyanoalkyl silicone gums are clear viscous polymers similar in appearance to dimethyl silicone gums. They can be prepared as fluids, pastes, solvent solutions and solids suitable for solution coating, moulding, calendering and extrusion; they find application as adhesives, solvent barries, encapsulants, cable component and automotive and aircraft components.

In general use of silicone as adhesives has not been extensive, but certain silicone resin and elastomer polymers have developed with sufficient adhesive properties for certain applications. They are suitable for continuous service up to 250^0 C, but have low initial adhesive strength. They may be used to improve the heat stability of other adhesive materials as epoxy and phenolic resins. These adhesives will be described in two sections, namely; silicone resins and silicone elastomers (rubbers).

Silicone resins are available as water white to straw coloured aromatic solvent solutions with a solids contents of about 60% or higher according to end use. Their shelf life at 20^0 C exceeds 6 months. They have good resistance to moisture and weathering with low water absorption. Their sunlight, ozone, biodeterioration, heat and oxidation resistance is excellent and service temperature range from -60^0 C to +250^0 C. Silicone resins withstand contact with many oils, chemicals, including dilute acids and bases, but are prone to dissolution in organic solvent media. They have good electrical properties with high dielectric strength and are resistance and low loss factor. They do not breakdown, and do not allow carbon tracking or current leakage.

These resins are used in pressure-sensitive tape manufacture. Typical backing materials include glass cloth, either plain or silicone-varnished, silicone rubbers, polyester film, PTFE, metal foils, synthetic fabrics. These tapes are used as insulation wrappings for electrial windings and coils for service up to 180° C. They are also used for bonding of mica and asbestos panel boards, and also as adhesive-sealant for exposed magnesium oxide (heating element) insulation.

For pressure sensitive adhesive tape applications, solvent is removed by drying coated adherends for 15-30 min. at 70-100° C. A tacky adhesive film is obtained, which may be contact bonded to another surface without further treatment. Some backing materials, other than glass cloth require the use of primer to improve adhesion, or a repellent to prevent migration of adhesive into the backing materials. A 2% solution of tetrabutyl titanate in white spirit, which is hydrolysed and dried provides the most satisfactory repellent. For certain fomulations a post cure for 5 min. at 250, or 5 min. at 125° C, where a peroxide or lead acetate catalyst is added up to 2% w/w, ensures optimum balance of cohesive and adhesive strength. For insulation material bonding and sealing, typical processing involves air drying followed by backing for 1 hr. at 100° C to remove solvent and then post curing for 1 hr. at 250° C to produce a hard and dry film.

Silicone Rubbers are used as solvent free white pastes in one or two part products, which cure to form flexible silicone elastomers or silastomers. These materials are essentially adhesive sealants. Their properties are consistent with silicone rubbers in gerenal; they are highly resistant to moisture, hot water, oxidation, ozone, corona discharge and weathering. They have good resistance to many chemicals including dilute acids and alkalies. Cured elastomers swell in the presence of hydro carbon solvents and fuels. They are heat stable over the range 75° C to 250° and retain good flexibility at low temperatures. Fluorosilicones, apart from all these properties, display excellent resistance to prolonged immersion in fuels, oils and solvents.

These silicone compounds are used for general purpose sealing, bonding and repair materials for caulking, water-proofing and insulating electrical and mechanical assemblies. They are used as sealant for seams and welded joints in automotive industive and for bonding between metals, glass, ceramics, wood and plastics requiring damaged silicone rubber surfaces in hot-air ducts, oven gaskets, encapsulants in electrical an electronic equipment, and wire or cable insulation. Silicone rubber compounds are used on natural and synthetic textile as coatings, e.g. for conveyor belts to give heat resistant and antistick surfaces. Fluorosilicone rubbers may be used for similar applications particularly where fuel and solvent resistance is required and also for bonding fluorosilicone rubber to any clean surface.

These one-part products (RTV type) cure at room temperature on exposure to atmospheric moisture. Thin films (0.6 mm) cure within 90 min. while thicker films (13 mm) are fully cured within 7 days. Two part products are cured by catalytic action; the pot life is dependent on catalyst concentration and ambient temperature. At 20° C and 1% catalyst the pot life is 10 hrs. while setting-time is 65 hrs. Curing is accelerated by temperature increase and retarded-by decrease in temperature.

Epoxy Silicone are binary systems consisting of epoxide resin adn silicones. Thus the resulting adhesive has the heat stability of the silicones and the mechanical strength of the epoxies. German Patent 9.56,711 describes a heat curable adhesive obtained by mixing 3 parts epoxy resin powder with 1 part of silicone polymer (obtained by heating dimethyl silicone with about 5% boric oxide for a few hours). This adhesive is particularly suitable for bonding metals.

Manufacture

Manufacture of silicone fluids involves following three important steps.

(1) Hydrolysis (2) Catalytic equilibration (3) Devolatization.

These fluids are preferably made in a batch process a weighed excess of water is placed in a glass lined jacketed reactor. Dimethylchlorosiliane is run through a dispersion nozzle and the contents are agitated well. The reaction is carried out under reflux. Although the reaction is endothermic, the absorption of hydrochloride gas evolved in the reaction generates enough heat to make the reaction exothermic and therefore it becomes necessary to cool the reactants. When the reaction is completed, the oily polymer layer is allowed to separate from the dilute acid phase which is then drwan off. The oil is then neutralized in a separate operation by washing with sodium carbonate solution. The neutral solution at this stage consists of cyclic and linear polymers. Cyclic polymers constitute 20-80% of the total products. In order to achieve a more linear polymer but with a random molecular weight distribution and also to stabilize the viscosity it is a common practice to equilibrate the fluid by heating with a catalyst such as dilute sulphuric acid. To check the degree of polymerization, chain stoppers such as mono-functional trimethyl chlorosilane is added. In practice for fluids of viscosities less than 1,000 centistokes, the equilibration reaction takes a number of hours at 100-150° C. The volatile low molecular weight products are finelly removed from the batch using a vaccum still.

A silicone elastomer stock is compounded and processed on the same type of equipment as used for organic rubbers. It can be mixed on a two-roll mill, in a Banbury or in a dough mixer. The curing agent should always be added on a mill to avoid premature set-up. Unvulcanized silicon elastomer is softer and weaker than organic rubber, and a scrapper blade attachment on the mill is recommended for removing the silicone compound. After compounding the next step is to cure rubber. The first stage of curing is carried out in a press, hot air chamber or steam vulcanizer, the process being referred to as set-cure. The second stage is carried out in an air circulating oven and is especially necessary in order to develop the optimum physical properties required for many applications and for maximum resistance to compression set.

Fully compounded silicone stocks may be moulded, extruded, laminated, calendered or applied from solvent dispersion. Conventional rubber processing machinery is used and should include a two-roll mill equipped with scrapper blades, a steam or electrically heated moulding process operating at temperatures between 100-150^0 C with provision for water cooling. A steam vulcanizer capable of operating at pressure up to 7 kg/cm2 should also be available. In addition, a forced air-draught circulating oven is essential to obtain an adequate final cure for optimum physical properties.

Application

RTV silicone are very much used in automotive industry. It is utilized to replace conventional gasketing material. RTV silicone is used as a formed in place gasket. They are used in value cover, oil pan, thermostat, rear axle cover, automatic transmission housing. Silicone sealants are used in aerospace industry. It is used as encapsulating material in electrical connectors and terminals. It is also used as construction sealants.

24

NATURAL RESIN BASED ADHESIVES

Adhesives were being prepared from natural polymers like gums, starch, casin, soya flours, etc. from the old days. Some of these adhesives are still in use. These adhesives are described below.

Starch Adhesives

Starch is a natural polymer. It is a polysaccharide abundantly available and is expensive and relatively stable in quality. As a polymeric polyhydroxy compound, starch yields adhesives with excellent affinity to polar substrates, such as cellulose. As a result of its origin, structure, hydrophlillic character and ease of dispersion, starch is water sensitive and prone to attack by microorganisms. These limitations can be controlled by chemical modifications.

Starch occurs is roots and seeds of plants, from which it may be recovered by dry or wet milling processes. Typical commercial starches are listed in the following.

Commercial starches

Starch	Corn	Wheat	Rice	Tapioca	Potato	Sago
Source	Seed	Seed	Seed	Root	Root	Pith
Granule size	5-26	3-35	3-8	5-35	15-100	10-70
Gelatinization:						
Temp °C	62-72	58-64	68-78	49-70	59-68	60-67
Amylose, %	28	25	19	20	25	26
Amylose (DP)	480	-	-	1050	850	-
Amylopecin (DP) 1	450	-	-	1300	2000	0

The common starches contain about 20-30% amylose and 70-80% amylopectin.

Modified starches are of three main classes: acid converted, oxidized and dextrins. Non degrading chemical modifications involves introduction of small amount of substituent groups into starch by ester and ether linkages. Typical groups includes carboxyl, aminoalkyl, hydroxyalkyl, cyanoethyl and acetyl. Their primary effect is that of weakening the granules and stabilizing the dispersions by preventing the molecules from aligning and retrograding.

Starch do not form a true solution, except after very high conversions and at extreme dilutions. The colsloidal dispersion normally obtained constitute various agglomerates of starch molecules, granule fregments and dissolve molecules. In the dispersed form, starch products products yield various degree of spreadability and filminess necessary for adhesion.

Raw or moderately converted starch with alkali yield heavy stringy and viscous dispersions. They maintain excellent bond of polar substrates with inherent moisture and humidity resistance. Bottle labelling is one of the largest use.

Gelatinization with alkali produces heavy paste from cereal starches and very clear adhesives from root starches and waxy type starches. The are useful as carries in paper corrugation as foil to paper adhesives and carbon or case, scaling adhesives. The simplest liquid adhesives are starch dispersion formulated with salts as calcium chloride, sodium nitrate or borax for better tack. Such pastes can be used in bill posting, bag making and tobacco seam gluing.

Adhesives formulated from heavy bodies starches or dextrins that have a short, soft with an appreciable degree of thixotropy are usually referred to as pastes. Many of the borated dextrins, formulated for short, nonthrowing properties, qualify also as paste. Generally pastes yield excellent adhesion to most paper stock.

Frequently dextrins are formulated with borax to obtain high tack at moderate concentrations and viscosities with good aging characteristics. Their colour ranges from off white to dark brown. Their applications are many, including case sealing, carton sealing, bag seams, tube winding, laminating etc.

Non-borated, highly converted dextrins are giving classification while nonborated lightly converted types are better classified as pastes. These types used when borax is objectionable. The solid content of the product may be higher than 65%. They are made mostly from canary dextrins and are usually tan to brown in colour. Their formulations are used in flat-gumming, envelop manufacturing, certain types of bottle labelling and whenever externally high initial tack is required.

Modified starches may be gelatinized and dried by running concentrated, aqueous starch suspensions over steam heated rolls. The resulting flakes are usually ground coarsely and freed of fines and reduces the tendency of these products to lump when dispersed in cold water. Their uses encopass adhesives for multiwall paper bags, wall paper, bill posting etc.

Some water resistance can be developed with starch-polyvinyl alcohol adhesives. To provide greater water resistance for paper corrugation or for cartons and fibre case adhesives use is made of additives, such as thermoset resins eg. urea formaldehyde or resorcinol formaldehyde. For best results a proper adhesive base and an accurately controlled pH for resin polymerization and hardening must be selected.

The corrugative adhesive consists of granular starch suspended in a dilute cook of (e.g.) corn starch. Sodium hydroxide is added to lower the gelatinization temperature and borax to increase th tack. The suspended starch should gelatinize immediately on contact with the heated fluting rolls and develop instant tack at 60-70° C. The following two component, two container formulation may be used for a non-weather proof pasts.

50 kg. of corn starch is added with mixing 200 kg, water followed by 8.5 kg, caustic soda solution in 15 litre water. The mixture is heated by steam to 71° C, agitated for 15 min. and diluted with 250 kg. cold water. This is a carrier starch.

8.5 kg. of borax is dissolved in 760 kg. water and 250 kg. starch is added to it. The earlier described adhesive part is slowly added with agitation until the viscosity reaches 35 sec. 1 kg. of formaldehyde is than added. Resorcinol formaldehyde condensate is added to the mix to make it water resistant.

Mix I	Water	1192	parts
	HAS	424	"
	Borax	6	"
	Bring to 54.4° C and add with stirring		
	NaOH	36.6	"
	Water	47.5	"
Mix II	Water	3480	parts
	Corn starch	1600	"
	Borax	28	"
	Thermosetting resin	91.2	"

I is added to II mixed for 20 minutes and then used by passing a wet strength medium for testing.

Normally three adhesives are involved in this application, seam, cross-pasting and bottoming. The following formulation shows approximate composition.

Water	339.5 kg
Dextrin	140 kg
Heat to 71 and add	
Borax	16.2 kg
Heat to 88 C and add	
Preservative	1.6 kg
Seam and bottom	
Water	336.5 kg
Corn starch	31.9 kg
Dextrin	122.5 kg
Soap	1.25 kg
Heat to 87^0 hold 20 min. cool to 57^0 C adjust to 25% solids	
and add Preservative	1.5 kg

An insolubilizing seam adhesive can be obtained by addition of a thermosetting resin such as urea-formaldehyde, according to the following formula:

Water	80.5 kg
White dextrin	350 kg
Soap	1 kg
Urea formaldehyde	35 kg
Cook with live steam to 93^0 C dilute with cold water	
to 1300 it. volume and add	
Ammonium chloride	7.5 kg

The resulting adhesive has a pH of 6.0. Seam adhesive should be thin flowing, nonstanding and have good tack. Converted type formulated with borax or caustic, clay, soap, tallow. They should not string not foam but have good tack and yield from non-brittle bonds.

Laminating adhesives must have good tack with sufficient open time. The following formulation shows the approximate amounts of ingredients used in these adhesives.

Water	215 kg.
Dextrin	105 kg.
Corn starch	20 kg.
Peptizing salt	160 kg.
Heat to 93⁰ C, hold for 20 min and add	
Preservative	1.6 kg.
and adjust to 50-55% solids.	

The following formula can be used for bottom and top carbon sealing.

Water	110	parts
White dexirin	80	"
Preservative	2	"
Borax	12	"
Antifoam	0.125	"
Cook to 85⁰ C for 20 min to 48⁰ C and add		
Water	10	"
NaOH	1.2	"

Paper to Glass Adhesives

Tapioca starch	125	parts
Glycerin	10	"
Water	150	"
Zinc chloride	2	"

Mix thoroughly and heat to boiling stirring vigorously. If tapioca is in lumps, the mixture should soak overnight before heating.

Office Use Adhesive

Starch	100	parts
Calcium chloride	47	"
Zinc chloride	36	"
Hot water	370	"

The two chlorides are mixed in 70 parts of water and heated to 65⁰ C. Starch is then added slowly with constant heating and stirring. A clear jelly is obtained; to this 870 parts of hot water is added. A denser opaque and cheaper adhesive is obtained by using sodium silicate.

Tapioca starch	100	parts
Caustic soda, 36 Be. diluted with amount of water	30	"
Sodium silicate, 35° Be	40	"
Hydrochloric acid, 22° Be	33	"
Formaldehyde	5	"
Water	500	"

Starch is suspended in water, diluted caustic is stirred into it. Hydrochloric acid is added ot neutralise the alkali partly, and to it 150 parts more water is added. Finally formaldehyde is mixed in. This adhesive is somewhat alkaline, hence is not suitable for some applications. Alum may be added to neutralize the remaining alkalinity. It also increases the viscosity of the product. Addition of more sodium silicate makes it gum like.

Wall Paper Paste

Water starch ratio 6.4.1

Water	220	parts
Starch	120	"
Calcium chloride flakes	140	"
Water	550	"
Borax	1.2	"
Formalin (30%)	1.8	"

Water and starch are mixed at 20° C and then $CaCl_2$ is added and mixed for 2 hours. Water, borax, formaldehyde mixture is then added slowly. Quantity of $CaCl_2$ can be reduced, very little alum is added, for example if 2 parts of alum is added then $CaCl_2$ may be reduced by 30 parts, and borax is eliminated also, the amount of water may be reduced by 50 parts.

Cheap Diluted Adhesive

Water starch ratio = 12:1

This adhesive is quite cheap and also meets a number of industrial requirements.

Water	950	parts
Sodium hydroxide	0.45	"
White Soap	0.50	"
Tapioca starch	80	"
Sodium fluoride	2	"
Formalin, 30 per cent	5	"
Water	3	"

Starch is mixed water, caustic soda and soap; it is heated to 85^{0} C; sodium fluroide, formalin and water are mixed for about 15 min. Stability of the paste is enhanced by the addition of small amount of caustic and soap. This cheap paste can be further diluted, if required.

Non Weather Proof Corrugated Board Adhesive

Concentrated adhesive water starch 3:1

This adhesive has quite low water to starch ratio, hence addition of calcium chloride is necessary to increase the translucent character and stability. As soap and sodium fluoride are precipitated by CaC1s, these are not incorporated. The quantity of $CaC1_2$ used is limited to 15 per cent of that of starch.

Water	854 parts
Bentonite clay	10
Caustic soda (in parts of water)	13
Corn starch	505
Borax mix	17
Formalin	2.7

25

DEXTRIN BASED ADHESIVES

The dextrins come second in importance among the basic materials of cold adhesives. They are not only cheaper than natural gums, but also almost equally soluble in water. As mentioned earlier dextrins are the degradation products of starches. This transformation is effected generally by heating the starch with a dilute acid or also by simple roasting of starch at high temperature. Dextrins are of three types are given below.

1. White dextrins
2. Canary or yellow dextrins
3. British gums

Manufacture

White, canary and British gum are made by heating starch in the dry state. For canary and white dextrins, starch is sprayed with acids and heated; for British gums heat is the principal factor, although relatively small propertions of acid may be used to shorten conversion times.

Dextrins are produced by roasting starch in the presence of acid to yield the solubility and colour desired. Solubility and colour can be varied by controlling the time and temperature of reaction along with the strength of acid. One more important point is that the starch acid mixture should be be uniform and therefore use of volatile mineral acids is recommended: usually hydrochloric acid is used. The amount and concentration of the acid should be so chosen that the acidulated starch contains about 25 per cent of water; acid strength up to 0.1 per cent are common. Water is evaporated to 2 to 8 per cent by vaccum drying. The dried starch is then roasted in roasters. Heating is effected by super-heated steam passing through the jacket of the roaster. Depending on the nature and percentage of acid, the temperature and duration of roasting white, yellow or deep yellow dextrins can be obtained. For white dextrins temperature is usually below 105^{0} C and the modification is accomplished in 8 hours or less. For yellow or canary dextrins higher temperatures are used. British gums are prepared by roasting starch at temperatures up to 150^{0} C without adding acid. Occasionally certain alkaline materials, such as sodium carbonate or sodium bicarbonate may be added in trace amounts.

When the desired degree of dextrinification of the starch has been obtained, the materials is cooled to stop the reaction. The cooled material is almost anhydrous and moisture has to be added again. This not gives the material accepted commercial strength but also improves its solubility; as anhydrous dextrin does not dissolve very easily and has a tendency to form lumps. Hydration can be brought about in a humidifier. A mixture of air and steam is blown upward while a stream of finely divided dextrin flows downward. Last step is bolting in which dextrin is passed through a vibrating sieve which removes impurities and outsize particles. Very small quantities of dextrins may be produced in a simgle mixer. This mixer consists of a vat jacketed on its both sides and bottom and fitted internally with a helicoidal agitator, which assures perfect scraping and mixing of the charge in both horizontal as well as vertical directions. The vat should be capable of being heated with steam at 10 kg/cm^2 pressure.

Dextrins are generally sold in powder from and should be stored dry and away from vermin. The characteristics of the dextrins are dependent upon the origin of the starch, from which they are prepared and the technique of the conversion. The percentage of glucose formed is usually held to a minimum, because glucose tends to increase hygroscopicity and decrease adhesiveness. Potato dextrins have better adhesiveness, clarity of pastes and stability. Sago and tapioca also show good paste clarity. Corn starch dextrins show poor paste clarity as compared to potato dextrins, but have good adhesive properties.

Dextrins do not have as good strength as the starch adhesives, though they are more soluble and set more rapidly. White dextrins are soluble to the extent of 25 to 75 per cent in cold water, slightly coloured dextrins are about 97 per cent soluble in cold water, while more highly coloured varieties are completely soluble. There are other dextrins, which are brown or pale and contain a higher percentage of glucose and are almost completely soluble in water. A distinclion between some of the highly soluble whites and a canary dextrin may be arbitrary, but generally, the latter will have a more stable viscosity at high solids than the former. The whites are characterised only by their lighter colour, but by their pastings tendencies. British gums give gummy, filmy colloids of relatively stable body at comparatively low solids concentrations; these are the strongest of the dextrin adhesive but are the slowest to make property.

Solubility of the dextrin in cold water depends on its glucose content, i.e. if more will be the glucose content higher will be solubility. Glucose content is dictated by the stage to which the starch conversion process is taken place; the further the starch conversion process is taken more glucose does the dextrin contain. The colour of a dextrin deepens substantially in proportion to the degree, to which its viscosity an thickening power diminishes. The pH of the dextrin solution has to be controlled to avoid further hydrolysis of dextrin. Dextrin films are always supported as in paper and textile coating and sizing, because they are brittle to be used alone. Glossy clear films are formed from tapioca dextrins, while corn dextrins tend to form more cloudy and brittle films. Remoistening films are prepared principally from tapioca dextrins although potato and waxy maize dextrins have been used.

Dextrin breaks down on heating in the same way as starch, and therefore, as little heat as possible, for as short a time as possible, should be used in preparing dextrin adhesives. A simple dextrin adhesive used as Photo Paste is given below.

Dextrin, white	24	kgs.
Water	24	litres.
Ginger grass oil	10	gms.

Dextrin is dissolved in the water with a gentle heat and the oil is then stirred in.

Dextrin is slightly acidic and in acidic solution clearer adhesives are obtained, but the adhesive strength is reduced. Addition of alkali darkens the solution, but makes it more viscous and sticky. For this purpose borax and caustic soda are used. Excess of caustic may have the the reverse effect of reducing the drying time, and also it improves the stability, while reducing the cost. Sodium bisulphite maskes the odour bleaches, and acts as a preservative. One such formulation is given below.

Dextrin	390	parts
Water	500	"
Borax	46	"
Caustic soda solution 36^0 Be	6	"
Sodium bisulphite	4	"

A thick paste of the dextrin and half of the water is made and rubbed, until all the lumps are gone. Rest of the water is then added, and the mixture is heated to 85^0 C. Sodium bisulphite is then added.

Dextrin films are frequently plasticized for moisture control with humectants, with solids such as urea, or for lubrication of a film using fatty material. Humectants may includde polyglycols such as glucose, sorbitol, glycerol or ethylene glycol, the latter two being most effective. These humectants slow the drying rate of the film and absorb moisture from the air, to allow a more plastic film. Urea forms a solid solution with a dextrin as does sodium nitrate. Ethanolamines act similarly. Film lubricants include fatty materials, such as sulphonated castor oil or turkey red oil and soluble soaps. Excessive amounts can reduce adhesiveness of a film.

Quick Setting, Machine Adhesive for Sealing Wrappers

Yellow dextrin	40	parts
Water	50	"
Borax	40	"
Sodium hydroxide	2	"
Phenol	0.1	"
Turkey red oil	0.5	"

Dextrin is dissolved in 45 parts of water applying heat if necessary. Borax is dissolved in with stirring. Sodium hydroxide is dissolved in 5 parts of water, and to it, dextrin is added with rapid stirring. The phenol and turkey red oil are then added. Wrapping paper is relatively impervious to the adhesive but in spiral tubes the paper is more absorbent and therefore the adhesive must be a little denser. A modified formula is given below which contains tapioca starch, partly replacing the dextrin. This gives cheaper adhesive, giving less brittle film. This adhesive has a water: dextrin ratio of 1.5.1.

White dextrin	180	parts
Water	600	"
Turkey red oil	2	"
Light yellow dextrin	150	"
Tapioca starch	60	"
Borax	46	"
Sodium hydroxide	6	"
Sodium bisulphite	4	"

A thick paste of dextrins and starch is made with 300 parts water, to this turkey red oil is added followed by 280 parts water. It is heated to 85° C with stirring. When the mass is gelatinised, borax is added, followed by sodium hydroxide dissolved in 20 parts water. The temperature is maintained at 85° C. Sodium bisulphite is added finally, and the mass is stirred until it has completely dissolved.

Neutral Conc. Adhesive for Coloured for Coloured Papers

The following adhesive has a dextrin to water ratio as 1.0.6. Coloured papers are very sensitive to alkali, hence, the adhesive is made neutral, and highly concentrate. Under these conditions, formaldehyde is used to reduce the viscosity to a workable condition.

Light dextrin	630	parts
Water	370	
Turkey red oil (90%) amm. salt	1.3	
Sodium hydroxide, 36^0 Be	3	
Formaldehyde (30%)	6.3	

The mixture of water, dextrin and turkey red oil is heated to 80^0 C. Just enough NaOH (36^0 Be) is added to neutralize the acidity of dextrin; determined by litmus. Formaldehyde is added last.

Library Paste

White dextrin	280	parts
Potato starch	280	"
Water	196	"
Glycerin	84	"
Phenol	2	"
Formaldehyde, 30%	3	"
Sessafras Oil	1	"

A smooth paste is obtained with dextrin, starch and half of the water. Remaining water is then added and heated on a steam bath until smooth. Glycerin, phenol, formalin and sassafras oil are then added.

Addition of soluble calcium salts produces a fatty paste. Both glycerin and calcium chloride make the adhesive slow drying, which is desirable for highly calendered papers, that are slow to wet out. The following white paste is of that type

Potato dextrin	100	parts
Water	150	"
Calcium nitrate	10	"
Phenol	2	"

Calcium nitrate is dissolved in water heated to 75^0 C. Slowly dextrin is added with stirring; when everything dissolves, phenol is added.

Clear White Highly Concentrated Adhesive

Usually sodium bisulphite is used as a decolouriser and deodouriser, but due to some reasons inorganic decolouring agent is to be avoided; then a very small quantity of high-class varnish-grade lithopone may be used, which makes the product almost almost clear white.

Water	340	parts
Turkey red oil, 90%	1.3	"
Lithopone, varnish grade	0.33	"
Dextrin, soluble	660	"
Sodium bisulphite	3.3	"
Formalin, 30%	6.6	"

The adhesive has dextrin to water ratio as 0.5.1.

Tube WInding Adhesive

Water	400	parts
Canary dextrin, 98% cold soluble	200	"
White dextrin, 175% cold soluble	100	"
Fine size clay	15	"
Sulphonated castor oil, 75%	1	"
Heat to 60° C and add borax	20	"
Heat to 90° C for 30 min, cool to 60° C and add caustic lye, 35%	12	"
Formaldehyde	1	"

Viscosity 1000 to 4000 cps. Clay reduces cost and prevents excessive penetration and improves adhesion.

Paper to Glass Adhesive Nonwater Proof

Water	40	parts
Canary dextrin (95% cold soluble)	60	"
Heat at 90° C unit dextrin is dispersed		
Corn syrup regular 43° Be	300	"
Phosphoric acid	0.5	"

Viscosity is adjusted to 10,000 to 20,000 cps, Phosphoric acid improves wetting and adhesion to paper.

Kraft Paper Envelope Gum

Tapioca dextrin	60	parts
Glucose	5	"
Phosphoric acid, 80%	1	"
Formaldehyde	0.2	"
Water	33.8	"

Water is heated and dextrin is added slowly with stirring, at 88° C till it is free from lumps. Glucose is added and cooled to 75° C. Finally formaldehyde and phosphoric acid are added.

Adhesives for paper and paper board are the largest outlet for dextrins. Frequently, blends of different dextrins are used and borax is added to increase tack. Bag and bottom pastes are usually made from white dextrins and British gums, to allow a reasonably high solids concentration. Borax is added to increase the rate of bonding and to minimise wetting and puckering. Bottom pastes are usually of higher viscosity than seam pastes; however good flow properties are required for a good bottom paste. Water resistance is obtained by using 5-15 per cent urea-formaldehyde resin in the absence of borax. Cartons require any of the more highly soluble dextrins; or British gums, in combination with borax, or alkali depending on the paper stock. Hand sealing will allow concentrations of 25 per cent to be used, while solids up to 50 per cent must be used for automatic machines. Sometimes clay is used as an inert filler in the carton or container paste. Envelope flaps require remoistening adhesives, which should be extremely fast drying, good colour, non objectionable flavour, gloss and smoothness. Tapioca canary dextrin of high solubility and light colour are most suitable. Envelope seams usually employ an adhesive from a highly soluble canary dextrin plasticized with urea or invert sugar. Solids of 60-50 per cent are used.

Envelope Gum for Remoistenable Front Seal

Water	150	parts
Canary dextrin, 95% cold water soluble	300	"
Tributyl phosphate	1	"
Heat to 90° C for 30 min,. and then cool to 60° C than add corn syrup reqular 43° Be	5	"

The viscosity is adjusted according to use, For plunger, wide range, rotary application equipments viscosities are adjusted to 10,000 cps. 7000 cps. and 5000 cps. respectively.

Stamps, labels and tapes all require high solids, light coloured canary dextrin with good remoistening properties. Tapioca dextrin is better. Cloth-backed tape may use urea plasticized dextrins. White dextrins with low solubility have been used in surface sizing of high grade papers, viscose rayon is sized with corn or tapioca dextrins.

Case Sealing

Water	300	parts
Tributyl phosphate	1	"
White dextrin (45% cold water solubles)	2000	"
Borax	30	"
Heat to 85 - 95° C with jacketed steam for 2 mins, and cool to 60° C and add		
Caustic soda, 40% lye	10	"
Formaldehyde	1	"

pH is checked after mixing for 10 mins. If pH is not between 9.1 to 9.4, enough caustic is added to make it so. Final viscosity is adjusted by addition of water.

Dextrins can be used in formulations with many different substances. They are compatible with animal glue, gum arable, gum tragacanth, latex emulsions of both natural and synthetic rubber, CMC, polyvinyl alcohol in low concentration, polyvinyl acetate resin emulsions of certain types and urea-formaldehyde resins. The latter three are used to aid in forming water resistant dextrin films.

Water-Resistant Multi wall Seam Gum

Water	1700	parts
White dextrin	700	"
Soap	2	"
Urea-formaldehyde resin	70	"

It is cooked in live steam at 95° C and cooled with water to about 2500 litres. Then ammonium chloride 14 kgs. is added. It becomes water resistant quickly, but because of low pH may set prematurely and cause trouble.

Gummed Label Adhesive

Water	600	parts
Extra Soluble Dextrin	400	"
Turkey red oil, 90%	0.4	"
Formaldehyde, 30%	120	"
Gelatin	20	"
Glycerin	40	"

Gelatin is soaked in 100 parts of water overnight and then heated to 80° C with stirring as the glycerin is slowly added. After the dextrin has been dispersed in water the gelatin solution is stirred into combination.

Corrugated paper board Adhesive

Dextrin	35	parts
Gypsum	45	"
Fish glue	6	"
Casein	10	"
Soda Ash	3	"

A homogeneous mixture of dextrin and gypsum is made. Another mixture of fish glue, casein and soda ash in is made. When adhesive is required, dextrin mixture is added in water, followed by the other powder.

Dextrins are also mixed with sodium silicate to form adhesives. The dextrins are made into a homogenous solution before other agents are added.

Water	90·	parts
White dextrin	30	"
Yellow dextrin	100	"
Glucose	20	"
Sodium silicate, 38-40^0 Be	25	"
Sodium bisulphite, 36-40^0 Be	50	"

Adesive for Bonding Aluminim Sheets

Dextrin, very soluble	16	parts
Sodium meta silicate, medium viscosity	4	"
Glucose	2	"
Water	25	"

Envelope Gum Remoistenable Front Seal

One of such formulas has been given before. Another formula for the same use utilises polyvinyl acetate resin emulsion; this is less affected by humidity and is non-curl and non-blocky.

Polyvinyl acetate emulsion, dextrin compatible	60	parts
Canary dextrin	25	"
Glycerin	5	"
Plasticizer	5	"
Water	5	"

These are added in the order given with agitation in a steam jacketed kettle. Heating is started and stirred, until dextrin has dissolved, and then cooled.

26

ACID MODIFIED OR THIN-BOILING STARCH ADHESIVE

Unmodified starch gives highly viscous pastes at comparatively low solids. It is necessary for some applications ot have high solid adhesives; at he same time the viscosity has to be suitable. Cooking of starch paste with acid below gelatinization gives an acid modified starch of reduced viscosity. These starches are known as acid-modified or thin-boiling starches. By varying the time, temperature, amount of acid and its kind various types of starches of different thinning and fluidity are obtained. Thin boilding starches are sued for surface sizing of paper, textile, warp sizing, laundry starches.

In making adhesives from cassava starch, the starch is treated with an equal weight of water, heating the combination to 55^{0} C and adding 2 to 3 per cent of sulphuric acid with agitation. Care is taken to avoid dissolving the starch. In 4 to 6 hrs. time, the mixture is neutralized and the starch dried. Treated in this manner, the water absorptivity of the starch is substantially reduced. This method of drying in the acid saves serious loss in solubles while making high fluidity starches.

The acid-modified starches are formed into adhesives in the usual manner. The addition of alkalies converts them into viscous liquid adhesive. They may be further modified or formulated with urea, inorganic salts, sugars, natural gums, clay, soap, urea-formaldehyde resins, formaldehyde etc. A simple starting formulation is given below.

Thin boiling cassava starch	200	parts
Water	205	"
Caustic soda	20	"
Water	30	"

Caustic soda is dissolved in some additional water, is slowly stirred in at room temperature until a viscous semi fluid consistency is obtained; adaptable to use in glue spreading machinery.

Water Resistant Seam Gums

Thin boiling starch	700	parts
Soap	3.8	"
Urea formaldehyde resin	105	"
Water	2000	"
Trisodium phosphate (TSP)	10	"

TSP is added after cooking and cooling: water-resistance develops very slowly over several months of bag storage.

Library Paste

Thin boiling starch	100	parts
Corn syrup regular 43° Be	15	"
Preservative	0.3	"
Water	220	"

Heat to 90° C for 20 minutes and package hot. It takes 2 to 7 for paste to set up depending on the rate of cooling. Oil of wintergreen is sometimes added to provide characteristic odour. It has 40 per cent solids, and sets up to stiff paste after being cooked. During application, when pressure is applied with a finger or a brush, the paste softens sufficiently, so that it will apply smoothly.

Lay Flat Paper Laminating Adhesive

Water	130	parts
Thin boiling starch, 20% cold water soluble	100	"
Sulphonated castor oil 75%	0.5	"
Hydrochloric acid, 10%	1.3	"
Heat to 60° C, and add sodium nitrate	40	"
Calcium chloride	40	"
Formaldehyde	0.5	"

Viscosity is about 5000 cps.

When curl is a problem, high solids adhesive are used for laminating.

27

CASEIN GLUES

Casein is milk protein, obtained from skimmed milk by precipitation with mineral or organic acid at pH of about 4.5. 100 litre of milk usually yield about 3 kgs. of casein. The precipitated casein is filtered, washed thoroughly, dried ground and screened to get 20 mesh of fine product for glue maufacture. Commercial dry casein contains about 80-90% of protein, 1-4% ash, 0-1.3% of butter fat, 7-10% moisture, 0-4% lactose and 0-3% acids expressed as lactic acid. The composition and amounts of impurities depend on among other factors, the method of manufacture.

Properties: Casein in an off-white powder. Its molecular weight is about 13000-19000. It is insoluble in water at its isoelectric point pH 4.6. Casein is more readly soluble in alkali. Casein powder has a shelf life of above 1 year at 20^0 C.

Casein adhesives are unsuitable for outdoor use although they are more resistant to temperature changes and moisture than other water-based adhesives. Casein adhesives are often compounded with materials such as latex and dialdehyde starch to improve durability.

A simple formula using lime and alkali is given below. It has good water resistance, good working life about 7 hours.

Casein	100	parts
Water	150	"
Sodium hydroxide	11	"
Water	50	"
Calcium hydroxide	20	"
Water	20	"

A sodium silicate containing casein glue formulations is given below.

Cupric chloride works as a inhibitor, cupric sulphate may also be used in place of cupric chloride.

Casein	100	parts
Water	150	"
Hydrated lime	20	"
Water	100	"
Sodium silicate	70	"
Cupric chloride	2	"
Water	30	"

As usual, wood flour, cellulose etc, are used as extenders in casein glues. Casein glues may be thickened by adding sodium sulphite, sugar or sodium hexametaphosphate.

The following is an emulsion type glue.

Polyvinyl isobutyl ether (medium viscosity)	100	parts
Casein	18	"
Stearic acid	0.6	"
Boric acid	1.8	"
Salicylic acid	1.8	"
Ammonia, 25%	6.9	"
Water	130.5	"
2,6 ditertiary butyl p cresol	0.3	"
N heptane	27	"

A hot solution of easein, water (48 parts) and ammonia (1.8 parts) are mixed with stearic acid, water (15 parts) and ammonia (3 parts). An 80% polyvinyl isobutyl ether solution in heptane is warmed to 50° C and added with agitation to the above mixture, a solution of boric acid, salicylic acid, remaining water, 2,6 ditertiary butyl p cresol and remaining ammonia is then finally added to it.

28

SOYABEAN ADHESIVES

A variety of adhesives of natural origin were and to some extent continue to be used by wood industry. These natural adhesives are alternate to the synthetic resin based adhesive systems. The plywood industries is a major consumer of these adhesives.

Soyabean contains approximately 40% protein, 20% oil, 35% carbohydrates and 5% other constituents. The oil and protein are both important commercial commodities.

The protein is an important constituent in the manufacture of adhesives. Soyabean protein isolate contains more than 90% protein. Soyabean flour typically contain 44% to 50% protein.

First the soybean flour is mixed with water, then sheared using efficient mixer to eliminate lumps. A suitable defoamer, usually pine oil, is added to prevent frothing. Alkaline materials (caustic solution) etc, are then added to give proper dispersion of the protein and being out is adhesiveness to the maximum. Various cross-linking or denaturing agents are then added, followed by the addition of mold inhibitors e.g. pentachlorophenol, copper naphthenate copper 8 quinolinolate, etc.

Soybean adhesives can be applied by almost any conventional system, including roll applicators, extruders, sprayers and curtain coaters.

Several sulphur based compounds such as carbon disulphide, polysulphided, ethylene trithiocarbonate, thiourea and potassium xanthate and tanning agents like metal salts of copper, aluminium, chromium and zinc are added to soyabean adhesives to improve their water resistance.

Soyabean adhesives are not resistant to mould and fungi growth, especially in humid surroundings. A variety of preservatives have been tried. This includes chlorinated phenols, pentachlorophenols, sodium pentachlorophenate, chloro 2 phenylphenol, tributyl tin oxide, copper-8 quinolinolate.

Applications & Formulations

Soyabean protein glues, as mentioned above, are suitable for interior grade plywood and softwood panelling and is also used as a component of blood albumin soyabean adhesives for interior plywoods based on softwood. Where maximum bond strength is not required, e.g. for applications such as paper and softwood lamination, cardboard base fabrication and particle bonding, the glue may be extended with fillers such as clays and wood flour, to reduce cost.

Soyabean protein	100	parts
Water, 30° C	400	"
Calcium hydroxide	15	"
Sodium silicate, 40° Be	25	"
Sodium hydroxide, 35% aqueous	15	"

Soyabean flour	30	parts
Water	120	"
Sodium hydroxide, 18% solution	13	"
Carbon disulphide	4	"
Calcium hydroxide	3	"
Sodium silicate	14	"
Copper sulphate	1	"
Water	5	"

Soybean flour 100 mesh	100	parts
Sodium phosphate	10	"
Sodium fluoride	5	"
Calcium hydroxide	7-10	"
Calcium carbonate	50	"
Copper sulphate	0.5	"
Water	510	"
Formaldehyde ammonia	5-10	"

All the solids are ground to 100 mesh and dissolved in water to which the reaction product of formaldehyde and ammonia is added giving a glue the consistency of which remians unchanged for 6 hours. Within 24 hours after the gluing of wood a shear strength of 25 to 35 kg/cm^2 is obtained in the dry state and 15 to 18 kg/cm^2 in the wet state.

Soybean flour	97	parts
Pine oil	3	"
Hydrated lime	12	"
Sodium hydroxide, 50% solution	14	"
Sodium silicate	25	"
Carbon disulphide	1.25	"
Carbon tetrachloride	0.50	"
Pentachlorophenol	4.25	"
Water	344	"

Soybean flour is mixed with 175 parts water at 20° C and to this pine oil is added and mixed for 3 minutes until smooth, 145 parts water is further mixed in followed by hydrated lime and 24 parts water. Sodium silicate is then mixed in followed by carbon disulphide solution solution in carbon tetrachloride and finally the inhibitor is added. The whole thing is mixed for 10 minutes. The glue is ready for use and its working life is about 6 to 10 hours depending on te storage temperature.

Phenol based inhibitor dissolve in aqueous alkaline glue dispersions, through the formation of their double salts; hence for this purpose 1% additional alkali per 5% inhibitor is required.

Soybean flour	57	parts
Casein	15	"
Hydrated lime	12	"
Wood flour	5	"
Sodium carbonate	5	"
Sodium fluoride	3	"
Pine oil	3	"

Gum Arabic

Gum arabic was known even 4000 years ago when it was shipped by Egyptians as a commercial commodity. It India this is known as East Indian or Indian gum. Gumghatti which is a different is also sometimes loosely used as Indian gum. It is available from the plant Acacia.

Gum Arabic is produced by unhealthy Acacia trees. Healthy trees do not produce the gum.

The gum production starts in breaks or wounds in the tree caused naturally and often artificially. Each season bark is torn from the tree in a different place gradually working around the trunk and not casuing harm to the tree. Trees are tapped when they are 6-7 years old when the gum yield is maximum.Annual yield ranges from 188 to 2856 g. with an average of

900 g per tree. Gum is collected manually, stored and transported to the marketing centre.

Gum Arabic is a neutral or slightly acidic salt of a complex poly saccharide containing calcium, magnesium and potassium cations. The molecular weight of gum Arabic is variable and varies between 250,000 to 580,000.

Hydrolysis of gum arabic produces L-arabinose, L-rhamnose, D-galactose and D-glucoronic acid.

Gum Arabic is insoluble in fats and non-polar organic solvents, but usually dissolves completely in hot or cold water forming a clear mucilaginous solution. The major use of gum arabic is in the food industry as an additive to improve viscosity, body and texture of the food. It is used in confectionery, dairy products, bakery products, pharmaceuticals, cosmetics, paints, inks, textiles and also in the lithography.

Gum Ghatti

Gum ghatti is a complax water soluble poly saccharide. It is a plant exudate that has been in long use in India. It is an amorphous translucent exudate of the anogeissus latifolia tree. The tree is large and found in dexiduous forests of India and Sri Lanka.

The gum has a glassy fracture and occurs in rounded tears normally less than 1 cm in diameter. The colour of the exudate vary from very light to dark brown. The higher the colour the better is the quality and grade.

After picking the gum is dried in the sun for several days. Processing of the gum consists of grinding and sieving.

Gum ghatti forms viscous mixture on dispersion in water to 5% or greater concentration gum ghatti is used in pharmaceuticals, food, beverages, oil drilling muds, cosmetics etc.

Gum Karya

Gum Karya is the dried exudation of the sterculia ureus tree. It exclusively available in India. The tree is a large bushy plant which grows to a height of about 9 metres. The best quality gums yield increases. After monsoon the gum collection again starte. Gum exudes from tapped sterculia trees. The dried tears are picked up and sent to the marketing centre. The tears are crushed and sorted. The gum is processed by powdering and flotation to remove loose barks. The gum is used in pharmaceuticals, paper making, in foods and also as textile sizing agents.

Gum karya absorbs water rapidly to form viscous mucilage at low concentration. Gum karya forms heavy non flowing gels above 2-3% concentration. The paste forms smooth films. At 25-30% concentration in water it shows strong adhesive characteristics.

Gum Tragacanth

Gum tragacanth is one of the widely used emulsifier and thickening agent available to the food, drug and allied industries. The gum forms a highly viscous liquid with water in solution. Gum tragacanth is the dried exudation of astragalus shrub. The plants are lonitudinally incised with sharp blade and the gum exudes spontaneously from the wound and dries or hardens as ribbons or flakes. The plants grow in Iran, Iraq. Syria and Turkey. Collected gums are transported to the marketing centre.

When tragacanth is mixed only soluble portion tragacanthin dissolves to give a colloidal hydrosol and the insoluble portion swells to gel. Chemically the gum is an acidic polysaccharide. Gum tragacanth has molecular weight near about 840,000. A 1% solution of the gum in water has a viscosity of 3600 cps. The gum is used in pharmaceuticals, foods, condiments, sauces, bakery, icecream, cosmetics and textile as sizers.

Guar Gum

Guar gum is derived from guar seeds (Cyanoposis teragonolobus family). It grows in India and Pakistan. Food grade guar gum is pure endosperm. It usually has a small residue of hull and gem. Guar gum is used as food additive and as textile sizing. A 1% solution in water has a viscosity of 5000 cps. It is also used as a frothing agent in flotation process, as a filter aid, in water treatment, in cosmetics, as a paper sizer in expliosives. Carbomethoxylated guar gum and other modified gums are excellent surface active agents.

29

ANIMAL GLUES

Animal glue is an adhesive of great versatility with broad acceptance in industry. This natural high polymer is an organic colloid derived from collagen, a protein constituent of animal skins, connective tissue and bones, principally of cattle origin. Animal glues better known as saresh in the market are more popular.

Its wide acceptance as an adhesive stem from its unique ability to deposit a tacky viscous film from a warm water solution, which on cooling a few degrees passes to a firm gelled state providing an immediate, moderately strong initial bond. Subsequent natural or forced air drying provides a permanent, strong, resilient bond between polar materials. Ease of preparation, ready applications, good machining properties relatively low cost and high speed operations are characteristics of prime importance and interest in its use.

Animal glue is commercially available in a number of forms including the dry granulated products for use as hot glues, cold liquid glues for immediate use and a wide selection of composition glues in cake or jelly form.

Animal glue is a protein derived from the simple hydrolysis of collagen which is a principal protein consitituent of animal hide. The approximate chemical composition of the glue is as follows.

	(%)
Carbon	51.29
Hydrogen	06.39
Oxygen	24.13
Nitrogen	18.19
	100.00

Animal glues are usually available as flakes, chips, powder or cake form. They are well preserved against bacteria or mold infection for their intended industrial application. These are odourless material ranging in colour from light amber to brown. The density of animal glue is approximately 1.27 g/cc moisture content is 10 to 14% and ash content between 2.25 to 4.00%. Animal glues are soluble in water, insoluble on oils, waxes, organic solvents and abosolute alcohol. An interesting property of animal glue solution is that the glue is transformed from a liquid to a gel state on cooling and reverting to a liquid on reheating. This property is of primary importance in many adhesive applications.

Manufacture

There are two types of animal glue hide glue and bone glue.

Hide Glue

Hide glue is prepared by initial cleaning of the raw stock by water washing followed by curing with milk of lime for the removal of non glue proteins. The cured stock is then acidulated with a mineral acid followed by removal of excess acid by additional washing with water. The treated stock is transferred to cooking kettle. Hot water is added to the kettle and a series of separate cooks are prepared under controlled conditions of temperature. Dilute glue solutions are drained from the cook kettle until the glue stocks are completely extracted of glue. The glue extraction liquor is then filtered, evaporated to 16 to 45% glue solids. The sticky mass is dried in noodle form in a continuous dryer in 2 hours time.

Bone Glue

Bone glue, is processed from the collagen content of the bones. Raw bone glue is produced from bones available from the cattle heads. Bone glue prepared from solvent extracted degreased bones are known as extracted bone glue. Bone glue is prepared by cleaning the bones in water and dilute acids, charging the clean bones to pressure tanks, and by a series of alternate steam pressure and hot water extractions. Dilute glue solution is removed from vessel. The dilute glue liquor is then filtered for removal of fatty substances. The solution is evaporated to high solids content. Usually hide or bone glues are supplied in the form of flakes.

Applications & Formulations

Animal glues have long been accepted as standard product which is economic and have, bond permanency, strength, ease of use and are versatile. They usually contains preservatives, foam suppressants, wetting agents and plasticizers such as glycerin, sorbitol, glycols, sulphonated oils, fats and waxes. These glue are used in book binding, labelling, wood work and paper boxes.

Book Binding Glue

Animal hide glue	30	parts
Water	29	"
Glycerine	30	"
Preservative	1	"

Paper Box Glue

Bone glue	45	parts
Water	15	"
Glycerine	39	"
Preservative	1	"

Formic acid, phenol and formaldehyde etc. are the suitable preservatives.

Can Lable Glue

Starch	100	parts
Water	700	"
Animal glue	10	"
Sodium silicate	100	"
Turpentine	50	"

Starch and part of water, gelatin and remaining water are mixed separately and dissolved, they are then mixed together and then sodium silicate and temperatine are added.

Water Resistant Glue

Animal glue	100	parts
Water	225	"
Oxalic acid	5.5	"
Paraformaldehyde	10	"

Glue	100	parts
Potash alum	10	"
Acetic acid	1.25	"
Denatured alcohol	1.25	"

Glue is dissolved in water. Acid and denatured alcohol are added and stirred.

Wood Working Glue

Animal glue	100	parts
Water	200	"
Urea	8	"
Glycerin	8	"

Labels & Stamps glue

Animal glue	25	parts
Trihydroxy ethylamine abietate	50	"
Polymerized terpenes	1	"
Water	170	"
Potassium hydroxide	1	"

Animal glues are usually applied at 25 to 50% concentration and at 60 C. In this state it has a paint like consistency and can thus be readily spread in the form of a thin continuous film. This film thickens on cooling permitting rapid development of desired tackiness and holds the adhesive at joint surface and this eliminates the danger of bleeding from the joint under pressure.

Fish Glues

Fish glue, as the name indicates, is obta obtained as a bye product of the fish skin industry. Some of the properties for which fish glue found importance commercially are its complete water solubility, good adhesion to metal, rubber, glass, cement, cork, wood and paper. High initial tackiness, ability of being used as remoistenable adhesive, similar to contact adhesive, Insolubility in organic solvents, does not soften at high temperature up to 560^0 C, as a metal coating it can be baked to provide a tough and tenacious film that is highly resistant to corrosion, hard enough to be sanded, can be made water resistant and insoluble in water, can be compounded to be thermoplastic and heat bondable and, can be used in photographic emulsions and coatings.

Manufacture

Fish glue is derived from fish skins. The skins are thoroughly washed to remove any salt or extraneous matter. The skins are cooked in water for sometime at elevated temperature. The broth is drained from the residue. The broth is concentrated in evaporator to the finished glue solids of approximately 45% solid content. Fish glue is a protein and care should be taken to prevent micro organisms coming in the glue phase. After evaporation an odorant is added to the finished glue to give it a characteristic smell. A bactericide is also added to increase its shelf life up to 2 years. A typical fish glue has the following properties.

Colour	- Light caramel
Odour	- Mild, characteristic of the odorant added
Viscosity	- 4000-7000 cps
Solide	- 43-50%
Temperature range	- 0 to 260^0 C
Shear strength	- 218 kg/cm^2
Weight/litre	- 0.8 kg

Upon cooling to 44 C or below, liquid fish glue sets to gel. This is reversible process. Fish glue films are brittle. They can be plasticized with glycerine or ethylene glycol to yield flexible films. Dried fish glue is insoluble in organic solvents. Although fish glue is soluble in water soluble, it can be made water resistant by the addition of polyvalent ion salts such as aluminium, ferric or chromium sulphate.

Applications & Formulations

Fish glue has good adhesion to many surface. Two non-porous surfaces can be bonded by using fish glues as a remoistenable adhesive.

Cans are pressure tested to check leaks. A rubber gasket is bonded, using fish glue to the pressure testing apparatus and makes the temporary pressure seal.

Embossing dies require a steel female die and a strawboard male die. The strawboard or counter die, must be held in exact register to its respective female die. Fish glue assures good adhesion and exact registration by preventing the counters from slipping or sliding.

Another application is in the gluing of labels to solvent cans. The labels withstand solvent spillage.

Fish glue can be applied by rollers in straight line gluing operations. In the manufacture of printing forms the glue sets quickly because of porous nature of the paper. Padding compounds can be made by the addition of glycerin which plasticizes the glue and gives a very flexible bond.

Fish Glue

Fish glue	100	parts
Water	0.22	"
Benzoic acid	0.22	"
Methylated spirit	0.75	"
Sassafras oil	0.15	"
Boiling water	8	"

Water Proof Fish Glue

Fish glue	100	parts
Water	10	"
Alcoholic solution of gum rosin	100	"
Methylated Spirit	35	"

Alcoholic solution of rosin such as rosin, estergum, lac enhances water resistant properties. This type of glue is used for setting jewellery, fixing precious stones to glass and metals. Carafully added small quantities of hydrochloric acid, acetic acid, benzoic acid tartaric acid etc. remarkably enhance the adhesive properties.

30

ROSIN ADHESIVES

Fish glue may be added to hot animal glue at slow rate to prevent cooling, the latter below its gel point, this is particularly usuful for making gummed tapes. Addition of fish glue to polyvinyl acetate emulsions improves the cold flow and creep resistance, heat resistance, heat resistance, initial tack, glue penetration and resistance to aliphatic solvents. Fish glues are incorporated latex adhesive for show industry to improve wet tack and adhesion.

Rosin or colophony, is a thermpplastic acidic product isolated by widely different procedures from exudates of live pine trees or the stumps of the wood. Rosin is a clear, pale yellow to dark amber, thermoplastic and friable solid at room temperature. It is insoluble in many organic solvents including alcohols, ethers esters, and chlorinated aliphatic and aromatic hydrocarbons. Rosin is an ethers esters, and chlorinated aliphatic and aromatic hydrocarbons. Rosin is an acidic resin and its acid number, measured by conventional means, is another property commonly used to characterise it.

Rosin is a complex mixture of mutually soluble, naturally occurring high molecular weight organic acids and related neutral materials. The acidic constituents that make up the major portion of rosin are known as resin acids. They are monocarboxylic acids of alkylated hydrophenanthrene nuclet. The reactions of rosin which yield derivatives that are used in the production of synthetic polymers and as additives or modifiers for natural and synthetic polymers, involves its carboxyl groups and double bonds.

Eserification of the carboxyl groups with short chain monohydric alcohols and with various polyhydric alcohols yields thermoplastic resinous esters having a wide range of softening point, compatibility and other useful properties for adhesive industry.

All types of rosin, especially modified rosin and their derivatives are used extensively in polymer base adhesives to impart tack or to enhance the inherent tack of the basic film forming ingredient. Adhesives which are formulated with rosin products for this purpose include water based, solvent based and hot melt systems. The rosin products used in such adhesives range in physical form viscous liquids to soft and medium hard to very hard friable solid resins. Then can be readily emulsified and have emulsified and have good to excellent resistance to oxidation and all possess inherent tack.

When rosin and rosin derivatives are used as tackifiers, the choice of the rosin product determines to a great extent the durability of the adhesives mass with respect to retention of its adhesive properties. The tackifier is selected for best suitability to the polymer to be used and the type of adhesive (latex, solvent or hot melt).

The tack of the resin rubber combination does not increase markedly until the resin concentration reaches 40-50% of the total composition. Tack increases rapidly thereafter, reaches a maximum for the harder resin between 60 and 70% and then drops rapidly to zero.

The film former in elastomer based solvent adhesives is generally a natural, reclaimed, or synthetic rubber and the tackifier resin is often a rosin derivative, which can also contribute to the bond strength of the adhesive.

Emulsion adhesives are primarily mixtures of a natural or synthetic rubber latex or other polymeric water based dispersion, with an aqueous emulsion or dispersion of a resin modifier, generally of rosin origin. Minor ingredients may include a protective colloed such as casein to provide emulsion stability, plasticizers and some times viscosity adjusters antioxidants and preservatives. Generally, the elastomer or other film former is a polymer (in latex form) such as natural rubber, styrene-butadine copolymers, polychloroprene or polyvinylacetate.

A typical commercial type finished emulsion adhesive may be prepared by blending a 40% solid resin emulsion, with natural rubber latex (usually 60-62% solids) to a resin rubber solid ratio of 1:1.

Hot melts adhesives are blends of a polymeric film former, a modifying resin, often of rosin origin miscellaneous ingredients to impart special properties. At room temperature they are usually tack free, but when heat is applied, they became sufficiently fluid to permit application. Solvents are not required in applying hot melts and no drying period is needed and the bonding is almost instantaneous. The modifying resin in hot melt adhesives, although functioning mainly a tackifire, also acts as a wetting agent and provides fluidity.

Rosin melted in a stainless steel reaction kettle with agitator, reflux condenser and temperature indicator and all the ingredients are added to it at about 75° C. Stirring is continued still a homogenous mixture is formed.

Reciaimed Rubber Dispersion with Asphlt

Whole tyre reclaim	100	parts
Surfactant	2	"
Caustic potash	1	"
Ester gum	20	"
Clay	30	"
Asphalt emulsion	175	"
Water	70	"

Pressure Sensitive Adhesive for Removal Labal Stock

Polyisobutylene rubber	100	parts
Methyl ester of hydrogenated rosin	35	"
Hydrocarbon resin	45	"
Polybutene	70	"
Additive	0.5	"
Hexane	to coatable viscosity	

Pressure Sensitive Adhesive for General Purpose Tape

Chlorobutyl rubber	50 parts
Styrene butadiene rubber	50 "
Pentaerythritol ester of partially hydrogenated rosin	30 "
Polyisobutylene	30 "
Ethyl antioxidant	0.5 "
Solvent	to coatable viscosity

Automotive Wind Shield Sealing Tape

Butyl rubber	100	parts
Silica	50	"
Carbon black	140	"
Polybutene	140	"
Zinc oxide	2	"
Penta ester of hydrogenated rosin	30	"
Magnesium oxide	0.4	"
Stearic acid	0.4	"

Pressure Sensitive Adhesive

Styrene butadiene rubber	100	parts
Penta ester of partially hydrogenated rosin	75	"
Antioxidant	2	"
Toluene	1003	"

Sprayable Adhesive

Styrene butadiene rubber (SBR)	100	parts
Polymerised rosin	100	"
Ester of hydrogenated rosin	40	"
Morpholine	2	"
Hexane	450	"
Methylene chloride	50	"

Sealant

SBR	120	parts
Polymerized rosin	19	"
Methyl ester of hydrogenated rosin	2	"
Aromatic plasticizer	17	"
Fibrous talc	10	"
Toluene	26	"
Xylene	12	"

Laminating Adhesive

SBR	100	parts
Sulphur and accelerator	20	"
Rosin	150	"

Cellophane Adhesive

Rosin	70	parts
Turpentine	20	"
Diethylene glycol ether	10	"

Polychloroprene Latex Adhesive

Latex	100	parts
Zinc oxide	15	"
Antioxidant	2	"
Terpene phenolic resin	85	"
Ester gum	50	"
Protein hardening agent	2	"
Defoaming agent	2	"
Stabilizer	2	"

Laminating Adhesive for Aluminium Foll to Paper

Acrylic modified rosin	95.5	parts
Natrosol	4.5	"

Adhesive for Glass

Rosin	75	parts
Congo resin	25	"

Flooring Adhesive

Rosin	100	parts
Castor oil	50	"
Bentonite	10	"

Sticky Fly Paper Adhesive

Rosin	100	parts
Benzene	60	"
Casor oil	3	"
Crepe rubber	2	"

Laboratory Cement

Rosin	60	parts
Asphalt	10	"
Rubber	30	"
Turpentine	10	"

Cutlery Cement

Rosin	60	parts
Sulphur	15	"
Iron fillings	25	"

31

VARIOUS OTHER TYPES OF ADHESIVES

Terpene Resin Adhesives

It is customary to consider the terpene as derivatives of isoprene. Terpene resins are paleamber, thermoplastic hydrocarbon resins manufactured by polymerisation of terpene hydrocarbons. Only a few terpene hydrocarbons polymerize to usuful resin. The resins are low molecular weight polymers, completely unlike long chain polymers of vinyl type.

Manufacture

All terpene resins are made by polymerization of terpenes hydrocarbons in a solvent with aluminium chloride catalyst. The usual terpene used are betapinene, alpha-pinene, alpha & beta pinene mixtures and thermally isomerized alpha pinene. Terpene resins range from viscous liquid to solid with ring and ball method softening points up to 135^0 C.

Polymerisation is traditionally carried out by mixing the beta pinene with a diluent such as toluene, xylene or naphtha and adding in aluminium chloride portion wise. This procedures is adopted to develop the highest molecular weight. A safer procedure is to stir the catalyst in the solvent and to feed in the pinene slowly.

Applications & Formulations

The largest use of terpene resins is in pressure sensitive adhesive. For this use, the terpene resins are compounded with natural or synthetic rubbers, modifiers and suitable antioxidants so that a composition of good stability to light, heat and air results. Hot melt adhesive is also an important derivative. In this application terpene resins are blended with copolymers of ethylene and vinyl acetate, waxes, antioxidants other resin and modifiers. Terpene resins are important in imparting the desired pot life to hot melt compositions.

Terpene resin is melted just 5^0 C above its melting point in a steam jacketed stainless steel kettle. Rubber compounds or phenolic resin as the case may be is added. Stirring is continued in nitrogen atmosphere till the mixture is homogenous. Antioxidant and others additives are added afterward. After one hour of agitation the mixture is cooled down and solvent is added to obtain the desired viscosity.

Pressure Sensitive Adhesive for Vinyl Floor Tile

Butyl rubber	100	parts
Modified hydrogenated rosin	20	"
Terpene resin	70	"
Solvent to coatable viscosity		

Butyl Latex General Purpose Adhesive

Butyl rubber	100	parts
Casein (ammoniated)	25	"
Terpene resins	50	"
Silica	25	"

Hot Melt Adhesives for Polyethylene

Ethylene vinyl acetate copolymer	40	parts
Phenolic resin	15	"
Terpene resin	25	"
Epoxy resins	20	"
Antioxidant	0.1	"

Lignin Adhesives

The most important noncellulosic portion of wood is known as lignin. It is the resinous material which binds the cellulose fibres in the tree. It is removed during the process of paper manufacture to disentangle the cellulose fibre. Lignin is a polymeric mixture as yet only partially characterised. It is available as a waste from the paper industry. It contains aromatic ring having methoxy and hydroxyl groups. It is a complex polyphenol derivative of propylglucol with molecular weight about 4000. Lignin has been found to be of value as a reinforcing agent for various elastomers and other adestives. There is large scale improvement of properties when lignin is coprecipitated with natural, GRS and nitrile elastomers. Tensile strength abrasion and tear resistance are substantially improved.

Lignin possesses sufficient formaldehyde reactivity to yield a cured adhesive with high insolubility in both dilute acids and bases. This lignin after hydroxymethylation and curing by acid catalysts, produce bonded woods with high water resistance with when polymerised with phenol. The incorporation of polyhydroxy compounds to suppress condensation reaction during hydroxymethylation permits an element of control over adhesive working properties and bond performance. The adhesive could be readily applied to wood surfaces, possess good shelf life and has good woking properties.

Formulations

Lignin is capable of forming water proof bonds on wood substrates after hydroxymethylation, precipitation at pH 5.5 catalysis with oxalic acid and hot pressing for 10 minutes at 10 kg/cm^2 and 150^0 C. The formulation consists of :

Moles	Molecular Weight	Ingredient	Total (g)	Solids (g)	Volatiles (g)
Basic components:					
1.0	180	Lignin (95%)	189.5	180.0	9.5
0.5	40	NaOH (50%)	40.0	20.0	20.0
1.0	30	Formalin (37%)	81.1	12.0	69.1
0.5	150	TEG	75.0	75.0	
20.0	18	Water	261.4	261.4	
0.5	60	Acetic acid	30.0	21.0	9.0
Additional component:					
0.4	126	Oxalic acid	50.4	36.0	14.4

It is advisable to use less formaldehyde and obtain complete hydroxymethylation under reasonable time temperature conditions. The fact that a 10 minute press time at 150^0 C and 15 kg/cm^2 required before high wet strength is achieved indicates that there is need for more energy t o cure lignin adhesive than was required for cure of a phenolic adhesive.

One method of reducing the energy requirements of cross linking of methylated lignin is to incorporate a difunctional material having much greater reactivity with methylal groups than they have for themselves and would, therefore, function as a crosslinking agent. Diisocyanates are such materials and they are available with blocking groups that allow their use in water system without premature reaction with water, alcohols, acids or other reactive materials.

Tannin Adhesives

Tannin is a widely distributed phenolic polymer. Tannin is mostly amorphous, astringent in taste and feebly acidic in character. Tannin occurs in the most parts of the vegetable kingdom and are more prevalent among the higher plants. Condensed tannins contain phenols which condenses with other chemicals during adhesive formation. Majority of the tree extracts can be represented by the flavone 3 ol catechin. A typical reaction for catechin would be a condensation reaction through the phloroglucinol A ring. The reaction between the phloroglucinol a ring of catechin and formaldehyde proceeds at a rate comparable to that of phloroglucinol and formaldehyde, although slightly lower. The catechol B ring in catechin is much less reactive toward formaldehyde than the A ring.

Formulation

A tannin based adhesive is developed at the following concentrations.

Tannin (28% aq. solution)	1 mole
Furfuryl alcohol (20% aq solution)	1.6 mole
Maleic acid (28% aq solution)	0.25 mole
Nitric acid (40% aq solution)	1.0 mole

Both tannin and furfuryl alcohol are capable of promoting a high strength wood bond. The tannin act as a plasticizing agent for the furfuryl alcohol polymer. Maleic acid promotes the polymerisation of furfuryl alcohol at room temperature and also enhance the shear strengths. The strengths values compare quite favorably with strength values for panels bonded with phenolic resins.

A distinct advantage of the Tannin-furfurylAlcohol-MaleicAcid system is minimal evolution of formaldehyde or other toxic chemical from the bonded product.

Cellulose Adhesives

Cellulose, the backbone of many important industrial adhesives is found in plant kingdom. Cellulose is a long chain polymer made by nature which is a series of glycoside rings joined by oxygen bridges. Esters of both organic and inorganic acids as well as ethers are used for adhesives and binders. For plastics, a relatively high molecular weight is more suitable, which have better solubility in solvents, a wide range of compatibilities with other resins and plasticizers. The following celulose derivations are used as adhesives.

A. Soluble in Organic Solvents	*B. Soluble in water*
1. Cellulose nitrate	1. Methyl cellulose
2. Cellulose acetate	2. Ethyl cellulose
3. Cellulose propionate	3. Carboxy methyl cellulose
	4. Ethyl hydroxy ethyl cellulose
	5. Hydroxy propyl methyl cellulose
	6. Hydroxy ethyl cellulose

Applications

Applications in cellulose derivatives and binders are numerous. Some of the most important applications are cited here.

A general purpose adhesive which can be used in a variety of applications is cellulose nitrate dissolved in suitable solvents. It is water resistant, clear, flexible adhesive for use with wood, metal, glass and leather. On non-porous surfaces such as glass, a thin coat is spread over each surface and then the two pieces are held together until the cement is dried. On porous surfaces such as wood, a thin coat is first applied and allowed to dry. A second coat is then applied and the two surfaces brought together and clamped until the adhesive has dried.

A representative composition is as follows.

Nitrocellulose	100	parts
Camphor	40	"
Acetone	75	"
Ethyl alcohol	300	"
Amyl acetate	165	"

Nitrocellulose adhesive are used in shoe manufacturing for attaching the sole to the body of the shoe. They are also used in cementing together the splice in leather power transmission belts. Typical good leather adhesive is shown below.

	Manufacturing & repairing shoe	Manufacturing & repairing driving belt	
Nitro cellulose	100	100	parts
Dibutyl phthalate	12	23	"
Tricresyl phosphate	12	-	"
Methyl acetate	300	440	"
Methanol	37	110	"
Ethanol	50	50	"
Acetone	50	-	"
Benzene	70	-	"
Decalin	-	38	"

Paper adhesives

	A	B	C	
Cellulose acetate butyrate	100	100	100	parts
Sulphonamide resin	100	100	-	"
Polyvinyl acetate	-	-	12.5	"
Hydrocarbon resin	-	-	37.5	"
1-methyl styrene	-	-	50	"
Tricresyl phosphate	-	-	10	"
Denatured alcohol	-	-	60	"
Isobutyl acetate	100	100	-	"
Toluene	300	300	215	"
Pyrolidone	100	100	-	"
Nitropropane	-	-	15	"

Hot melt adhesives

	A	B	C	D	
Cellulose acetate butyrate	100	100	100	66	parts
Ethyl acetate butyrate	-	-	-	34	"
Nowport V-40	57	-	-	-	"
Alkyd resin	-	-	-	41	"
Polyvinyl acetate	-	-	9	-	"
L methyl styrene	86	-	27	-	"
Plasticizer	-	-	45	-	"
Dioctyl phthalate	43	66	-	-	"
Tricresyl phosphate	-	-	-	91	"
Chloro wax	-	-	-	49	"
Titanium dioxide	-	33	-	7	"
Calcium carbonate	-	134	-	-	"
Antimony oxide	-	-	-	44	"

A-Glass adhesive; B-Fibre board adhesive; C-Paper adhesive; D-Cloth adhesive

Adhesive based on ethyl cellulose are water resistant, free from discolouration in sunlight, also have resistance to deterioration by heat, are resistant to alkalies and exhibit low flammability. Such adhesives may be of the solvent type or the hot melt type. Typical formulation are presented in the following.

	Solvent type	Hot melt	
Ethyl cellulose (T-100)	100	-	parts
Ethyl cellulose (N-10)	-	100	"
Archor	80	-	"
L methyl styrene	20	-	"
Octyl phenol	4	10	"
Hydrogenated rosin ester	-	300	"
Castor oil	-	100	"
Toluene	300	-	"
Denatured ethyl alcohol	100	-	"

32

BLOOD ALBUMEN GLUES

The use of animal blood as an adhesive reaches backward into antiquity. There are three general categories of dried blood used in adhesives. They are based on the severity of the drying treatment. These are soluble, partially soluble and insoluble. The preliminary steps before drying are the same in each case. Fresh liquid blood is collected from slaughter house over a period of hours or even days. The fibrin or clotting substance is removed by mechanical agitation or acid precipitation and preservative is generally added.

The first and most important category of dried blood adhesives is soluble blood which includes products with about 80 to 85% cold water solubility. The second category of dried blood is partially insoluble or denatured blood, which have solubility between 15 to 80% and covers a broad range of adhesive behaviour. The third type of dried blood is totally insoluble and completely denatured. This material is generally intended for fertilizer rather than adhesive uses.

The source of animal blood has a large influence on its behaviour and adhesive properties. Blood differ considerably among species of animals and also from one animal to another in a given species due to variations in age, condition, feed etc. The uniformity is brought about by drying blood stocks from different species of animals separately and blend large quantities of blood from a single species to get uniform product.

All the soluble dried bloods are fre-flowing medium density powders ranging in colour from dark red to almost black. As the degree of insolubility increases, the colour becomes browner and the bulk density tends to decrease. All dried bloods are bygroscopic and are protected from moisture.

The primary adhesive constituents in soluble dried blood are its proteins, serum albumin and globulin. Dried blood protein dissolves readily in water to yield a moderately adhesive colloidal solution, but the full adhesive potential of its complex structure is developed only through alkaline dispersion. Blood protein appears to become strongly adhesive at a lower pH then vegetable protein, but some strong bases such as sodium, potassium, or lithium hydroxide are usually necessary to develop its full adhesive potential.

Controlled application of heat can be employed to thicken a blood glue, alter its consistency, lengthen its working life, improve its cold bonding properties, or cure it irreversibly. This sensitivity to heat is mainly responsible for the popularity of blood glue.

Aldehydes are useful for increasing the water resistance, viscosity, working life and water requirement of blood glues, while modifying the consistency to any degree from gelatinous to completely granular. Compounds frequently used for this purpose are paraformaldehyde, formalin, dimethylol urea, sodium formaldehyde bisulphate, hexamethylenetetramine, tris (hydroxy methyl) nitromethane, monomethylol dimethydantion and urea or melamine formaldehyde resins. Only small quantities (0.1 to 1.0%) of these materials are required with sodium hydroxide dispersions of blood protein to yield gross modifications. As the dispersing pH is reduced from approximately 13 to 10, proportionately larger qunatities of aldehyde are needed to yield corresponding effects They are usually added after the blood is in solution and most frequently after alkaline dispersion.

All phenolic resins impart mold resistance characteristic to blood glues when added in quantities of 10% or more of resin solids based on the weight of dry glue. Blood glues must be hot-processed to gain the full measure of protection from phenolic resin additives.

Water at 15-21° C	300	parts
Low solubility dried beef blood	75	"
Wood flour	21	"
Pine oil or equivalent defoamer.		
mix 3 min or until smooth	4	"
Water at 15-21° C, mix 2 min	330	"
Hydrated lime in	10	"
Water at 18-23° C	20	"
50% sodium hydroxide solution mix 10 min	16	"
Sodium silicate solution mix 5 min	35	"

Water at 15-21° C	175	parts
Low solubility dried beef blood	50	"
Soluble dried beef blood	25	"
Fir wood flour	22	"
Pine oil or equivalent defoamer.		
mix 2 min or until smooth	3	"
Water at 15-21° C, mix	400	"
Hydrated lime in	6	"
Water mix 1 min	12	"
Sodium silicate solution, mix 1 min	45	"
50% sodium hydroxide solution mix 5 min	16	"
50% solids phenolic adhesive resin mix 3 min	27	"

Water at 37° C	75	parts
Soluble dried beef blood	75	"
Fir wood flour	12	"
Wheat flour	10	"
Diesel oil, mix 5 min	3	"
Water at 37° C	250	"
Pine oil, mix 2 min 6 "		
Sodium silicate solution, mix 10 min	150	"
Cold water	150	"
40% solids phenolic adhesive resin	200	"
50% sodium hydroxide solution, mix 5 min	50	"

Water at 21° C	190	parts
Extender, mix 2 min	70	"
50% sodium hydroxide solution, mix 1 min	40	"
Sodium carbonate, mix 15 min	18	"
Diesel oil, mix 1 min	3	"
Dried soluble blood, mix 5 min	30	"
40% solids phenolic adhesive resin, mix 5 min	500	"

Water at 21° C	120	parts
Urea resin hot press catalyst, mix 1 min	10	"
Soluble dried beef blood	10	"
Wheat flour	100	"
Pine oil, mix 5 min	1	"
65% solids urea bonding resin, mix 5 min	100	"

Inorganic Adhesives & Cements

Inorganic bonds which have lasted for conturies are common. Many building stones are formed from aggregate bonded with siliceous composition, both crystalline and amorphous. Inorganic cement and adhesives are widely known as well as the facts that they are economical, fire resistant and usually resistants to water and many other chemicals.

Soluble silicate are relatively low cost adhesives and they are flame resistant. These siliceous bonds are attached by alkali. This can be avoided by using additives which react with silicates to form insoluble compounds.

Properties. The commercial silicate adhesives have no yield point and are composed of colloidal electrolyte particles with negative charges and becomes just electropostive as the pH approaches to zero. These colloidal characteristics give their films the property of deformability which is necessary for a good adhesive bond. The presence of alkali ions may be ocnsidered as stabilizing the silica micelles until time of contact when bonds from.

The viscosity of silicate solution to be used in adhesive application varies from a few centipoises to several thousand centipoises to several thousand centipoises depending upon the condition of the surface, temperature, humidity and time available for setting. The viscosity can be increased by adding a neutral salt such as sodium chloride. Sugar, glycerin, sorbitol tends to retain moisture and thus increase its flexibility. They usually reduce the viscosity but at the same time increase the tackiness, the setting time and the toughness f the film.

The wetting rate can be increased by adding a small amount of a more alkaline silicate or by diluting the silicate. The viscosity can be maintained by adding fillers such as clay which also increases the drying rate.

Inorganic alkaline adhesives resist the growth of molds and fungi as well as attack by ants and other cellulose destroying insects.

Applications

Dilute solution of potassium silicate binds phosphorus to the surface of television tubes. An adhesive formed by heating 40 parts by weight of 37 Be 3.22 sodium silicate with 1 part by weight of fine filament glass wool for about 2 days at 60 to 70^0 degree is recommended for optical work such as the bonding of leases or the preparation of multilayer shatter proof glass. Glass lined equipment may be patched with thin layer of sodium silicate solution at about 30^0 Be, dried by radiant heat.

The soluble silicates bond decorative sheets of copper to wall, plywood to steel, aluminium foil to paper. Soluble silicate are odourless, non-poisonous, fire resistant, non-corrosive to soft metal and resistant to vermin and moulds. Tetrafluoro ethylene coatings are bonded to metal without cracking by in terposing a layer of potassium silicate solution. The development of glass to metal bonding has achieved rapid progress with sodium silicates. A high temperature adhesive which fuses and welds to stainless steel at 927° C but will not flow at 1100° C for a short period has been formed form a silicate with stainless steel filler.

A good bond can be obtained with most of the wood surface with silicate adhesives. Pressure is usually required. Soya flour adhesive frequently contain soluble silicates for the improvement of its wetting characteristics, viscosity bond strength and water resistance. The usual formula involves mixing soybean flour, lime caustic solution and sodium silicate.

An important application of soluble silicate adhesives is that of bonding paper. Sealed box flaps, wound cans and tubes use silicate adhesives.

Latex silicate adhesives have used among other in shoe soles and trim, foxing on tennis shoes, gauze bandages, fabric layers and palletizing. Dimethylourea is mixed with soluble silicates to form an adhesive for flexible abrasive coated material.

Applications: Soluble silicate adhesives are used as refractory cements for laying refractory bricks. Ready mixed cements of silicon carbide, fire sand, raw fine clay and powdered hydrated sodium silicate are used as mortar. A simple acid proof cement is made from a fine, pure quartsy sand and 3.7 ratio sodium silicate in equal proportions. The coloured pigments which brightens the roots of many housing developments are bound to inert granules by silicate adhesives which permit a life expectancy of 25 years or more.

Three types of chemically setting silicate mortars have been differentiated. The first types sets by drying in air; the second group, in which silica is gelled by the slow hydrolysis an organic ester, the third comprises a reaction with the fluoro silicates.

Silicate cements are used primarily for fillings of teeth. The brittle mixed silicate zinc phosphate cement are utilized as translucent cementing material.

Phosphate cements

The principal metal phosphates are the zinc phosphate bonds in dental cements and household appliances. A mixture of ZnO powder and H_2 PO_4 react with considerable hat development when mixed but small amount of dental cement are spread on a chilled stab so that temperature is kept down to that of the body tissue.

An oxide bond is formed with phosphoric acid and aluminium, matured at 300° C, are relatively insoluble in water. This phosphate bond decomposes and converts to a sintered aluminium bond with excellent thermal stability and strength at high temperatures. Cements for ramming, gunning may be formed by mulling phosphoric acid with alumina. For cementing castings in very deep wells a cement which sal off contamination is formed by mixing bauxite, calcium fluoride and a filler such as coal with water and 85% phosphoric acid.

Acid phosphate cement may be prereacted or formed in situ by reaction of acids with oxides, hydroxides or salts of basic elements. Acid phosphates which form reaction bonds include the aluminium, calcium, copper, chromium, iron, copper and tin. Phosphoric acid with asbestos probably forms a magnesium acid phosphate as a bond. Phosphorous pentoxides and ethyl alcohol with magnesia makes a gelatinous refractory bond which may be an acid phosphate.

Hydraulic cements

The principal types of cements which set by hydration are calcium silicates or portland cement, calcium aluminium cement, pozzuolana cement, slag cement, natural lime-silica cement, barium silicate and gypsum cement.

The essential constituents of portland cement are $3CaO. SiO_2$ and $3CaO. SiO_2$ with some minor proportions of $3CaO. Al_2O_3$. $4CaO. Al_2O_3$ and Fe_2O_3. The dry powder is made by sintering limestone and clay in to a clinker which is finely pulverized with about 5% gypsum. The cement is used in construction.

Lime cement

Sandlime bricks and other calcium silicate products resistant to high temperature result from the reaction of calcium oxide and sand under pressure and hat in the presence of steam. They are usually improved by incorporation of sodium silicate. Calcium silicate refractories will withstand temperatures of 650° C.

Slag cement

Slag cements or cement sursulphates are made of granulated blast furnace slag, usually mixed with portland cement.

Pozzolana cement

Pozzolana is a loosely consolidated siliceous rock of volcanic orgin which imparts to portland cement an improved resistivity to corrosive waters. The trass cements with high dimensional stability and small exothermic reactions, are especially valuable for dams, bridges and walls.

Lime mortars

These are mixers of sand and hydrated lime. A lime putty is formed with water, aged and mixed with sand as needed. A lime mortar usually contains about, port of hydrated lime to 3 ports of sand and many contain from 0.3 to 1 part of cement with additional sand. Lime plasters are made with 1 volume of lime putty, 2 volume of plastering sand and 3.5 kg. of fibre.

Plaster of Parls

Plaster of Paris is also known as wall plaster. There are hard finish plasters for flooring and tilling such as Keene's cement and parian cement. The best known of these is Keene's which is made by burning gypsum at about 110^0 C to form the hemi hydrate, dipping in a solution of papermaker's, alum and then reburning to 400^0 C. In pottery industry plaster of Paris moulds re used for slip casting various forms of potteries.

High alumina

Calcium aluminate cements have been developed for refratory concrete applications. Calcium aluminates prepared from limestone and alumina by sintering their mixture is used above at 1200 to 1300^0 C.

Sorel cement

A sorel cement is a basic salt of a heavy meal, usually magnesite. It is a magnesium oxy chloride based product. It is suitable for dry locations. Magnesium oxy chloride cements are made by reacting magnesium oxide with magnesium chloride. This cement resist damage by cooking fats and greases, repel vermin and prevent growth of mould and bacteria. They also conduct static electricity.

Metal powder cements

Sealing compositions containing iron powder are of increasing use in automobile radiators, iron covers and connecting lines. The setting appears to occur by corrosion of the iron and crystallization of solids which provides adhesion between the adherend and the remaining iron particles.

Litharge cements

Mixtures of glycerin and litharge are used as a lining to protect digesters for cellulose against acids and as paints resistant to hydrocarbons, as well as for the repair of tubes and sinks, pipe valves, glass; stoneware and ammonium gas conduits.

Sulphur cements

Sulphur cements resist mixtures of nitric acid andhydro fluoric acid. A sulphur cement adheres well to metals, particularly well to copper.

33

PRESSURE SENSITIVE TAPES & LABELS

An adhesive tape is composed of a backing element in a long strip upon which is applied an adhesive, the function of which is to attach the carrier backing to some secondary surface. The attachment is made by activating the adhesive with solvent, heat or finger pressure.

Gummed tapes, stamps etc. are the most commonly known variety of solvent activated tape, that is, the adhesive is activated by wetting with water. For certain industrial applications, an organic solvent-activated-adhesive is used. A second type of adhesive tape is the thermoplastic or heat activated variety. In this construction, the adhesive is made sticky by the use of heat and pressure.

The most rapidly growing line of adhesive tapes is the pressure-sensitive variety. This type of tape can be applied with hand pressure in the absence of solvents or heat and sticks aggressively to most common surfaces. Because of its extreme ease of application, it has gained wide acceptance.

Cloth, paper, films, foils, strand reinforced backings as well as many laminates have been employed as tape backings. They are always thin and flexible to conform readily to the surfaces upon which they are applied.

The most commonly used films are cellophane, polyvinyl chloride, polyester, polyethylene, polypropylene and the cellulose acetate films. Aluminium and lead foils are used for speciality tapes. Films and foils are generally coated with a very thin anchor coating called a primer to improve the bonding of the adhesive to backing. Hydrophilic backings can be primed with a mixture of a water soluble gum in water and a natural rubber or GRS latex, whereas hydrophobic backings may be primed with a solution of a buna-N rubber combined with GRS or a similar polymer. A butadiene - styrene acrylonitric terpolymer plus resin has also been reported to be a good primer for hdyrophobic film surfaces. The films are often coated on the opposite side with release agent to reduce the adhesion of the adhesive to the back side of the next layer of tape when in roll form. Cured dimethyl silicone coatings provide excellent release.

Cloth backings can be used without further treatment or they may be sized with starch or other organic binders to help bind the fibres together. The cloth may be coated with nitro-cellulose, plasticized polyvinyl chloride, polyethylene or other film formers on the back side of the cloth to improve its appearance, unwind characteristics and reduce its moisture vapour transmission.

Paper backings used with pressure sensitive adhesives are almost universally impregnated with some sort of rubbery material to improve the improve the internal strength (ply strength or delamination resistance) of the backing. Without the necessary ply strength, the paper backings would split when unrolled from a roll and the adhesive would be sandwiched between two layers of paper, thus making the tape useless. The first paper impregnent consisted of glue plasticized with glycerin. This has been replaced by paper saturants based on solvent-based rubber solutions and sythetic rubber latices. The back side of the tape is coated with a film forming polymer to improve its appearance, increase its solvent resistance and reduce the adhesion of the adhesive to the backing. In addition, a release coat may be applied with or over the back-size coat to reduce the unwind tension. As described previously, the release materials may consist of a polymeric chain to which are attached linear long chain alkyl groups (C_{12}-C_{24}).

For very low levels of release, silicone coated papers are most commonly adopted. These release papers are generally used as interliners on double faced tapes or on tapes which must pass through equipment requiring tack free surfaces. The silicone release agent is reported to be a curd reaction product of a alkoxyl or hydroxyl terminated polydimethyl siloxane and a methyl hydrogen polysiloxane using the tin salt of an organic acid as a catalyst.

Lable stock is sold universally in roll or sheet form on a release liner. For most applications, the face stock or backing which carries the adhesive consists of an unimpregnated paper stock which is coated on the backside with a printable high gloss clay coating. Where good weatherability, flexibility and toughness is required, an impregnated sheet is used. Such applications include the transfer address labels on the internal revenue forms and identification labels on tape reels for computers. The release liner consists of a densified kraft paper, a glassine paper or a polyethylene paper laminate. The release surface is coated with a silicone composition.

Laminated backings consist of a film or foil bonded to cloth or paper with a rubbery type adhesive such as a pressure-sensitive adhesive. Here again, the paper is impregnated in order to resist the delaminating forces when a roll of the tape is unwound. Strand reinforced backings are made by bonding a plurality of strands in a lengthwise direction to a film, impregnated paper or cloth by means of rubbery adhesive. Glass strands are used where highest tensile tensile strength and lowest elongation are required. Rayon is used where high impact strength is needed and where the tensile strength requirement is somewhat lower.

A gummed tape coated with a water activated animal glue coating is quite boardy and shows a great tendency to curl. To overcome this deficiency, the tape, before slitting into narrow rolls, is pulled over a series of breaker bars which produces fine diagonal hairlike cracks in the adhesive surface. This minimizes the tendency to curl and provides a more flexible construction.

Adhesives activated with organic solvents have not received wide acceptance because of the fire and health hazard involved and the inconvenience of activating with solvents. They are used in certain applications where a pressure sensitive adhesive tape cannot supply the bond strength, solvent or heat resistance required.

Heat activated adhesives

Heat-activated adhesives are used on tapes which can be applied with heat and pressure. They can be made from a wide variety of thermoplastic materials such as waxes, polyethylene, cellulose esters and ethers, nitrocellulose, polyvinyl acetate, polyvinyl chloride and many rubber resin combinations. One of the widest applications of this type of adhesive tape is in garment repair. A fabric mending tape normally consists of a plasticized polyvinyl chloride adhesive applied upon a cloth backing.

A stay tape used in box manufacturing consists of a kraft paper coated with a thermoplastic adhesive consisting essentially of plasticized polyvinyl acetate.

Heat-activated adhesives provides a very high, irreversible bond. No fire or health hazards are involved in their application. One disadvantage, particularly in industrial applications, is the need for special high temperature presses to apply this type of adhesive.

Pressure-sensitive Adhesives

Pressure-sensitive adhesion can be defined as those adhesives which will adhere tenaciously upon application with only light finger pressure. Tapes with these adhesives have gained wide acceptance because of their ease of application and their ability to be removed cleanly from the surfaces on which they were applied. They, of necessity, produce a bond of a much lower order of magnitude than the two previously mentioned adhesives.

Pressure-sensitive adhesives normally are composed of a rubbery type elastomer combined with a liquid or solid resin tackifier component. A mixture of resins may be used to provide a balance of properties which cannot be obtained with either resin alone. Fillers are often added to change the rheological properties of the adhesive or to add colour. Antioxidants are used to stabilize the adhesive against oxidation and heat and light degradation.

Adhesives for high temperatures use or for electrical applications sometimes contain a minor amount of a heat-curing oil-soluble phenolic resin. An alkaline filler or zinc resinate is added as a catalyst to promote the reaction between the phenolic resin and rubber. The adhesive is cured by the application of heat. Van der Mer has postulated that crosslinking occurs through an intermediate quinone methide structure. Compatibility seems improtant since the higher alkyl phenolic resins are much more effective than the lower alkyl analogues. Sulphur-curing systems are not used in electrical tapes since they cause chemical corrosion of copper wires. Similarly, sulphur-curing systems are undesirable in masking tapes because sulphur and its derivatives stain light coloured painted surfaces. Light coloured resins and nonstaining adhesives. For masking tapes which must withstand high temperature drying and baking, adhesives containing oil-soluble heat curing phenol formaldehyde resins, as described above, are applied and cured to the backing during its manufacture.

Typical ingredients used in pressure-sensitive adhesives are listed.

Elastomer

Milled natural rubber
Reclaimed rubber
SBR (styrene butadiene rubber)
Polyisobutylene or butyl rubber
Buna-N(butadiene acrylonitrile rubber)
Polyvinyl ethers (ethyl or higher)
Polyacrylate esters (ethyl or higher)
Block copolymers
(styrene-butadiene-styrene)
(styrene-isoprene-styrene)

Tackifiers

Polyterpene resins
Gum rosin
Rosin esters and other rosin derivatives
Oil-soluble phenolic resin
Coumarone indene resins
Petroleum hydrocarbon resins

Plasticizers

Mineral oil
Liquid polybutenes
Liquid polyacrylates
Lanolin

Fillers

Zinc oxide
Titanium dioxide
Aluminium hydrate
Calcium carbonate
Clay
Pigments

Antioxidants

Rubber antioxidants (preferably nonstanding)
Metal dithiocarbamates
Metal chelating agents

Pressure-sensitive adhesive formulations

Adhesive A

Milled pale crepe	100	parts
Poly-beta pinene resin (mp 70°C)	75	"
Petroleum oil	5	"
Polymerized trimethyl dihydr quinoline	2	"

Adhesive B

Milled smoked sheet rubber	100	parts
Zinc oxide	50	"
Dehydrogenated rosin	75	"
Sym-di-beta-naphthyl para phenylene diamine	2	"
Lanolin	10	"

Adhesive C

Butadiene styrene copolymer (70:30 ratio, Mooney value 50)	50	parts
Milled smoked sheet rubber	50	"
Ester of hydrogenated rosin	50	"
Polymerized trimethyl dihydroquinoline	2	"
Petroleum oil	20	"

Adhesive D

Polyvinyl ethyl ether (intrinsic viscosity = 2.37)	100	parts
Hydrogenated rosin	50	"
Phenyl alpha naphthylamine	0.35	"
Polyethylene glycol 400 diricinoleate	11.5	"

Adhesives E

Polyisobutylene (high molecular weight polymer)	100	parts
Polyisobutylene (viscous liquid)	70	"

Adhesives F

Crude rubber	50	parts
GRS	50	"
Octyl phenol formaldehyde heat curing resin	20	"
ZnO	60	"
Diethylene glycol of dehydroabietic acid	110	"
Antioxidants	2	"

Control of the amount of cure is necessary for optimum performance. Insufficient cure will cause shear failures at elevated temperatures or may result in mass transfer on removal. Overcure will result in the loss of some of the pressure-sensitive tape properties.

The recent introduction of block copolymers has broadened the scope of available-pressure sensitive adhesives. Relatively low molecular weight polymers may be used which through the styrene domains provide a heat and solvent sensitive physical crosslinking. Because of the low molecular weight of the block copolymers (i.e. 100,000 - 124,000), adhesive manufacturers are able to formulate high solids pressure sensitive adhesives or formulate extrudable adhesives that can match the quality and performance of pressure-sensitive adhesives based on conventional high molecular weight polymers. Likewise, hot melt pressure sensitive adhesives that provide better performance than prior art hot melt adhesives are being offered commercially.

Pressure-sensitive acrylic adhesives are being used on many speciality tapes. The acrylic adhesives have the advantage of water clarity and extremely good resistance to changes due to oxidation. The acrylate pressure sensitive adhesives are normally a copolymer of a higher alkyl acrylate such as 2-ethyl hexyl acrylate copolymerized with a small amount of a polar comonomer. Typical of the polar comonomers are: acrylic acid, acrylamide, maleic anhydride, diacetone acrylamide and long chain alkyl acrylamides.

Typical acrylate copolymer adhesives can be made from the following monomer mixtures using polymerization techniques given in reference:

Monomer mixtures for acrylate copolymer adhesives

	Adhesive A	Adhesive B	Adhesive C
Fusel oil ester of acrylic acid	95	-	-
2 ethylexyl acrylate	-	75	50
Vinyl acetate	-	18	43
Acrylic acid	5	-	2
Maleic anhydride	-	2	-
Diacetone acylamide	-	5	5
3 methacryloxypropylrimethyl silane	-	0.05	-

34

PERFORMANCE & APPLICATION OF ADHESIVES

Adhesives are formulated chemicals with a wide range of components used in them. They stick a widely different range of substrates. It is virtually possible to design an adhesives which will suit to any particular purpose. The detail characteristics, performance and applications are given in tabular form in this chapter. The basic type of adhesives, the number of packs required to produce the product to be applied, mode of application, the substrates on which they are applied with best results, the condition of curing etc. are given in the table.

Performance & Application of Adhesives

Type of adhesive & No. of components		*Colour*	*Physical form, consistency*	*Working life*	*Method of application*	*Processing*		*Service temp. range °C*	*Main uses*	*Adherends*
						Curing cycle	*Bonding pressure N/cm²*			
Acrylic	2	Trans parent	Syrupy liquid	Viscosity dependent 2 wk for syrup at 20°C in the dark	Brush Spatula	2 h at 55°C+ 8 h at 80°C or 5 h exposure to u.-violet radiation	Contact to 4	-60 to 80	Structural work requiring maximum joint strength. Outdoor applications. Bonding rigid acrylic sheets to other materials	Acrylic materials Polymethylmethacrylaterubber Polymethylmethacrylate-polymethylmethacrylat
Acrylic	1	Trans-parent	Liquid	Solvent evaporates in 1 h at 20°C	Brush Spatula	20 h at 20°C to 6 h at 80°C	Contact to 4	-60 to 80	Acrylic sheet bonding requiring moderate strength with limited gap filling	Acrylic materials Polymethyl-methacrylate-polymethylmethacrylate
Acrylic+ other resins	2	- -	Liquid	For 2% catalyst, varies from 3 h at 5°C to 40 min at 30°C. For 5% catalyst, varies from 2 h at 5°C to 25 min at 30°C	Spatula	For 2% catalyst, 2 d at 15°C to 1 h at 80°C. For 5% catalyst, 2 d at 15°C to 25 min at 80°C	Contact to 70	-70 to 120	Metals, rigid plastics, ceramics and similar hard materials employed for large structures exposed to the weather. Building applications, roofing, aircraft components	Aluminium/ Copper/ Magnesium Aluminium/ Silicon/ Magnesium alloy CS, SS, Brass Aluminium

Type of adhesive & No. of components		*Colour*	*Physical form, consistency*	*Working life*	*Method of application*	*Processing*		*Service temp. range °C*	*Main uses*	*Adherends*
						Curing cycle	*Bonding pressure N/cm^2*			
Animal (glue)	1	Pale brown	Stiff jelly	- -	- -	Melted at 70-75°C Sets on cooling	Contact	- -	Woodworking Carpet materials Paper Bookbinding	Paper Wood Textiles
Animal (hide) (glue)	1	Pale brown to brown	Fine/ coarse powder or cake	- -	Applied as water solution, 0.8 kg/1. Sets on cooling and drying	- -	Contact	- -	Woodworking Paper Porous materials	Paper Wood Textiles
Bitumen	1	Black	100% w/w solids solution	Indefinite	Dip coat	Applied as melt at 60-65°C	Contact	-20 to 32	Bonding of expanded polystyrene and other low melting points expanded plastics to surfaces	Polystyrene (expanded) to brickwork, concrete, asbestoscement, metals. Porous surfaces (primed with Colset 183)
Bitumen-latex emulsion	1	Brown-black	Thin emulsion	Indefinite	Spreader	Dried to tacky state at 20°C and bonded	Contact	- -	For fixing wood mosaic tiles to concrete	Wood Concrete
Fish glue	1	Yellow	Thick liquid 50% w/w solids	Open time $^1/_2$ h at 20°C	Dispensed from container	Dries at 20°C in 1 h	Contact	- -	General purpose adhesive for bonding absorbent materials	Paper Leather Fabrics Wood-wood

Type of adhesive & No. of components		Colour	Physical form, consistency	Working life	Method of application	Processing: Curing cycle	Processing: Bonding pressure N/cm^2	Service temp. range °C	Main uses	Adherends
Fish glue	1	Pale buff	High viscosity liquid	Open time $^1/_2$ h at 20°C	Brush machine	Dries at 20°C in 1 h	Contact	60	General purpose glue for porous materials	Wood Chipboard Paper
Butyl rubber	1	Off white	Heavy paste	20 min at 20°C	Spatula Trowel	Contact bonded when wet	Contact	- -	Ceramic tile adhesive. Inflammable, Flash Pt. 46°C, coverage, 1.8 $m^2/1$	Ceramic tile Wood Plaster (primed) Concrete Brickwork
Casein	1	White	Powder	7 h at 16-21° C to 3h at 26-32°C	Stiff brush Mech-anical spreader	Cold setting after 20 min standing period on mixing	14 to 35 for 4-16 h at 19°C	- -	Laminated timber arches and beams, plybox beams, and timber engineering work	Timber with moisture content 8-18% w/w
Casein+ 60% latex	2	White	Powder+ emulsion	3 h at 20°C	Brush, Roll spreader	Cold setting after 20 min standing period on mixing	Contact to 14 for 8-12 h	- -	Bonding of dissimilar materials to give flexible, water resistant bond	Aluminium Wood Phenolic formaldehyde (rigid) Leather Rubber
Cellulose acetate in solvents	1	Clear	0.26 Solids content 10% w/w	Open time indefinite (min at room temp.	Brush	Wet bonded and allowed	Contact to 4	- -	Bonding cellulose acetate to itself and porous substrates	Cellulose acetate Cellulose materials Paper board Leather, Fabrics

Type of adhesive & No. of components		Colour	Physical form, consistency	Working life	Method of application	Processing: Curing cycle	Processing: Bonding pressure N/cm²	Service temp. range °C	Main uses	Adherends
Cellulose nitrate in mixed	1	Colour-less	Liquid 8 Solids content 30% w/w	Unspecified	Spatula	Sets by solvent loss	Contact to 4	- -	Domestic applications, model building	Metals, Glass, Cellulosic plastics, Acrylics, Wood-wood (beech)
Nitro-cellulose in ester solvent	1	Trans-parent	Low viscosity liquid	Open time $^1/_2$ h at 20°C	Brush	- -	- -	- -	Labelling	Cellulosic materials Paper
Cellulose ether	1	Trans-parent	Liquid	- -	Brush	Dries in air	Contact	- -	Interior decorating applications	Paper Polystyrene (foam) Plaster Aluminium (foil)
Sodium carboxy-methyl cellulose in water	1	Trans-parent	Liquid	- -	Brush	Dries in air	Contact	- -	Decorating and general purpose	Paper Corrugated board Multi wall sacking
Modified methyl-cellulose	1	Trans-parent	Liquid	- -	Brush	Dries in air	Contact	- -	Heavy duty adhesive. Decorating paper and plastics	Vinyl coated paper Polystyrene (foam)

Type of adhesive & No. of components		Colour	Physical form, consistency	Working life	Method of application	Processing		Service temp. range °C	Main uses	Adherends
						Curing cycle	Bonding pressure N/cm²			
Cyano-acrylate	1	Trans-parent clear	Liquid 0.09-0.12	Sets under pressure in joint	Dispensed from container or automatic applicator	15s to 10 min at 20°C Substrate dependent	Contact to 4	-80 to 80	Rapid assembly of metal, glass, plastics, rubber components. Light engineering applications; instrumentation	Steel-steel Aluminium-steel, Aluminium-aluminium, Phenolic-butyl rubber Butyl-butyl Neoprene-neoprene, Rubber-rubber (natural), Nylon-nylon, Acrylic-acrylic, Neoprene-neoprene, Steel-steel, Aluminium-aluminium.
Cyano acrylate	1	--	Medium viscosity liquid 0.06	--	--	15 s to 1 min at 20°C Substrate dependent	--	-80 to 80	as above	Steel-steel
Cyano acrylate	1	--	Liquid 0 04	--	--	1-6 s at 20°C Substrate dependent	--	-80 to 80	Especially suitable for rubber bonding	Steel-steel

Type of adhesive & No. of components		*Colour*	*Physical form, consistency*	*Working life*	*Method of application*	*Processing*		*Service temp. range °C*	*Main uses*	*Adherends*
						Curing cycle	*Bonding pressure N/cm²*			
Cyano-acrylate +additive	2	- -	Liquid 0.04 +solid additive	- -	Dispensed from container	6 h at 20°C (maximum). Handling strength in 10 min at 20°C and ~ 80% of ultimate strength in 30 min	- -	-80 to 120	Bonding of metals, alloys and heat-resistant plastics required to operate at elevated temperatures	Steel-steel, Aluminium -aluminium, Polycarbonate-polycarbonate
Dextrine	1	Brown	Semi-liquid	Indefinite	Brush	Air drying	Contact	- -	General purpose glue for absorbent materials	Paper, Cardboard, Leather, Wood, Pottery
Dextrine	1	White	Thixo-tropic paste	Indefinite	Brush Machine	Air drying	Contact	- -	Bag sealing and board lining. Bookbinding	Paper
Dextrine	1	Buff	Thick paste	Indefinite	Brush Machine	Air drying	Contact	- -	Labelling silicone treated bottles in Pharmaceutical industry	Glass (treated) Paper
Epoxy resin +catalyst	2	Amber	4.6 at 25°C	35 min at 25°C 60 g mass	Spatula Roller Extruder	16 h to 9 d at 20-22°C to 1 h at 100°C	Contact to 20	- -	Metals, plastic laminates and ceramic mouldings	Polyester-glass fibre (sheet) Epoxy-glass fibre Phenolic (lam.) -Glass, Wood, Aluminium(alloy) - Aluminium

Type of adhesive & No. of components		Colour	Physical form, consistency	Working life	Method of application	Processing		Service temp. range °C	Main uses	Adherends
						Curing cycle	Bonding pressure N/cm^2			
Epoxy resin +catalyst	2	Grey	Medium thick liquid	2-2$^1/_2$ h at 25°C	Spatula	3 d at 18°C to 1 h at 50°C	Contact to 20	100	Metals	Steel-steel, Wood-wood, Glass-glass, Tile (unglazed)-tile, Aluminium-aluminium,
Epoxy resin +catalyst	1	Yellow	Liquid 25% solids in xylene	Open time 15 min at 24°C	Brush	1 h at 176°C or 2 h at 190°C	10-70 or 27-35 for trans-ducers	150 (static) to 176 (dyna-mic)	Strain gauge adhesive, coating for transducers	Metals Transducer materials
Epoxy resin +catalyst	2	Amber	Paste	16 h at 20°C	Spatula	8 h at 121°C to 1 h at 204°C	Contact to 20	-54 to 260 For short expo-sures 370	High strength adhesive for elevated temperature use. Formulated for bonding fluoro-carbons to various materials.	Polytetrafluore-thylene Wood Ceramics Steel Glass Aluminium-aluminium
Epoxy resin +catalyst	2	Orange	Thixotro-pic paste	45 min at 20°C	Spatula	24-48 h at 20°C to 45 min at 93°C to 10 min at 150°C	Contact to 20	-40 to 121	Bonding of fluorocarbon materials	Polytetrafluore-thylene Wood Steel Glass Ceramics Aluminium-aluminium

Type of adhesive & No. of components		Colour	Physical form, consistency	Working life	Method of application	Processing		Service temp. range °C	Main uses	Adherends
						Curing cycle	Bonding pressure N/cm^2			
Modified epoxy with aluminium powder filler	2	Brown	Paste	2 d at 20°C	Brush	Dried for 30 min at 60°C. Cured for 30 min at 150°C under pressure. Pressure released, on cooling at 50°C	69	-40 to 150	Metal bonding structural assemblies at elevated temperatures	Aluminium(alloy) - aluminium
Elasto-meric modified epoxy	1	- -	Film supported on nylon carrier	- -	Brushed primer+ press curing of film	Primer air dried, 30 min at 20°C+60 min at 100°C. Film cured 60 min at 177°C under pressure. Pressure released, on cooling(50°C)	17	-40 to 125	Metal bonding for structural assemblies at elevated temperatures	Aluminium(alloy) - aluminium
Epoxy	2	Grey	Putty	1 h at 21°C	Spatula	4.6 h at 20°C to 30 min at 65°C to 15 min at 100°C	Contact	- -	General purpose bonding agent. Defect repairs in sheet metals, castings, tanks, concrete, building applications	Glass, Ceramics, Wood, Steel-steel, Aluminium-aluminium, Concrete-concrete

Type of adhesive & No. of components		*Colour*	*Physical form, consistency*	*Working life*	*Method of application*	*Processing*		*Service temp. range °C*	*Main uses*	*Adherends*
						Curing cycle	*Bonding pressure N/cm²*			
Epoxy+ amine catalyst (Ancamine LT)	2	Pink	Liquid 1.2-1.4	75 min at 25°C (25 g mass)	Spatula	2-7 d at 20°C for 33% w/w catalyst content	Contact	-5 to 60	Repair of concrete, roads and stone surfaces	Concrete Stonework
Modified epoxy resin with amine hardener	2	Blue	Medium paste. Sp. gr. = 2.3 g/ml	Exceeds 4 h at 25°C	Spatula	45 min at 120°C or 4 h at 73°C or 24 h at 60°C	Contact to 4	- -	For instrument applications where high thermal conductivity is required. Bonding of noble and other metals	Gold-gold (plated steel) Silver-silver (plated brass) Brass-aluminium Copper-copper Solder-solder (63%Sn+37%Pb) Aluminium-aluminium
Epoxy	2	Light Brown	Paste	4 h	Trowel	Cold curing in 24 h	Contact to 7	- -	Building applications	Concrete Masonry
Epoxy	2	Green on mixing	Pourable slurry. May be sand filled ($BS^{25}/_{200}$ grade)	Initial set in 4 h after mixing	Trowel	12 h at 20-25°C 24 h at 10-15°C	Contact to 7	- -	Pile jointing and repair work under outdoor conditions	Concrete-concrete
Epoxy polysulphide	2	Grey	Non-flow thixotropic paste	1.5-2 h at 20°C	Pressure gun Spatula	16 h at 20°C Optimum cure after 24 h	Contact	-30 to 75	Cold curing adhesive sealant for interior and exterior usage	Glass Metals Concrete Wood

Type of adhesive & No. of components		Colour	Physical form, consistency	Working life	Method of application	Processing		Service temp. range °C	Main uses	Adherends
						Curing cycle	Bonding pressure N/cm^2			
Epoxy polysulphide	2	Light grey	Paste Sp. gr. 1.45	25 min for 454 g mixture	Spatula Trowel Automatic equipment	Sets at room temp. Handling strength 4th. Full strength 3-7 d	Contact	-35 to 93	Adhesive-sealant for caulking joints based on metals, masonry, insulation materials. Roof bow assembly; aluminium and wood channelling and frameworks. Double-glaze window manufacture	Wood Glass Ceramics Aluminium-aluminium
Phenolic resin modified with butyral	1	Orange to Brown	Liquid	Indefinite	Brush	Dried for $^1/_2$-2 h at 60-80°C then cured for 18 h at 100°C to 20 min at 149°C under pressure	40-70	100	Phenolic stoving cement for metals, plastic laminates and inorganic substrates. Metal foil to plastic laminates as in printed circuit boards	Wood Graphite Asbestos Phenolic (laminate), Copper Steel-steel Aluminium(alloy) -aluminium
Polyfunctional epoxy resin +liquid epoxy resin and catalyst (powder)	3	Brown	Thick liquid	2-3 h at 100°C	Spatula Roller	Applied to surfaces at 100°C. Cured 3 h at 180°C	Contact	240	Hot setting adhesive with high resistance to heat. Metals, ceramics and heat resistant materials. Strain gauge attachment	Adherends listed for AralditeATI grade

Type of adhesive & No. of components		*Colour*	*Physical form, consistency*	*Working life*	*Method of application*	*Processing*		*Service temp. range °C*	*Main uses*	*Adherends*
						Curing cycle	*Bonding pressure N/cm²*			
Ethylene vinyl acetate co-polymer+ resins	1	Yellow	Solid in block form	6 mth at 5-25°C	Special equip-ment available for appli-cation of molten adhesive. Roller applicator Extruder Hot spatula	Applied as a melt at 160-190°C which sets on cooling	Contact to 20	- -	General purpose adhesive for use at ambient tempera-tures. Metals, plastics, rubber and textiles	Cotton (duck)-cotton, Rubber-rubber, Rubber (gum stock)-resin rubber, Polyvinyl chloride, (flexible)-PVC, Leather (chromic)- -leather (tan), Wood-wood, Aluminium-aluminium, Steel(mild)-steel, Polypropylene (rigid)-polypropylene, Polythene-polythene, Acrylic (sheet)-acrylic, Glass-glass
Synthetic thermo-plastic resins	1	Light brown	Strip material 100% solids 100 at 200°C	Indefinite	Machine	Applied as a melt at 200-220°C	Contact to 4	- -	General purpose edge veneering and lipping using wood vencers, plastic laminates and thermoplastic edgings	Wood Plastics (decorative laminates)

Type of adhesive & No. of components		*Colour*	*Physical form, consistency*	*Working life*	*Method of application*	*Processing*		*Service temp. range °C*	*Main uses*	*Adherends*
						Curing cycle	*Bonding pressure N/cm²*			
Thermo-plastic synthetic resins	1	White	Emulsion 16 to 17 solids content 52% w/w	Indefinite	Manual or machine	Joint assembly after 5-10 min at 20°C	14-69 cold or hot pressed	- -	Designed for usage with high speed machinery in wood bonding, lamination, etc.	Wood-wood (beech) Plastic laminate -wood Wood-wood (beech), Plastic laminate -wood (beech), Veneer-wood Plastic laminate - wood
Ethylene vinyl acetate copolymer + resins	1	Cream to yellow	Cylindri-cal solid sticks 100-120 at 195°C	6 mth at 5-25°C shelf life	Edge veneer machinery spatula	Applied as melt at 190-200°C	Contact to 20	- -	Edge veneering applications using wood, melamine laminates or polyester veneers. Maximum service temperature 70°C	Melamine laminate-plywood
Polyester	2	Brown	Liquid 10 70% w/w solids	Pot life 1 d at 20°C	Nip roller	Up to 7 d at 20° C	Contact to 4	-30 to 150	Laminations of plastics materials for electrical insulation and other purposes	Polyethylene tereph-thalate (Melinex) to Polyimide (Kapton) Cellophane Cellulose acetate Polyethylene (treated) Polypropylene (oriented) Copper foil

Type of adhesive & No. of components		*Colour*	*Physical form, consistency*	*Working life*	*Method of application*	*Processing*		*Service temp. range °C*	*Main uses*	*Adherends*
						Curing cycle	*Bonding pressure N/cm²*			
Ethylene vinyl acetate copolymer+ resins	1	Pale Yellow	Solid in film form	Indefinite 6 mth at 5-25°C	Heated nip rolls or hot iron	Film transfer at 70-80°C followed by bonding at 150-160°C	Contact to 20	60 or 1 h at 90	Metals, laminated plastics and textiles. Fabrication of leather goods. Specialised adhesive for acrylic assemblies and lamination work	Cotton (duck)-cotton Resin rubber-leather Melamine laminate-plywood, Steel (mild)-steel, Acrylic (sheet)-acrylic
Ethylene vinyl acetate copolymer+ resins	1	Cream to Yellow	Solid in cylindrical stick form 100-120 at 195°C	6 mth at 5-25°C	Edge veneering mechinery Hot spatula	Applied as a melt at 190-200°C	Contact to 20	70	Edge-veneering applications using wood, melamine laminates or polyester veneers	Cotton (duck)-plywood, Melamine laminate-plywood
Aluminium phosphate +silica filler	1	Green	Paste	20 min at 20°C	Spatula Brush	Dried 1/2 h at 20°C then 1/2 h at 70°C+ 1/2 h at 100°C+ 1 h at 250°C. Repeat for 2 over coatings and finally cure 1 h at 350°C	Contact	750°C	Strain gauge attachment to heat resistant metals. Heater element bonding	Steels (low alloy) Iron Brass Titanium Copper Aluminium

Type of adhesive & No. of components		*Colour*	*Physical form, consistency*	*Working life*	*Method of application*	*Processing*		*Service temp. range °C*	*Main uses*	*Adherends*
						Curing cycle	*Bonding pressure N/cm²*			
Inorganic	1	- -	Paste	20 min at 20°C	Brush	Dried for 1/2 h at 77°C and cured 1/2 h at 100° C + 1 h at 200°C+ 1 h at 250°C. Post cured 1 h at 350°C	Contact	816	Strain gauges, temperature sensors for elevated temperature work	Metals
Ceramic based	1	- -	Paste	Up to 24 h at 20°C	Spatula	24 h at 20°C to 2 h at 400°C	Contact	400	Chrome-nickel alloy strain gauges for elevated temperatures	Metals Concrete
Silicate	1	Off White	Fine gained paste	Indefinite	Spatula Trowel	Sets on heating	Contact	Up to 1650	Jointing of insulating bricks. Protective surface coating for refractories	Alumina Magnesia Brickwork Asbestos
Silicate	1	Off White	Very soft paste Bulk density is 1970 kg/m³	Indefinite	Brush	Sets in 8 h at 20°C on drying	Contact	10 to 430	Lagging asbestos cloth on high temperature insulation. Dense thermal insulations such as amosite, magnesia and asbestos block, to porous surfaces	Asbestos Magnesia

Type of adhesive & No. of components		*Colour*	*Physical form, consistency*	*Working life*	*Method of application*	*Processing*		*Service temp. range °C*	*Main uses*	*Adherends*
						Curing cycle	*Bonding pressure N/cm²*			
Sodium silicate with filler	1	White	Paste	Indefinite	Dip coat Spatula Spray gun	Dried at 80°C before heat exposure	Contact	0-1000	High temperature applications involving jointing, sealing embedding, and repair of heat resistant and other materials	Glass, Ceramics, Asbestos, Wood, Fibrous materials-paper board, Metals
Silicate with china clay filler	1	White	Paste	Indefinite	Brush Trowel Spray gun	Dried at 80°C before exposure to heat	Contact	-180 to 1500	General purpose cement for bonding refractory materials and metals. Furnace repairs and gas tight jointing of pipework. Heat insulating materials	Asbestos Ceramics Brickwork Glass Silver Aluminium Steel (mild)-steel
Sodium Silicate	1	White	Liquid 0.5 at 20°C 43.2% w/w solids	Indefinite	Brush	Dried at 20-80°C before exposure to heat	Contact	0 to 850	Close grained cellulosic board bonding. Metal foil to paper laminating	Aluminium (foil) Paper
Sodium Silicate+ china clay filler (25% w/w)	1	White	High viscosity, thixotropic liquid 0.25-1.2 at 20°C	Indefinite	Brush	Dried at 20-80°C before exposure to heat	Contact	0 to 850	Insulation materials to steel pipes and tanks	Glass fibre Steel

Type of adhesive & No. of components		Colour	Physical form, consistency	Working life	Method of application	Processing: Curing cycle	Processing: Bonding pressure N/cm^2	Service temp. range °C	Main uses	Adherends
Bitumen/ latex emulsion	1	Brown black	Liquid	15-30 min open time at 20°C	Trowel Spreader	Dried in air to a tacky state	Contact to 7	0 to 66	Light weight thermal insulation boards, and preformed sections to porous and non-porous surfaces. Building applications	Cork Polystyrene(foam) Polyvinyl chloride Concrete Asbestos
Latex	1	White	Low-medium viscosity liquid	- -	Brush Machine	Air dried 15 min and contact bonded	Contact to 7	65	Bonding plastics porous materials. Carpet bonding. Automobile trim work	Polyvinyl chloride (rigid) Nitrocellulose Plywood Hardboard Fabrics
Synthetic latex-resin in aqueous media	1	Yellow	Liquid 50% w/w solids	Indefinite	Trowel	Sets by drying 40-60 min drying period	Contact to 4	-15 to 75	Bonding tile materials for interior flooring applications	Linoleum Cork, PVC Concrete, Timber
Natural rubber latex	1	White to clear when curred	Ammoniacal aqueous solution of low viscosity. pH exceeds 10	Indefinite	Brush Roller Machine Stencil	Dried at room temp.	Contact to 4	- -	For self-seal bonding of cartons and paper. Rapid assembly adhesive for carton stencilling machines in packaging industry. Envelopes and stationery applications.	Paper board materials

Type of adhesive & No. of components		Colour	Physical form, consistency	Working life	Method of application	Processing		Service temp. range °C	Main uses	Adherends
						Curing cycle	Bonding pressure N/cm^2			
Natural rubber-resin in mixed hydrocarbon solvent with filler additive	1	Black	Liquid, Solids content 65% w/w	Open time 20-30 min	Brush Roller Trowel	Dried to touch dry state and bonded. Porous materials are amenable to 'wet' assembly	Contact to 4	-50 to 70	General purpose adhesive for porous and non-porous materials	Wood Cork Metals Linoleum Felt
Natural rubber	2	Light Brown	- -	- -	Brush	Air dried 20 min at 20°C and heat cured 5 min at 140°C	Contact	- -	Vulcanising cement for rubber bonding to textiles and rubbers	Rubber (styrene-butadiene) Rubber (latex) Aluminium Cardboard Leather Cotton
Rubber latex-casein	1	White	Thick paste	- -	Brush Roller machine	Air dried	Contact	- -	General purpose adhesive for labelling and combining work with metals and plastics	Wood, Textiles, Parchment, Varnished surfaces
Rubber latex-acry-lonitrile blend	1	Off White	Paste	5-8 min at 20°C	Spreader	Contact bonded when wet	Contact	- -	Bonding vinyl plastics to floor surfaces	Polyvinylchloride Wood Concrete Asphalt Plaster

Type of adhesive & No. of components		*Colour*	*Physical form, consistency*	*Working life*	*Method of application*	*Processing*		*Service temp. range °C*	*Main uses*	*Adherends*
						Curing cycle	*Bonding pressure N/cm²*			
Rubber latex	1	White	Liquid	Several hours at 20°C	Brush Spreader	Air drying within 15 min	Contact	- -	Bonding textiles, papers, packaging materials. Carpet bonding	Canvas, Paper, Fabrics, Cellulosic materials
Styrene-butadiene rubber latices	1	Light Brown	Medium viscosity	15-25 min at 20°C	Brush Trowel Roller coater	Air drying	Contact	- -	Bonding poly-styrene foams to porous surfaces	Polystyrene(foam) Wood Hardboard Asbestos Brickwork
- -	1	White	Semi-liquid	Indefinite	Spatula application of warm liquid at 90°C	Sets on air drying	Contact	- -	China, ceramics, pottery, glass carpets, leather	- -
Natural rubber in petroleum	1	Pale Cream	8-10 at 20°C	Tacky in 5-15 min	Brush Scraper	Contact bonding after drying at 20°C for 15 min	Contact to 20	- -	Bonding plastic insulation tiles to plaster, masonry. Natural and synthetic foams, metals	Rubber, Concrete, Wood Linoleum, Polyurethane (foam), Leather, Fabrics Chipboard
Reclaim natural rubber in petroleum	1	Black	37.5-60 at 20°C	Tacky in 15-30 min	Stiff brush of scraper	Contact bonded after drying at 20°C for 20 min	Contact to 20	- -	General purpose rubber cement	Plaster Aluminium Hardboard Latex (foam) Polyurethane (") Polystyrene (") Rubber, Wood

Type of adhesive & No. of components		Colour	Physical form, consistency	Working life	Method of application	Processing		Service temp. range °C	Main uses	Adherends
						Curing cycle	Bonding pressure N/cm^2			
Chlorinated rubber	1	Light tan	Liquid	15 min at 20°C	Brush	- -	Contact	- -	Priming solution for cold setting or heat curing in conjunction with neoprene or nitrile cements	Wood Metals Rubber
Acrylo-nitrile rubber+ phenolic resin	1	Brown	- -	1 h at 25°C	Brush	Dry for 1 h at 20°C or 20 min at 90°C then cured at 150°C for 25 min	90 to 140	150	General purpose adhesive	Steel (mild)-rubber, Wood-rubber, Cement-polyvinyl, chloride (rigid), Wood-leather, Steel-leather, Wood-cork, Steel-cork, Aluminium alloy-phenolic laminate, Aluminium alloy-polyester/ glass fibre, Steel (mild)-polyvinyl chloride Steel (mild)-polyvinyl chloride Copper (foil)-phenolic laminate Steel (mild)-wood (oak)

Type of adhesive & No. of components		*Colour*	*Physical form, consistency*	*Working life*	*Method of application*	*Processing*		*Service temp. range °C*	*Main uses*	*Adherends*
						Curing cycle	*Bonding pressure N/cm²*			
Acrylo-nitrile rubber+ phenolic resin	1	Yellow Brown	Film supported on glass cloth (0.25 mm thick)	- -	Brushed primer+ press curing of film	Primer air dried 60 min at 20°C. Film cured 60 min at 175°C under pressure. Pressure released, on cooling at 50°C	130	-40 to 120	Metal bonding for structural assemblies at elevated temperatures	Aluminium(alloy)- to DTD 746
Phenoxy resin	1	White	Cylindrical pellets, $^1/_8$ in dia	Indefinite as pellets	Dissolve pellets in any common organic solvent, then brush on, or rollers, or spatula. A 'film' form can be obtained on request	Varied; 10 s at 340° 3 min at 260° or 30 min at 190°	Enough to maintain alignment only	-70 to 120	As a fast bonding material for metals, wood and paper. Also for cloths, foils etc. For pipes and automobiles too	Aluminium-aluminium Birch-birch
Epoxy-nylon	1	Silvery	100% solids, a paste	6 mth at 25°C	Spatula, spreader or very stiff brush	40 min at 121°C	Light pressure	-60 to 170	As a flexible combining with good peel properties	Aluminium-aluminium Steel-steel

Type of adhesive & No. of components		*Colour*	*Physical form, consistency*	*Working life*	*Method of application*	*Processing*		*Service temp. range °C*	*Main uses*	*Adherends*
						Curing cycle	*Bonding pressure N/cm²*			
Polyimide	1	Olive green	As a filled resin on a glass cloth i.e. a leathery consistency contains 14% volatiles	6 mth if kept below -20°C or 2 wk at R.T.	Cut out the amount required and sand-wich in joint	30 min to heat up to 280°C, then 90 min at 280°C	280	-40 to 300, but for short spells up to 350	As a high tempe-rature structural adhesive; in Bonds metals, and many other materials	Steel-steel
Epoxy/ phenolic resin+ aluminium powder filler	1	Grey	Film supported on glass cloth (0.38 mm thick)	12 d at 20°C	Press curing of film	52 N/cm² applied at 20°C; heated to 165°C in 40 min under pressure. Pressure released on cooling, at 50° C	52	-40 to 150	Metal bonding for structural applications at elevated temperatures	Aluminium(alloy) - aluminium
Phenolic formalde-hyde	1	Yellow	Paper based films (various) 60-80% resin content of thickness, 0.06-0.1 mm	Indefinite	Films sand-wiched between adherends	Film thickness dependent 3 min at 157°C to 9 min at 130°C under pressure	Up to 1600	150	Furniture manu-facture. Veneering and waterproof plywood fabrica-tion. Bonding of decorative plastic laminates to wood. Aircraft and boat-building	Polyvinyl chloride (rigid) Plastic laminates Chipboard Plywood Wood (birch)-wood

Type of adhesive & No. of components		*Colour*	*Physical form, consistency*	*Working life*	*Method of application*	*Processing*		*Service temp. range °C*	*Main uses*	*Adherends*
						Curing cycle	*Bonding pressure N/cm²*			
Melamine/ urea formaldehyde blend	1	Yellow	Paper based films (various) 75% w/w resin (0.09 mm thickness)	Indefinite	Film sandwiched between adherends	2 min at 95°C to $^1/_2$ min at 130°C	69 to 450	130	Bonding and surfacing veneers, plywood and chipboard. Plastic decorative laminate bonding	Plywood Chipboard Hardboard Plastic laminates
Resorcinol formaldehyde+ catalyst	2	Brown	Liquid	8 h at 16°C to 20 min at 38° C	Brush Spatula Mechanical spreader	Cured at 16°C to 80°C under pressure	Contact to 70 5 min at 82°C or 4 h at 21°C or 10 h at 16°C		Constructional laminates for marine craft. Building and Timber applications. Aluminium-plywood bonding. Laminated plastics	Wood, Asbestos, Aluminium, Phenolic laminate Polystyrene(foam) Polyvinyl chloride Polyamide (rigid)
Urea formaldehyde	1	White	Powder	Curing temperature dependent	Brush Roller Spreader	9 h at 10°C to 1 h at 21°C after mixing powder with water (22%)	4-40 for 18 h at 10°C to 3 h at 21°C		Wood gluing and bonding of plastic laminates to wood. Plywood, chipboard manufacture. Boat building and timber engineering	Wood Phenoliclaminate
Melamine formaldehyde (plasticised)	1	White	Powder, added to solvent to give 0.03-0.05 solution	- -	Dipper Spreader	For laminates 135-145°C under pressure	For laminates 690 to 1030 for 18-20 min	180	Manufacture of post-forming laminates	Paper, Wood fibre boards Chipboard

Type of adhesive & No. of components		Colour	Physical form, consistency	Working life	Method of application	Processing: Curing cycle	Processing: Bonding pressure N/cm²	Service temp. range °C	Main uses	Adherends
Urea formalde-hyde+ catalyst	2	- -	Liquid 2-3 at 25°C	Pot-life varies from 10 min at 10°C to 10 h at 32°C for catalyst used	Brush Spreader Roller	Cured under pressure 10-82°C	Upto 70 Press times vary from $1\frac{1}{2}$ min at 82°C to 15 h at 10°C for catalyst used	- -	General purpose wood adhesive	Cellulosic mater. Hardboard Chipboard Plywood & vencer Timber (moisture content between 5 and 15% w/w)
Polybenz-imidiazole	1	Green	As a filled resin on a glass cloth	3 mth at RT longer if refriger-ated	Cut out the amount required and sandwich in joint	Varied, depending on area being bonded, e.g. Heat to 370°C apply pressure and leave for 3 h cool Post-cure.	Max. of 1400 Min of 400	-40 to 550, but for short spells up to 650	As a high tempera-ture structural adhesive; in aircraft, missiles, etc.	Steel-steel
Polychloro-prene	1	- -	Syrup $9.5x10^{-3}$ m^2/s at 18°C	Open time is 35 min at 20°C	Brush	Contact bonding within 35 min of drying in air. Heat reactivate 2 min at 90°C	15 s at 45	- -	Footwear manu-facture, leathers, rubbers and plastic coated fabrics	Leather (chrome)-leather Leather (chrome)-resin rubber Leather (chrome)-latex blend Leather (chrome)-rubber (SBR)

Type of adhesive & No. of components		*Colour*	*Physical form. consistency*	*Working life*	*Method of application*	*Processing*		*Service temp. range °C*	*Main uses*	*Adherends*
						Curing cycle	*Bonding pressure N/cm²*			
Polychloro-prene-resin in hydro-carbon solvent	1	Buff	Medium viscosity liquid	Tack life for one-way wet bonding 1-5 min; two-way wet bonding 5-10 min; two-way dry bonding with solvent activation 15-40 min	Brush	Sets by drying at room tempera-ture. Bonding by wet, semi-wet activation of dried coatings depending on substrate	Contact to 4	- -	Adhesives for use automobile industry Car-trim application for porous and non-porous ahderends	Steel (painted) Natural rubber Neoprene rubber Canvas PVC Wood
	1	Light Brown	Liquid 7 Solids content, 36% w/w		Brush Sticker Roller coater				1 GA 186-general purpose adhesive 1 GA 516 severe 1 GA 585 temps. up to 150°C for short periods	
Polychloro-prene-resin in hydro-carbon/ ester solvent	1	Light brown	Liquid 3 30% w/w solids		Brush Scraper Pressure equipment					
Neoprene rubber in solvent blend	1	Gold/ green	Medium viscosity syrup	Indefinite	Stiff brush or scraper	Dried for 20 min at 20°C and joint made by contact bonding	Contact to 4	- -	General purpose impact adhesive	Porous materials Leather Rubber Wood-wood Steel-steel
Chlorinated rubber in solvents	1	Light brown	9 Solids content 29.0% w/w	Open-time is 30 min	Brush Spreader	Dried at 20°C for 10 min	Contact to 4	- -	A general purpose contact adhesive joining plastics to non-metallic substrates	Polyvinyl chloride Polystyrene ABS plastics Wood Rubber (natural)

Type of adhesive & No. of components		*Colour*	*Physical form, consistency*	*Working life*	*Method of application*	*Processing*		*Service temp. range °C*	*Main uses*	*Adherends*
						Curing cycle	*Bonding pressure N/cm²*			
Polyvinyl ester in mixed ester solvent	1	Colour less	Liquid 3 35% w/w solids	Unspecified	Brush	Sets by solvent loss and optimum strength after 24 h	Contact to 4	- -	Domestic applications and purposes. Service temperature 70°C max	As for UHU Hard adhesive
Polyester resin+ catalyst	2	- -	Paste	30 min after mixing	Spatula	Cold curing in 330 min	Contact to 7	- -	Metal frames and edges to stone flooring	Aluminium Steel Concrete Ceramics
Polyester resin +hardener catalyst	3	- -	Liquid	2 h at 25°C	Spatula	60°C for 1 h and then slowly increased to 140°C and held for 1 h. Post cured for 1 h at 10°C above service temp.	Contact	170	Strain-gauges based on copper-nickel alloys	Metals
Polyester resin+ catalyst	2	- -	Liquid	20 min at 20°C	Spatula	2-3 h at 20°C to 2 h at 100°C	Contact	180	Strain gauges based on copper-nickel alloys with polyester or cellulosic carrier material	Metals Polyesters Wood

Type of adhesive & No. of components		Colour	Physical form, consistency	Working life	Method of application	Processing: Curing cycle	Processing: Bonding pressure N/cm^2	Service temp. range °C	Main uses	Adherends
poly-sulphide rubber in ketone solvent and catalyst	2	Buff	Thixotropic paste 88% solids	2-3 h at 25°C	Extruder gun Brush Spatula	3 d at 25°C	- -	-50 to 130 With stands higher temps for short periods	Sealant for fuel tanks and pressur-ised cabins in aircraft, where good weather-proof and water-proof properties are required	Metals
Poly-urethane	2	Black	Liquid 31000 cps	47 min	Spatula Trowel	24 h at 25°C	Contact	120	Repair of rubber rolls, hoses, belting, casting and caulking. Metal bonding	Iron Steel Aluminium Wood Rubber Glass Canvas
Poly-urethane	2	Black	Liquid 2400 cps	30 min	Spatula Trowel	24 h at 25°C	Contact	94	As above	As above
Poly-urethane	2	Black	Liquid 3000 cps	25 min	Spatula Trowel	24 h at 25°C	Contact	66	As above	As above
Polyure-thane in hydro-carbon solvent	2	Brown	Liquid 0.33 23% w/w solids	Pot life 8-16 h	Brush Roller coater	3-7 d at 20°C	Contact	Up to 100	Bonding plastics materials and fabrics when high heat resistance is required	Nylon (fabrics) PVC Polyurethane foam

Type of adhesive & No. of components		Colour	Physical form, consistency	Working life	Method of application	Processing		Service temp. range °C	Main uses	Adherends
						Curing cycle	Bonding pressure N/cm²			
Poly-urethane +catalyst	2	Black	25	5 h at 24°C	Spatula Extrusion gun	5 d at 24°C to 6 h at 82°C	Contact to 20	-62 to 149 For short per-iods, 204	Applications requiring flexible, cold flow resistant rubber with good electrical properties. Metals, rubbers and plastics	- - PR1527 (cured)-aluminium PR1527 (cured)-cadmium PR1527 (cured)-Neoprene PR1527 (cured)-polyvinyl chloride
Polyvinyl acetate maleate copolymers in ethanol	1	White	7-11 at 25°C 55% w/w solids	Indefinite	Brush	- -	- -	- -	Lamination of plastic films to metal foils	Polyurethane (fm) Polystyrene Polyester (film) Cellulose acetate Polyvinyl chloride (foam) Aluminium (foil) Fabric Aluminium (foil)-aluminium
Polyvinyl acetate emulsion with plasticiser	1	White	Liquid with 50% solids content	Indefinite	Spatula Trowel	24 h at 20°C	Contact to 4	- -	General building industry requirements	Porous materials, concrete wood-wood (beech)

Type of adhesive & No. of components		*Colour*	*Physical form, consistency*	*Working life*	*Method of application*	*Processing*		*Service temp. range °C*	*Main uses*	*Adherends*
						Curing cycle	*Bonding pressure N/cm^2*			
Polyvinyl acetate	1	White	Emulsion 51% w/w solids	Open time 5 min at 20°C	Brush Spreader	Sets by drying. Optimum strength 12-24 h at 20°C	Contact to 4	-20 to 70	General purpose adhesive for gluing variety of substrates in building and other trades	Wood Concrete Plastics Metals Asbestos
Polyvinyl acetate	1	White to clear when cured	Aqueous emulsion of high viscosity pH = 4--5		Brush Roller	Wet assembly and pressure until set within few hours at room temp.	20-35	- -	General woodwork, assembly and veneering with wood and plastic laminates	Wood, Chipboard materials, Melamine laminate
Polyvinyl acetate	2	Pale pink	Liquid 8-10 at 25°C Solids content 57±1%	Shelf life is 3 mth at 20°C. Usable life is 24 h at 20°C	Brush Spreader	1 h at 20°C to 30 min at 30°C or hot pressed for 1.5 min at 95°C to 0.5 min at 115°C	34-120	- -	Wood gluing of cabinets, doors, furniture	Wood (moisture content between 5 and 15%)
Polyvinyl acetate+ catalyst	1	White	Liquid 4 at 20°C 48% w/w solids	24 h at 20°C	Brush Spreader	Cold press 20-40 min at 20°C or Hot press 1-10 min at 65-150°C	10-20 or 70 for hot cure	100	Wood gluing. Decorative laminate bonding	Timber (with water content less than 12% w/w) Wood (birch, pine, fir) Plywood

Type of adhesive & No. of components		Colour	Physical form, consistency	Working life	Method of application	Processing: Curing cycle	Processing: Bonding pressure N/cm²	Service temp. range °C	Main uses	Adherends
Poly-urethane in solvent +2% catalyst	1	Trans-parent	Liquid	10 d at 20°C	Brush	Dried in air 1 h at 20°C then heat activated 40s at 85°C	55	60	Vinyl plastics to porous materials for footwear manufacture	Fabrics Rubber Leather (chrome)-polyvinyl chloride
Poly-urethane in solvent +catalyst	2	White	Liquid	45 min at 20°C	Brush	Dried in air 1 h at 20°C and cured 24 h at 20°C to 1 h at 80°C	Contact	70	Bonding to metals, rubbers and synthetic textiles. Protective coating lacquer	Aluminium Polyamide textiles (nylon) Polyurethane coated fabrics
Poly-sulphide polymer+ catalyst	2	Alum-inium	Liquid 1.3	2 h at 24°C and 50% relative humidity	Spatula Extrusion gun	72 h at 24°C or Heat cure up to 48°C	Contact	-54 to 107	Applications requiring tough rubber adhesive/ sealant with good weathering properties up to 3 year	Aluminium, Cadmium, Acrylics, PR 340 (cured)-aluminium, Aluminium -aluminium
Poly-sulphide polymer+ catalyst	2	Tan	Medium viscisity liquid 93% w/w solids	90 min at 25°C	Spatula Extrusion gun	24 h at 25°C	Contact	-54 to 82	Bonding and sealing of low voltage electrical equipment against moisture and corrosive agents. Aircraft	- -

Type of adhesive & No. of components		Colour	Physical form, consistency	Working life	Method of application	Processing: Curing cycle	Processing: Bonding pressure N/cm^2	Service temp. range °C	Main uses	Adherends
Silicone rubber	1	White	Paste	Tack-free time is less than 1 h at 20°C	Spatula Dispenser pack Mastic gun	Exposure to airr. 0.6 mm films cure in 90 min 3 mm films cure in 24 h	Contact	-75 to 250	Flexible heat stable bonds between metals, ceramics, plastics, wood, etc. Repairing silicone rubber moulds. Electrical and electronic equipment. Furnace and refrigerator doors. Plastic pipe bonding	Metals (tinned and galvanised) Polychloroprene, PVC (primed) Acrylics, Ceramics, Glass, Epoxide resins, Polystyrene, Wood (oak), Aluminium-. aluminium, Steel (mild)-steel Copper-copper
Silicone rubber	1	Red	Paste 250	Tack-free time, 15-30 min	Cartridge pack, Dispenser, Dipping Spraying Spatula	Exposure to air. 3 mm films cure in 24 h. 0.3 mm films may be heat cured at 120°C	Contact	-60 to 250	Flexible heat stable elastomeric adhesive and sealing agent. Electronic component bonding and caulking. Coating cloth for anti-stick surface, conveyor belting. Repair of wire and cable insulation. Hot air ducting assembly	Steel Aluminium Copper, Brass Tinplate Glass Wood Phenolic resins Polyester resins Polyamide Nitrite rubber Polychloroprene Silicone rubber Concrete

Type of adhesive & No. of components		*Colour*	*Physical form, consistency*	*Working life*	*Method of application*	*Processing*		*Service temp. range °C*	*Main uses*	*Adherends*
						Curing cycle	*Bonding pressure N/cm²*			
Silicon resin in xylene	1	Trans-lucent	70-150	Indefinite	Brush	5 min at 150°C (cata-lysed) or solvent loss at 94°C to tacky state	Contact	-73 to 290	Used primarily for manufacture of pressure sensitive tapes with wide variety of backing materials. High temperature electrical insulation moisture and corrosion resistant wrappings	Glass cloth (either plain or silicone varnished) Silicone rubbers Polyethylene terephthalate PTFE Polyimide Aluminium foil
Silicone rubber	1	Black	Uncured rubber. No sag or flow	<1/2 h Tack-free time	Spatula Trowel	24 h at 20°C (20% R.H.) Full cure in 5 d	Contact	-65 to 260	General purpose bonding and sealing application. Adheres to metals, glass, ceramics, painted surfaces. Adhesive/sealant for situation where material expected to support suspended weight. High pressure exposure conditions	Aluminium Titanium Steel (stainless) Glass Cork, phenolic bonded, Silicone rubber Cured rubber-aluminium Cured rubber-titanium Cured rubber-steel (stainless) Aluminium-alum. (2024 Alclad) Cork-cork (phenolic bonded)

Type of adhesive & No. of components		Colour	Physical form, consistency	Working life	Method of application	Processing		Service temp. range °C	Main uses	Adherends
						Curing cycle	Bonding pressure N/cm^2			
Silicone rubber	1	Trans-lucent	Non-sag Uncured rubber	<1 h Tack-free time	Spatula. Extrusion from capsule	72 h at 20°C for 20% R.H.	Contact	-66 to 230	Adhesive/sealant for metals, glass, natural and synthetic fibres. Sealant for oven doors; bonding gaskets in heating and refrigerating units, insulation	Silicone rubber-silicone rubber, Silicone rubber-fluorosilicone rubber, Silicone rubber-neopren, Silicone rubber-glass, cloth, Silicone rubber-steel (stainless), Silicone rubber-aluminium, Silicone rubber-copper, Silicone rubber-PTFE, Silicone rubber-aluminium
Silicone rubber	1	Trans-lucent	Self-levelling rubber 35	Tack-free in 30 min at 20°C	Brush Spray Extruder gun	Cures on exposure to air at 20°C in 24 h	Contact	-65 to 150	Thin film rubber coating of electrical and electronic components	Steel (20 mesh screen) - copper, Steel (20 mesh screen) - alumin., Steel (20 mesh screen) - glass Steel (20 m.s.) - acrylic (rigid) Steel (20 m.s.) - steel (stainless) Steel (20 m.s.)-aluminium

Type of adhesive & No. of components		*Colour*	*Physical form, consistency*	*Working life*	*Method of application*	*Processing*		*Service temp. range °C*	*Main uses*	*Adherends*
						Curing cycle	*Bonding pressure N/cm^2*			
Starch	1	White	Paste 9 at 20°C 29% w/w solids	- -	Brush Machine	Dries at 90-150°C	- -	100	Aluminium foil laminating Packaging industry	Aluminium (foil) Paper Cardboard
Synthetic rubber latices+ synthetic resin with inorganic fillers	1	Off White	Stiff cream 54-58% w/w solids in water	30 min at 20°C	Spreader Trowel	Contact bonding within 15-30 min	Contact	7 to 60	Covering and panelling of expanded poly-styrene parts to vertical and horizontal absor-bent surfaces	Cement Hardboard Plaster Polystyrene (foam) - wood Polystyrene (foam) - concrete
Synthetic rubber latices+ synthetic resin with inorganic fillers	1	Off White	Stiff cream 54-58% w/w solids in water	30 min at 20°C	Spreader Trowel	Contact bonding within 15-30 min	Contact	7 to 60	Covering and panelling of expanded poly-styrene parts to vertical and hori-zontal absorbent surfaces	Cement Hardboard , Plaster Polystyrene (foam) - wood Polystyrene (foam) - concrete
Synthetic resin/ rubber latex with inorganic fillers	1	Off White	25-40 at 20-30°C 40% w/w solids	15-25 min at 20°C	Spreader Trowel	Contact bonding within 15-30 min	Contact	7 to 50	Bonding flooring materials	Linoleum Asphalt Cement Hardboard PVC flooring - wood/concrete PVC flooring - wood/concrete

Type of adhesive & No. of components		Colour	Physical form, consistency	Working life	Method of application	Processing: Curing cycle	Processing: Bonding pressure N/cm^2	Service temp. range °C	Main uses	Adherends
Rubber/ resin in petroleum	1	Black	Thick liquid	Tack free time is 30 min	Brush Spray gun Extruder Trowel	Contact bonding after air drying	Contact to 4	-47 to 71	General purpose adhesive for porous and non-porous materials	Rubber Cork Linoleum Felt Wood Aluminium
Rubber/ resin in hydro-carbon solvent	1	Dark Brown	Medium viscosity liquid	Tack free time is 15 min	Brush Trowel Spray gun	Contact bonding after air drying	Contact to 4	-18 to 100	General purpose bonding - as above	As above
Synthetic rubber/ resin in ketone solvent+ catalyst	1	Trans-parent	Medium viscosity liquid 31+2% solids	8 h at 20°C	Brush	Dried 10 min at 20°C and cured 3 d at 20°C or 16 h at 70°C	Contact to 20	-5 to 100	Used in vacuum covering process of wide range of articles such as cases, cabinets, automotive components	Wood, Canvas, Acrylonitrile rubber, Polyvinyl chloride (rigid, flexible), Polyamide, Glass, ABS plastics, Polystyrene (rigid)
Synthetic rubber/ resin in ketone solvent	1	Trans-parent	- -	Tack free time of dry film is 20 min	Brush Extruder Roller coater	Dried 10 min at 20°C and contact bonded	Contact to 7	-5 to 32	Bonding plastic foams, laminate sheets, and porous materials. Motor car headlining materials	Polyurethane (foam), Polyvinyl chloride (foam)

Type of adhesive & No. of components		*Colour*	*Physical form, consistency*	*Working life*	*Method of application*	*Processing*		*Service temp. range °C*	*Main uses*	*Adherends*
						Curing cycle	*Bonding pressure N/cm²*			
Synthetic rubber	1	Trans-parent	medium viscosity liquid	- -	Brush	Air dried 15 min at 20°C	Contact	- -	Pressure sensitive adhesive for labelling. Auto-motive trim work. Laminating of packaging films	Polythene (film) Paper Metals
Synthetic rubber	1	Golden Brown	Heavy syrup	2-40 min at 20°C	Brush	Air dried up to 40 min at 20°C	Contact	- -	Bonding laminated plastics to metals and rigid materials. Decorative plastics	Polyester (lamin.) Wood Metal (painted, unpainted) Concrete
Synthetic polymer	1	Yellow to brown	Liquid 25% w/w solids	Open time 3 min at 20°C	Brush	Air dried 1-3 min at 20°C and contact bonded	Contact	155	Bonding foam insulation to metals and painted surfaces for elevated temperature use	Polyurethane (foam) - metal
Polystyrene in solvents	1	Clear	10 Solids content 33.5% w/w	Open time indefinite (minutes at 20°C)	Brush	Wet bonded and allowed to set at room temp.	Contact to 4	- -	Bonding poly-styrene to itself and porous substrates. Insulating lacquer and coating for electrical components such as capacitors, coils, cables	Polystyrene (film)

Type of adhesive & No. of components		Colour	Physical form, consistency	Working life	Method of application	Processing: Curing cycle	Processing: Bonding pressure N/cm^2	Service temp. range °C	Main uses	Adherends
Synthetic rubber/ resin in ester solvent	1	Off White	Medium viscosity liquid	Indefinite	Brush Spray gun	Dried 1 h at 50-70°C & cured for 4 h at 100°C to 5 min at 250°C under pressure	Up to 110	-50 to 250	Bonding brake linings to metal shoes in automotive industry	Asbestos (rigid) Steel
Synthetic rubber/ resin in alcohol	1	Amber	Thin liquid	Indefinite	Brush	Dried 1 h at 27°C and cured 20 min at 141°C	Contact to 20	-40 to 300	Fabrication of hot air ductings for aircraft conditioning units. Metals, plastic sheets	Steel Aluminium Polyvinyl butyral (sheet) Glass cloth
Polyester resins+ catalyst+ filler	3	Grey	Slurry to paste according to filler content	15 min at 20°C	Trowel Spreader	Cold setting in 25 min at 4-27°C according to grade	Contact	- -	Jointing applications in building and civil engineering Bonding pre-cast concrete and setting in dowel bars and bolts	Concrete Brickwork Timber Steel Asbestos
Phenolic-polyvinyl formal	2	White powder+ transparent liquid	Liquid with powder	30 min drying period. Prepared substrates can be stored for 3 d before assembly	Brush or roller to apply liquid. Wet substrate is then dipped into powder	Cured for 30 min at 150±5°C Pressure removed when joints cooled to 70°C	17 to 70 depends on substrate	Up to 120	Bonding metals, alloys, wood, thermosetting plastics, friction materials, rubbers in aircraft and industrial applications	Aluminium/alloy Steel, Wood Magnesium/alloy Natural rubbers Polychloroprene Steel-steel (mild) Steel (stainless), Titanium, Alclad-Alclad.

35

TEST METHODS AND STANDARDS

There are a number of general factors that require consideration in the evaluation of an adhesive pertaining to the behaviour of an adhesive from the time it is made to the moment the ultimate bond is accomplished. They are commonly referred to as the working properties and include such characteristics as viscosity or consistency, storage life, working life, coverage, blocking, tack, penetration and curing rate or rate of strength development. Their importance becomes apparent when one seeks to obtain the same adhesive from batch to batch with respect to its physical properties and application. Several standard test methods are available for obtaining this information. Unless otherwise specified, the atmospheric conditions surrounding the specimen prior to an during the test shall be 73.5 + 2° F and 50 + 4% relative humidity.

Consistency (viscosity)

Adhesive materials are not simple fluids. In general they consist of polymers, usually in solvents and often compounded with powders of various physical or chemical properties. It is not surprising therefore that adhesive materials do not exhibit Newtonian flow and the characterization of the rheological properties of adhesives requires more than one measurement. To characterize fully the rheological properties of a non-Newtonian adhesive for practical purposes, it may be necessary to plot curves of strain rate vs shear stress and thixotropic shear stress vs time, in addition to accumulating a family of curves at various temperatures and degrees of cure. Obviously, except for special circumstances, this procedure would be too time consuming and costly when many adhesive materials are involved. Instead, devices which are flexible in their operation and adaptable to a wide variety of measurements are used.

There are a number of test methods available for evaluating the flow properties of adhesives. ASTM test method D-2556 describes the apparent viscosity of adhesives having shear rate dependent flow properties. The principle of measurement is based on reversible isothermal change in apparent visocsity with change in rate of shear. Measurement is performed is performed with a spindle, disk, T-bar or coaxial cylinder rotational viscometres under standardized conditions with rigid control of time intevals of measurement.

ASTM test method D-1084 is intended for determining the viscosity of freeflowing adhesives. Four methods are covered of which the first is applicable only to adhesives that will deliver 50 ml in the steady uninterrupted stream in from 30 to 100 sec. at standard conditions. The apparatus consists of a set of four consistency cups, each having an orifice of one of four diameters ranging from 0.07 to 0.25 in. Consisting of a Brookfield viscometer, the second method is ranging from 50 to 200,000 cp. The third method is intended primarily as a control method for determining the consistency of adhesives which have or approach Newtonian flow characteristics. The apparatus consists of a Stormer viscometer with a double flag paddle-type rotor actuated by a falling weight. This method is limited, however, to self-levelling adhesives thereby eliminating thixotropic and plastic materials, the viscosity of which is a function of rate of stirring and previous history of the adhesive. The fourth method is intended for determining the viscosity of materials which have an equivalent viscosity no greater then 3000 cp. The apparatus consists of a set of live Zahn cups so designed to allow a sample to flow through a calibrated orifice in approximately one min or less.

Storage Life

When an adhesive is stored for a considerable length of time under extreme temperature conditions, physical and chemical changes may occur. Storage life of an adhesive is the time during which an adhesive can be stored, preferably under controlled conditions and remain suitable for use. ASTM method D-1337 provides a means for determining the storage life of an adhesive. This is realized by requiring the measurement of either the consistency of an adhesive or the bond strength, or both, before and after storage at a specified temperature and for various periods of time. The adhesive and all of its compounts, if there are any, are stored in their original and unopened containers.

Some adhesives may be seemingly impaired by exposure to low temperature but can be restored to satisfactory service by slight warming and agitation. Some solvent based adhesives, for example, separate at temperatures 0 to 5^0 C but can be reconstituted by stirring at room temperature. The undesirable effects of low temperature are not limited to water-based adhesives. Although adhesives may be apparently unaffected by being frozen and thawad once, they may be effected by repeated cycling.

Often it may be impractical to conduct extensive room temperature storage tests. The only alternative is to conduct the test at elevated temperatures.

Accordingly, it is not uncommon to expose adhesives to a temperature of about 40° C for 30 days. Although an accelerated test of this nature will shorten the storage life test from 6 months or a year to 30 days or so, it may also cause changes in the adhesive which may not occur at room temperature. Generally, it is advisable that the adhesive be stored at a temperature close to actual service conditions and the time when changes in the adhesive occur be observed. To determine these changes both the consistancy test and bond strength test should be periodically conducted.

Working Life

The working life of an adhesive is the time elapsing between the moment an adhesive is ready for use and the time when the adhesive is no longer usable. Pot life is another term commonly used for working life. ASTM method D-1338 covers two procedures applicable to all adhesives having a relatively short working life. This method purports to determine whether the working life conforms to the minimum specified working life required of an adhesive by determining the change in consistency or bond strength or by both. The method applies to self contained liquid or paste adhesives, to adhesives requiring addition of a catalyst, hardener, filler, thinner, etc. or combinations of two or more of these materials just prior to use, as well as to powdered or flaked adhesives which are dissolved in water or other solvents and are used as liquid or paste adhesives.

Coverage

Coverage is that property of an adhesive which determines the extent to which an adhesive can be uniformly spread over an area to be bonded with an unit weight or volume of adhesive. Two ASTM methods exist. D-898 describes a procedure for determining the quantity of adhesive solids applied in a spreading or coating operation, whereas D-899 describes a procedure for determining the quantity of liquid adhesive applied in a spreading or coating operation. The amount of spreading or coating weight is expressed in pounds per thousand square feet of surface area to be bonded and is the solvent-free gross weight of the adhesive on the surface, whether resulting from a single spread, double spread (spread on both contacting surfaces) or multiple applications of adhesives.

Blocking

Blocking is the undesirable adhesion between touching layers of similar or dissimilar materials such as that which occurs under moderae pressure or during storage. In some applications, adhesives are applied to one or both of the surfaces to be bonded and stored until ready for use or assembly.

It is essential that the coated surfaces do not bond or block during storage even if subjected to slight contact pressure or minor variations in humidity or temperature. Adhesives will block in various degrees, from none at all to complete bonding. Invariably impairment of the adhesive will occur when an attempt is made to separate memebers which have completely bonded.

ASTM method D-1146 is intended for determining the blocking point of a coating of potentially adhesive material i.e. those materials is substantially nonadhesive state which may be activated to an adhesive state by application of heat or solvents. Since some potentially adhesive materials are both thermoplastic and hygroscopic, this method provides means for estimating both thermoplastic and hygroscopic blocking since some requirement are more strict than other. Two varying degrees of blocking are defined. First degree blocking is an adherence between surfaces under test to such an extent that when the upper specimen is lifted, the lower specimen will cling thereto but may be parted with no evidence of damage to either surface. Second degree blocking is an adherence between surfaces to such an extent that when the surfaces under test are parted, one surface or the other will be found to be damaged. The two types are referred to as cohesive and adhesive blocking, the former being blocking between two similar, potentially adhesive faces and the latter being the blocking of a potentially face and a standard test surface.

Tack

Tack is that characteristic of an adhesive which causes one surface coated with an adhesive to adhere to another on contact. Essentially it is the stickiness of an adhesive. An adhesive having this characteristics to a high degree is spoken of as having quick tack or an aggressive tack: moreover, it is one of the most important properties in determining the suitability of an adhesive for particular applications. Associated with tack are dry tack, which is the property of certain adhesives to adhere on contact to themselves, at a stage in the evaporation of volatile constituents even though they seem dry to the touch and tack range, which is the period of time in which an adhesive will remain in the dry tack condition. The measured value of tack may vary with time, temperature and film thickness.

Many tackmeters have been produced over the years. Tackmeters dependent on metal contacting a rubber surface have mainly the concern of manufacturers of adhesive tapes. Tackmeters which are concerned with rubber-to-rubber contact have been of interest to rubber technologists and particularly of interest to the tyre manufacturing industry.

Penetration

The control of adhesive penetration into porous materials is important to manufacturers of asphalt laminated kraft paper, multi-layer corrugated board, fibreboard, grocery bags and multi-wall shipping bags. The foremost requirement for an adhesive is to wet or intimately contact both surfaces to be bonded. An adhesive which penetrates far below the surface of the material being coated contributes nothing to the bonding of two materials and is wasted. When excessive substrate penetration occurs, adhesive costs are increased; further more, a starved glue line or adhesive layer may result and a wet or soggy product may be obtained which could lead to warpage, reduced production speeds and processing delays.

ASTM Method D-1916 is intended for the determination of penetration under pressure of an adhesive where at least one of the adherends is porous. It is particularly adaptable to use with starch or starch base adhesives commonly used in the paper converting industry. The method consists of applying a measured quantity of adhesive, normally 0.1 ml, to the centre of the bottom end of a hammer and 30 sec. after the adhesive is applied, the hammer is released allowing it to fall freely onto five disks of filter paper, stacked one on top of another and located on an anvil at the bottom of the tube.

After the assembly is removed from the press, each sheet of filter paper is examined for depth of penetration. As an aid in detecting the presence of adhesive on each of the papers, special techniques are used, such as an iodine staining solution for use with starch adhesives or phenolphthalein solution for silicate and other alkaine adhesives being evaluated.

Curing rate

Many adhesives require curing by either the application of heat or the addition of catalyst, or both, with or without pressure for specified periods of time. Since it is often desirable to know the variation in bond strength with rate of cure. ASTM has issued a recommended practice, D-1144, which provides a means of determining the rate of strength development of adhesive bonds when cured at time intervals of 2/5, 3/5, 4/5 and 1 1/5 the time prescribed by the adhesive manufactures. The specimen used for determining the strength properties of the adhesive bonds may be either the tensile specimen (D-897) or the lap shear specimen (D-1002).

Evaluation of the chemical, physical and other characteristics of adhesives helps in predicting the performance and reliability of an adhesive bond. Testing provides a measure of quality control of the adhesive material, adequacy of the bond formed, acceptability against specifications and other criteria of economic importance.

Perhaps more than most other classes of materials, evaluation of adhesives requires specialised test methods. In testing, not only is the adhesive material evaluated but also the bonding technique which includes preparation of the surface, application of the adhesive and the curing of the adhesive.

The accuracy and reproducibility of test results will depdend on the conditions under which the bonding process is performed. Before starting any evaluation the individual conducting the tests should have complete information on each of the following variables.

1. Procedure for preparing the surfaces prior to application of the adhesive, including the moisture content of wood, the cleaning and drying of metal surfaces and special surface treatmants.

2. Complete mixing directions for the adhesive.

3. Conditions for applications of the adhesive, including the rate of spreading, thick of film, number of coats to be applied, whether to be applied to one or both surfaces and the conditions of drying where than one coat is required.

4. Assembly conditions before application of pressure, including the room temperature, per cent relative humidity and whether there should be any open or closed assembly time.

5. Curing conditions, including the amount of pressure to be applied, the length of time under pressure and the temperature of the assembly when under pressure. It is should be known whether this temperature is that of the glue line or of the atmosphere at which the assembly is to be maintained.

6. Conditions procedure before testing, unless a standard procedure is specified, including the length of time, temperature and relative humidity.

Strength Properties

Specialised testing methods are required for the evaluation of the strength properties of adhesives. In addition to joint strength determination these methods provides a means for checking the effcacy of the processes used to make the bonds. The joint strength is invariable dependent on bonding technique factors such as adhesive application, adherend pretreatment and the adhesive curing conditions. Bonding conditions also determine the reproducibility of test results and complete information on a number of variables is, therefore, necessary before undertaking an adhesive evaluation. The following particulars are essential for the fabrication of reliable test specimens.

1. Instructions for the preparation of the adhesives.
2. Adherend surface pretreatment procedures recommended for the adhesive under consideration.
3. Adhesive application and processing before bonding.
4. Manufacturers specified conditions for joint assembly.
5. Adhesive curing conditions relating to bonding temperatures, pressures and times.

Test specimens required to give reproducible failing strength need to be carefully designed and prepared; unsatisfactory bonds will result from the faulty execution of any stage in the assembly process. Most of the standard test methods employ test specimens of definite shape and size which have to be machined to specified tolerances. Most methods specify the number of specimens to be tested in order to obtain a reliable result because testing factors and slight differences between adhesive batches prepared under identical conditions lead to joint strength variations. Ten or more specimens may be required to give meaningful data. The equipment used for testing is important and will influence the reliability of strength values obtained. Some variations in the performance between machines of the same type are to be expected. Often, test machine accuracy is greatest over a limited working range of the loading capacity (usually 10-90%) and test specimens should fail at loads within this span. The rate at which test specimens are stressed is another factor influencing the strength values obtained for adhesive bonds. Standard test methods generally specify the testing rate although it may be better to adopt a rate which more closely resembles the stressing rate that an actual assembly is likely to experience.

The data obtained from test methods is useful for comparing the performance of several adhesives prior to the selection of one for a particular assembly job. It must be emphasised that the test specimen rarely simulates the actual configuration of an assembly and that the data cannot therefore be relied upon the predict the performance of the assembly in service. The same limitation applies to test specimens removed from an assembly; these are unlikely to represent the behaviour of the whole structure. Short of testing an assembly under service conditions it is necessary to adopt a test specimen and method which simulate the assembly and its working environment as closely as is practicable. The testing procedure finally employed must produce results that are likely to show a good correlation with the results that would be obtained in tests on assemblies. In this respect, selected standard test procedures are frequently employable without modifications.

Summary of strength properties and tests

Strength property	Test specification	Adherend materails
Shear	ASTM D1002-64	Rigid materials such as metals wood, reinforced plastics
Shear	ASTM D906-47 BS 1203: 1954	Plywood
Shear	ASTM D905-49	Wood & similar materials
Tensile	ASTM D897-49	Wood, metals
Tensile & rubber		Metals to metal
Tensile		
Tensile	ASTM D2095-62T	
Impact	ASTM 950-54	Metals, wood
Cleavage	ASTM D1062-51	Rigid materials such as metals. reinforced plastic, hard woods. Unsuitable for flexible extensive adherends
Shear		Rigid materials

Strength property	Test specification	Adherend materails
Peel	ASTM D903-49	Flexible materials fastened to rigid or flexible materials. Plastics, rubbers fabrics, leather etc. to thermselves or metals, wood, glass
Peel	ASTM D1876-61T	Materials slightly less flexible than those employed for 180 peeling. Plastic rubber composities, leather metal foils
Peel	ASTM D 773-47	Rubber from metal or glass plates
Peel	ASTM D1781-62	Laminated material having a member flexible enough to bend over the drum and resistant to peeling forces. Metal laminates. honeycomb sandwich structure where the core is bounded by metal skins
Flexural	ASTM D1184	Laminates based on metals, wood. reinforced plastic. Honeycomb sandwich Structures sandwich the core is bonded by metal skins

Tensile Strength

An adhesive is in tensile loading when the acting forces are applied perpendicularly to the plane of the adhesive. The tensile strength of an adhesive bond is the maximum tensile load per uniarea required to break the bond. It is expressed in psi or kg/cm2. ASTM method D-897 is intended for determining the comparative tensile properties of adhesives when tested in standard shape specimens and under defined conditions of pretreatment, temperature and testing machine speed. The mothod described spool-type specimens for both wood-to-wood and metal-to-metal adhesives. The test specimens are similar in shape except that in order to minimize the probability of wood failure, the bond area is reduced proportionally to the cross-sectional area of the adjacent wood. The specimen is loaded by means of two-U shaped grips which fit over the annular boss at the end of each half of the specimen.

Either the wood or metal specimen can be adopted for determining the tensile strength of adhesives between dissimilar materials and this is readily accomplished by interposing the dissimilar materials between the two adherends. Thus by applying adhesive to both sides of a thin material such as rubber, plastic, leather, or glass and sandwiching it between the two wood or metal adherends the bond strength of two different materials can be determined. This technique is particularly advantageous when one of the materials to be bonded cannot be used as an adherends either because of lack of strength e.g. rubber, or a material difficult to machine such as glass.

A variation of the sandwich specimen for dissimilar materials just described is a specimen for determining the bond strength between two low strength or difficult to machine materials. Thus, for example, by bonding a 1 in. square of glass cut from a microscope slide to one metal adherend and a thin sheet of rubber to the other metal adherend, bond strength determinations can be obtained for glass-to-rubber adhesives, the only limitation is that the bonds between the glass and metal and between the rubber and metal be greater than the adhesive bond between the glass and rubber. Similarly, tensile bond strengths between glass-to-glass, plastic-to-plastic, rubber-to-rubber etc. can be determined.

One major difficulty arises with the spool type tensile specimens. Cleavage is introduced in testing the specimen, which results in substantially lower strengths. However, when a nonrigid or low modulus adhesive is used, the difference between the spool type and the centre-loaded specimens is not large.

ASTM method D-1344 describes cross lap specimens for determining the tensile properties of adhesives. The test was especially designed for the adhesion of glass either to itself or to other materials. The glass block (1 by 1 1/2 by 1/2 in) is easily cut from plate glass; the cross-lap consists of two glass blocks assembled at right angles to provide a 1 sq. in. of bonded area. Self-aligning grips holding at the extending edges of each block pull the specimen apart in testing. The maximum tensile load is expressed in pounds per sq. in.

Shear Strength

Shear stresses are those forces which act in the plance of the adhesive layer and reflect the total stress exerted by the adherends along the adhesive plane which tend to slide the adherends in opposite directions. A pure shear stress acutally cannot be attained with specimens commonly used in adhesive tests, but since pure shear stress is rarely encountered in adhesive assemblies, conventional test specimens are adequate for most purposes. The shear strength of metal-to-metal adhesives is determined by ASTM method D-1002. This method is intended for determining the comparative shear strengths of adhesives for bonding metals when tested on a standard specimen and under specified conditions of preparation and testing.

The recommended length of overlap for most metals of 1.62 mm (0.064 in) in thickness is 12.7 + 0.25 mm (0.5 +0.01 in). The maximum permissible length of overlap between metal strips may be computed from the following relationship;

$L = Fty\ t/r$

where,

L = length of overlap (in).

Fty = yield point of metal (for stress at proportional limit). psi

t = thickness of metal, in. and

r = 150% of the estimated average shear strength in adhesive bond, psi.

This formula also may be used some nonmetallic adherends where the yield point of the material will permit its use. It is underirable to exceed the yield point of the adherend in tension testing. A variation in thickness of the metal and the length of overlap will influence the test value and make direct comparison of data questionable.

Bond strength of lap shear specimens are directly proportional to the width of the specimen, but as the length of overlap increases, the unit strength decreases dur to stress concentration at the edges of the overlap.

In lap specimens an optimum film thickness exists. Bond strength will decrease when films are very thin or thick. For maximum bond strength the optimum will very with adhesives of diffierent moduli. The thickness varies from about 0.05 mm for high modulus materials to 0.15 mm for low modulus materials.

Lap shear specimens can be used for determining the shear strength of dissimilar materials in a manner similar to that which was presented for the tensile specimens. Thin and inherently weak materials such as plastics, leather and fabrics are sandwiched between the metal adherends and tested. It is important to maintain the thickness of the overlap to a minimum in order to reduce deflection in the specimen during testing.

Wood-to-wood specimens are tested in shear by tensile loading in a plywood construction as outlined in ASTM method D-906.

Shear strength of adhesives can be determined also by compression loading, rather than tensile loading. ASTM method D-905 describes a standard specimen for determining the compression shear strengths of adhesives for wood and other similar materials. An adhesive will demonstrate higher bond strengths when tested in compression shear specimens than when using tensile lap shear specimens. The higher bond strength is ascribed to better strees distribution.

Peel Strength

The peel test involves the stripping of a flexible member of an assembly that has been bonded with an adhesive to another member that may be flexible or rigid. For example, cloth bonded to cloth or cloth bonded to metal may be tested in peel. The test consists of pulling the flexible member at an angle of 90 or 180 so as to induce peeling. Failure may occur in the flexible member, in the adhesive, or in the rigid member. The 180 test for peel or stripping strength of adhesives is described in ASTM method D-903 and strength is expressed in pounds per square inch of width.

The stress distribution in a peel test are complex and the force required to initiate and maintain stripping is influenced by the width of the specimen, the mechanical properties of the adherends and the strength of the adhesive. In testing the flexible adherend is bent sharply (180) on itself causing deformation as its yield point is exceeded and resulting in undue stresses in the exposed adhesive layer. A small change in adhesive strength or thickness of adherend will result in a large variation of the peel force. For this reason the avarage force over a 5 or 6 in. length pull is taken area as an indication of the feel strength. An alternate method is to calculate the under the stress vs distance curve as a measure of the work done or the strength of the bond.

Another precaution is necessary in the 180 peel test. The flexible member is rubbed on itself as the test is performed. To reduce the friction created, a suitable fluid may be used such as oil, glycerin or soap solution, provided it does not deleteriously affect the adherends or the bond. When the flexible member is a porous material such as cloth, the thickness of the adhesive layer and the degree of penetration of the adhesive into the cloth are difficult to control. This is another source of variation in peel strength. When one considers all the conditions which require careful control, it becomes apparent that the peel test is a very sensitive method for the determination of bond strength.

The T-peel test is a frequently used test because of the simple configuration of the test specimen and its ease of fabrication. The T-peel test is defined in ASTM method D-1876. The objective of the test is to determine the relative peel resistance of an adhesive bond between two flexible adherends. The specimens are 1 in. wide and 12 in. long but bonded only over 9 in. of their length. The test is performed on a standard tensile testing machine and readings are reported directly as pounds per linear inch.

Another peel test is the climbing drum test used extensively in the airplane industry for determining the peel resistance of adhesive bonds between metal facings and sandwich cores and between metal laminates when one member is flexible. The test apparatus cosists of a 2 in. flanged drum with flexible loading straps and suitable clamps for holding the test specimen. This test is described in ASTM D-1781. It should be noted that the results obtained from this test include the torque required to break the bond and to bend the flexible member. The average peel torque is reported in inch pounds per inch width of specimen.

A recently developed ASTM recommended practice, D-2918 makes use of a T-peel specimen of assessing the durability of adhesive joints while being exposed to any desired exposure medium e.g. air, water, aqueous solutions or relative humidity at various temperatures. The apparatus used in this test method is portable and self-contained. It can be exposed outdoors or placed in an environmental chamber.

Impact Strength

The standard method of evaluating the impact strength of adhesive is described in ASTM method D-950. The specimen consists of two blocks, which may be made of wood or metal, bonded together. In testing, the lower and larger block is held in the vice like grip of the machine and the upper block is struck by a pendulam hammer traveling at a velocity of 11 ft/sec. and in direction parallel to the plane of the adhesive layer. The impact energy absorbed by absorbed by the specimen is reported in foot-pounds per sq.in.

The shear impact specimen has been found to give reproducible values and it is quite generally used despite one limitation. Frequently the bond at the moment of failure actually is being stressed in cleavage, with the back of the specimen being lifted. Impact strengths increase with film thickness over a range of 0.25 to 0.75 mm. This was ascribed to the greater deformability of the heavier films.

The impact strength of adhesives may also be tested in tension. Several types of specimen can be used, of which a modified spool-type specimen (D-897) is the most generally employed. Another common specimen is the butt-jointed rods with gripping ears at the extreme ends.

Cleavage Test

The cleavage test is conducted by introducing a prying force at one end of a bonded specimen to split the bond apart. A suitable cleavage test is described in ASTM method D-1062. The test specimen is pulled apart by tensile loading and the cleavage strength is specified in terms of pounds per inch of width. Specimens are ordinarly made of metal, but other rigid materials can be employed as well. With low modulus adhesives, a lap length of 1 in. is sufficient. The stress distribution in a cleavage test is complex and the forces required both to initiate and continue separation are considerably influenced by the dimensions of the specimen, the mechanical properties of the adherends as well as the strength and elastic characterising of the adhesive.

Creep Test

The deformation or dimensional change occurring in an adhesive-bonded specimen under stress and over a period of time is referred to as creep. It is customary to determine creep by subjecting a bonded specimen to a constant load for a given period of time and at a specified temperature. The length of time for conducting such as test depends on the properties of the adhesive and the service requirements for which it is being evaluated. Thermoplastic adhesives may be tested for weeks or months until either failure occurs, or the test is terminated after a specific amount of deformation. Creep performed at room temperature is usually referred to as cold flow.

Periodically it is desirable to determine the rate of creep, in which case the dimensional change occurring in a bonded specimen is determined regularly during the length of the test. Usually the test is performed at various temperatures because the effect of temperature on creep is appreciable. Bonds made with rigid thermosetting adhesives possess no creep or negligible creep under strees. Highly plasticized adhesives are more apt to creep than rigid adhesives.

By unloading the specimen and allowing it to remain unstressed one can determine the amount of relaxation or recoverability of an adhesive. Direct numerical correlation between creep and relaxation is not available; therefore, relaxation design of adhesive bonds is not yet on a sound basis.

ASTM test method D-2293 determine the creep properties of adhesives in shear by compression loading and D-2293 determines the creep properties of adhesives in shear by tension loading. Both methods made use of metal to-metal specimens similar in description to the lap shear specimen described in ASTM D-1002. The apparatus in both methods permits testing the specimen over a wide temperature range and stress conditions. Creep is determined by observing the displacement of five razor scratches across the centres of both sides of the lap joints with a calibrated microscope.

Fatigue Test

The repeated application of a given load or deformation imposed on an adhesive specimen, which is known as fatigue testing, is a measure of the ability of an adhesive specimen to resist failure. This test does not measure mechanical properties such as elastic modulus or damping characteristics; furthermore, it may be used for comparing the behaviour of bonded assemblies under repeated loading and for evaluating the effects of environmental conditions on the ability of a specimen to withstand repeated loading without failure.

A variety of fatigue testing machines have been developed for determining the fatigue endurance limits of materials, of which several types may be used for adhesive specimens. In these machines a suitable specimen is held in such a manner that a cyclic axial load is applied or an alternating bending stress is applied. Since fatigue life is known to be dependent on frequency, amplitude, temperature and mode of stressing as well as the magnitude of the stress, these varigables must be controlled and specified. An adequate fatigue strength test is described in Method 1061 of Federal Test Method Standard No. 175.

Loads are selected such that failure occurs within a range varying from at least 5000 cycles to not more then 10 million cycles. A cyclic axial load is applied and the maximum rate of cyclic loading is 3600 cycles per minute. Although the standard lap shear specimen given in ASTM method D-1002 is generally used for fatigue testing, other bonded specimens may be used. Some may require modification for suitability in fatigue testing. The number of cycles to failure and the corresponding loads, calculated in psi are recorded and plotted on stress-log cycles coordinates. The point at which a smooth curve connecting the points of minimum stress crosses the 10 million cycle ordinate is referred to as the fatigue strength.

Flexural loading Shear Strength

ASTM method D-1184 is intended for determining the shear strength of adhesive bonded strips (8 strips of 0.01 in. thick) of metal or wood by testing as a simple beam loaded at mid span. The span-to-depth ratio is 8:1. The maximum shear stress is developed at the neutral surface approximately midway between the top and bottom of the specimen, therefore, delamination or failure will occur in the centre layer of adhesive.

The shear strengths obtained by this method are usually much higher than the values obtained with lap shear specimens (D-1002) or with compressive loaded blocks shear specimens (D-905). The reason for this is that substantial compressive stresses normal to the adhesive layer exist which increase the resistance of the adhesive to failure by shear.

Nondestructive Tests

One principal difficulty associated with mechanical testing of adhesive bonds has been that the structure (or specimen) is destroyed in tests made to determine its properties. The advantage of nondestructive testing is that complete inspection of bonded assemblies can be made. The ultimate strength of bonds cannot be measured by nondestructive techniques; however, some useful properties such as the dynamic elastic, viscous or complex moduli, as well as dielectric constants can be measured nondestructively. The dynamic moduli and dielectric constants may be used to differentiate between bonds of high and low tensile strength; thus they can be used to determine the deteriorating effect of prolonged heating. There is no standard test method at present. The problem is not the need for new methods or techniques, but that the present methods need more research and improvement. Nondestructive testing of adhesive bonds is realistic and in the near future will be mandatory by absolute necessity, especially for the entire aerospace industry.

Permanence of bond

No test or series of tests is known to exist which will accurately foretell the service life of an adhesive bond. There are, however, a number of tests which may be used to measure the effects of various destructive or deteriorating influences, thereby helping to ascertain which adhesives will survive best under various conditions. Oxidation, water, oils, chemicals, sunlight, mold and temperature changes are factors which can be measured, thus giving definite indications that an adhesive will be satisfactory for specific periods under controlled conditions. Strength tests with any of the test specimens described in the previous section can reveal quantitative changes. The selection of the test specimen will depend on the information being sought.

Chemical Factors

Chemical factors may affect the permanence of an adhesive bond in the ways that chemicals affect the properties of the adhesive or the adherend and the adhesive may react and affect the adherend. The resistance of adhesives to chemical reagents may be determined by exposing films of adhesives or by exposing bonded specimens to a chemical environment. The exposed films can be used to determine qualitative effects only; whereas strength tests on the bonded specimens will yield quantitative data.

ASTM method D-896 described certain standard reagents in which strength test specimens are soaked for 7 days at room temperature. The most commonly encountered reagents are water, sea water, oil, gasoline and hydraulic fluid. The concentration of the reagent is important because some adhesives may be resistant to diluted reagents and vulnerable when exposed to the concentrated form of the reagent; however, the degree of deterioration may not be proportional to the concentration.

An adhesive bond can be affected by chemical reagents in other ways. External chemical reagents may attack an adhesive bond by action on the adherend, e.g. when glass assemblies are in contact with water, the glass may hydrate and cause adhesive failure. Some adhesives may be affected by chemical constituents contained n the adherends. For instance, vinyl compounds or rubber compositions may contain plasticizer which will migrate to the adhesive-adherend interface and cause loss of adhesion. Similarly, plasticizer in the adhesive may affect the bond by migration to the adhesive-adherend interface, Plasticizer or other ingredients of the adhesive may cause crazing in plastic adherends. A simple test can be used to determine whether crazing in acrylic plastics will occur, i.e. an adhesive is applied to a stressed specimen of an acrylic under controlled atmospheric conditions. After 4 days the specimen is examined for crazing.

Service life

Expectancy of an adhesive can be determined by exposing test specimens for specified periods of time to all the conditions which the bonded assembly would be expected to enounter in service. Tests of this nature are usually long, often impractical and sometimes impossible. There are some tests which can be utilized for judging and predicting the performance of a bonded assembly under various predetermined conditions, of which typical tests consist of exposure to light, water, salt spray, bacterial attack etc. Judicious care must be expercised in using these test methods, e.g. light may have little effect on adhesive specimens which are protected by light-impervious adherends such as metal. Light, however, is an important factor with glass and other transparent or translucent materials. ASTM method D-904 provides a means for determining the effect of artificial and natural light on the premanence of adhesive assemblies. ASTM method D-1828 provides a means for the uniform operation of an accelerated weathering apparatus which exposes specimens to intermitted light and water spray. However, considerable research has shown that laboratory artificial weathering tests do not give consistently good correlation with outdoor exposure tests.

The extent of deterioration can be measured quantitatively by determining the change in bond strength of exposed specimens using any of the standard specimens such as the tensile specimen (D-897), the peel specimen (D-903), or the lap shear specimen (D-1002).

Salt spray tests are usuful for evaluating specimens which are intended for use in coastal areas or which are to be shipped overseas. A standard salt spray atmosphere test is described in ASTM method B-117 for exposing specimens in a salt spray apparatus.

Exposure to an atmosphere of high ozone concentrations can have a deteriorating effect on adhesive specimens. A standard test method for ozone resistance is not available; however, it is the general practive to expose adhesive films on specimens to ozone concentrations of up to 50 parts per hundred million in air. Deterioration is known to occur more rapidly when the specimens are stressed during exposure.

Long-term exposure of test specimens to actual weathering is generally considered to be a reliable indication of the durability and premanence of the bond. Unfortunately, such serive information is often difficult or impossible to interpret accurately because specimens are subjected to uncontrolled exposure and wide variations over extended periods of time. In fact, results may not be repeatable due to natures varying behaviour from time to time. Also results in one locality may be different from those obtained elsewhere; nevertheless, exterior weatherings represents a useful service type test. A continued program of supervised and properly recorded service testing is an important requirement to more adequately understand the durability of adhesive bonding, since the results of such a program would be expected to serve as a standard for correlation with all other durability tests.

Accelerated test procedures whereby the time of exposure is reduced from years and months to days and hours are highly desirable to both the adhesive manufacturer and the consumer. Obviously, the reliability of accelerated tests is dependent on the degree of correlating that can be established with long term service tests and on the degree to which they adequately simulate the pertinent factors influencing durability of the adhesive bond.

Under laboratory conditions the Weatherometer is commonly used to expose materials to various cycling weather conditions. The cycle which consists of a combination of simulated rain, sunlight and dry heat serves to provide information in a comparatively short time for general evaluation and study. The Weatherometer can be used for testing bonded assemblies of dissimilar adherends to determine the variation in stress and endurance caused by the differing coefficients of thermal expansions. Cyclic testing, which should also include a study of the effects of extremes of temperature on the durability of the adhesive bond, can be adapted to evaluate wood bonds. Wood is susceptible to dimensional change with variations in moisture content depending on the surrounding atmosphere. ASTM method D-1183 contains a group of cyclic tests of varying severity for evaluating the resistance of wood adhesives. High and low temperatures as well as high and low relative humidities under laboratory conditions are specified. The extent of deterioration is ascertained from the change in strength properties of plywood shear specimens (ASTM 906) as a result of exposure to the test conditions.

A test method for determining the quality of adhesive bonds in laminated wood products when subjected to continuous exposure at specified conditions of moisture and temperature is presented in ASTM method D-1151. The performance is expressed as a percentage based on the ratio of strength retained after exposure to the original strength.

At elevated temperature a number of changes may take place which can affect the adherends as well as the adhesives, thus influencing bond. The adhesive or the adherend may decompose at elevated temperatures. Long exposure to moderately high temperatures may cause changes in degree of polymerization of the adhesive physical as well as chemical change, which may occur, can result in stresses at the adhesive-adhered interface which will influence the bond strength; moreover, these reactions can occur in days, weeks, or years. The best tests for evaluating the permanence of bonds are those which reflect service temperatures. Exposure tests conducted at temperatures substantially higher must be considered on a comparative basis rather than an absolute one.

Whatever test method is employed, it must be recognised that no accelerated procedure for determining deterioration of a bond corrlates perfectly with actual service conditions and that no single or small group of laboratory test conditions will simulate all actual service conditions. Consequently care must be exercised in the interpretation and use of data obtained in tests.

Biological Stability

Adhesives composed of dextrin, soybeen, casein or protein etc. may be subject to attack by mold, fungi and bacteria as well as by rodents and insects. Accelerated mold tests can be quite useful in evaluating the performance of casein and soybean adhesives in adhesives in plywood under mold conditions and that they appeared to correlate well with long term exposures at high relative humidities. The accelerated mold tests consisted of impregnating birch veneers with a diluted casein adhesive and inoculating them with mold organisms. Plywood shear specimens were made an maintained in a closed chamber over water at 22 to 26^0 C. Significant losses in bond strength were observed after 14 days of incubation. Since this early work, standard laboratory methods have been developed to determine the effect of these deteriorating agents on the the strength of bonds. The tests appear to be useful also in evaluating the relative effectiveness of preservatives for protein adhesives.

ASTM method D-1286 is intended for evaluating the effect of mold contamination on the permanence of adhesive preparations by determining the change in viscosity of adhesives and the comparative bond strengths of contaminated and uncontaminated specimens when tested under defined conditions. The organisms used are Aspergillus niger. A. flavus and Penicillium luteum, the incubation period is 28 days with weekly inspection.

ASTM method D-1174 is intended for evaluating the effect of bacterial contamination on the permanence of adhesive preparations and bonds as determined for the mold contamination test just described. The organisms used are Pseudomonas fluorescens, Bacillus subtillis and Proteus vulgaris and the incubation period is 28 days with weekly inspection.

ASTM method D-1338 describes a procedure for evaluating the susceptibility of dry adhesive films to attack by laboratory bred, starved, white, male rats. Danage is determined by calculating the per cent destruction (weight loss) of the test specimen. Comparison is made between adhesive-impregnated filter paper and blank filter paper.

ASTM method D-1382 describes a procedure for determining te extent to which adhesive impregnated filter paper, compared to blanks, is damaged by starved male and female Periplaneta americana roaches. As in the previous test with rodents, damage is determined by calculating the per cent weight loss of test specimens.

Radiatino Test

Polystyrenes are resistant to radiation showing less than 50% reduction in shear, impact and tensile strengths after exposure of 3 x 10^{10} rad. Polymethyl methacrylate, on the other hand, shows 50% reduction in shear and impact strength after only 10^8 rad rad exposure and a 50% reduction in tensile strength after 5 x 10^7 rad exposure.

An acrylonitrile rubber phenolic and a vinyl phenolic adhesive have usable properties after exposure up to 10^9 roentgens. An epoxy can withstand temperatures up to 250^0 C and gamma dosages up to 10^9 roentgens.

ASTM recommended practice, D-1879 is available defining conditions for exposure of polymeric adhesives in bonded specimens to high energy radiation by gamma or X-ray radiation, electron or beta radiation, neutrons and mixtures of these, such as reactor radiation. Procedures are described for exposure at ambient conditions, controlled temperatures in a medium other than air and under load.

Durability Test

The specimens described previously may be used to determine the effects of various adverse environments on an adhesive bond although no single test (or series) exists which will enable the user to predict its service life. A suitable test will provide information on the permanence of the bond when it is exposed to deteriorating circumstances such as temperature changes leading to oxidation, thermal degradation or softening of the adhesive. Other destructive hazards include low temperatures, sunlight and radiation water, chemical reagents, oils and biodeterioration. Test specimens and procedures should be selected to simulate the type of service conditions envisage for the bonded assembly. Consideration must be given to the adherend material for certain tests e.g. for the evaluation of the acid resistance of an adhesive, certain metals would be unsutable as adherends. Some of the environments which often provide the basis for unfavourable long term conditions of exposure for adhesive bonds are discussed here.

Temperature Resistance

Adhesives and adherends are affected by high, low and varying temperatures. Elevated temperatures may decompose adhesive materials by oxidation or thermal degradation. Long exposure to moderate temperatures often leads to polymerisation changes in adhesives. Displacement of bonded surfaces occurs whether high or low temperatures accentuate differences between the thermal coefficients of expansion for adherends and adhesives; stresses and set up at the interface which influence bond strength. Low temperatures embrittle many adhesives causing a reduction in their peel and cleavage strength.

Test chembers with heating or cooling units can be employed or environmental simulation. Adhesive durability is best determined at the service temperature; higher test temperatures should be regarded for their comparative value only. Destructive temperature effects may become apparent in hours or years.

Weathering Test

The long term ageing or weathering properties of bonded structures are difficult to predict since there are no standard short term permanence tests. Actual long time weathering is usually a reliable guide to adheisve durability although variations in exposure conditions over long test periods can make data difficult to interpret. Rainfall, humidity and temperature vary widely with locatity. Acceterated weathering tests designed to reduce the long exposure periods are useful if the results can be correlated with actual weathering. Several tests have been adopted in the UK for providing a uniform testing procedure for military equipment. Referred to as ISAT (Internsified Standard Automating Trials), these tests are claimed to be equivalent to prolonged storage under clamined to be equivalent to prolonged storage under existent weather conditions. A typical cycle test representative of 9 wk, continual tropical storage is the following.

ISAT Series B Cycle

46^0 C, 95% R.H. 2 days then 60^0 C 60% R.H. 1 day afterwards cooled to ambient temperature 1 day after that 75^0 C without moisture addition 8 hours. The samples are then cooled to ambient temperature kept for 16 hours; 46^0 C 95% R.H. 1 day; Cooled to ambient temperature 1 day.

The 1 week cycle is repeated as often as desired. Other cyclic tests have been developed which incorporate temperatrue, sunlight and moisture changes. One such cyclic which resembles weather cycling without the duplication of any specific weather cycle is described here.

Light, corresponding to sunlight, 2 hours, Rain 5 min; dry heat at 38^0 C to complete 24 h cycle.

Many factors influence test results and these must be assessed before testing. Adherends, adhesive and exposure period need to be appraised before cyclic tesing. Thus, thick porous adherends may require longer exposures than thin ones where moisture absorption is the adhesive hazard. For metal adherends the adhesive layer may not be exposed to moisture, a cyclic test involving moisture would be of dubious value.

Chemical Resistance

The permanence of a bond may be affected by exposure to external chemical agents or by the latent chemical mreactivity of the adhesive for an adherend.

Several tests have been specified to evaluate adhesive bond strength on exposure to reagents such as acids, alkalies, water, sea water, petrol organic solvents and lubricating oils. The deterioration in adhesion is sometimes dependent on reagen concentration. Temperature adn exposure period should also be considered as test factors. Other tests are concerned with the effects atmospheric constituents which are known to cause adhesive deteroration, e.g. salt spray or ozone.

Chemical constituents in the adherends, such as plasticizers, can migrate into the adhesive an destroy adhesion. Additionally the byproducts of an adhesive curing reaction may attack the adhered at the interface and cause loss of adhesion.

Visual inspection

The appearance of the bond and whether there is sufficiently of adhesive at the joint edges, or between adherends (transparent), determines its adequacy. The technique might include spot checks with a micrometer on glue-line thickness over a bonded area. More recently, photoelastic properties of adhesives and joints have been studied by observing stress patterns in transparent bonds with polarised light. Variations in the colour pattern producted by liquid cholesterol crystals on a substrate are dependent on the heat transmission properties of the joint. Certain areas correspond to deficiency of adhesive and may be detected visually.

36

SUPPLIERS OF PLANT, EQUIPMENTS AND MACHINERY

BOILERS

D. N. Reddy, MD
A P MOTRONIX PVT LTD
3-18-3, Pragathi Nagar,
Ramanthapur, Hyderabad-500013,
Andhra Pradesh
Phone: 040-27038560
27031929
Email: apmotronix@satyam.net.in

Saz Boilers
Plot No. 44, Swami Vivekanand Indl. Estate, Sasane Nagar,
Hadapsar, Pune - 411028,
Maharashtra, INDIA
Tel. No.: + 91-20-26970840,
Telefax: + 91-20-26970420
Mobile: + 91 - 98220 36995
Email: response@sazboilers.com,
sales@sazboilers.com
Visit Also: www.sazboilers.com,
www.sazboilers.in
www.steamboilersindia.com,
www.thermalfluidheaters.net
www.sazboilers.co.in, www.hotwater-generators.com

A V U Engineers Pvt Ltd
K. C. Rana, MD
A-15, A.P.I.E., Balanagar,
Hyderabad-500037,
Andhra Pradesh
Phone: +91 40 237 73235
+91 40 237 72343
Email: avuhyderabad@rediffmail.com

EVAPORATORS

Airfrige Industries
Mr. Harmeet Singh (Dir)
10/65, Kirti Nagar Indl. Area
New Delhi-110015
Phone: 011-25931909
011-25931972
011-25927219
Email: airfrige@vsnl.com;
afi@del3.vsnl.net.in

Anmas Ahlstrom Ltd
S. Muthaiah,
Executive Personal Officers
304 - 305, IV Floor,
Guna Buildging,
Anna Salai, Teynampet
Chennai-600018,
Tamil Nadu
Phone: +91 44 24338050
24338051
Email: eal@md2.vsnl.net.in

FILLING & SEALING MACHINE

Authentic Designers
Address:No. E-138, Sector-63
Noida - 201 301,
Uttar Pradesh, (India)
Mobile: +(91)-9811272160
9810179173
Phone: +(91)-(120) 4331071
+(91)-(120) 4227713
E-mail : authentic_pooja@rediffmail.com,
authenticdesigners@rediffmail.com

Swastik Systems & Services
A-12, Gali No. 3, Hardev Puri,
100 Feet Road,
Shahdara, New Delhi - 110093,
Delhi, India
Mobile: +(91)-9810895623
Phone: +(91)-(11)-22819019
+(91)-(11)-65374623
Fax: +(91)-(11)-22801664
+(91)-(11)-22819019
Email: info@weighingsystems.in
dayanand.swastiksystems@gmail.com

MIXER/BLENDERS

Renders
Mr. Dinesh Katkar (Director)
Survey No. 232/2,
Atlas Metal Compound,
Opposite Rupee Bank,
Near Elca Lab,
Nashik-Pune Road, Bhosari,
Pune - 411039,
Maharashtra, India
Mobile: +(91)-9822026536
+(91)-9552536955
+(91)-9689863411
phone: +(91)-(20)-27110227

Darshini Engineers
Mr. Prabhudas R. Aghera (CEO)
Plot No. 5227/A, Vatva
Ahmedabad - 382445, Gujarat, India
Mobile: +(91)-9375040318
+(91)-9825901490
Phone: +(91)-(79)-65436946
+(91)-(79)-65456412
Fax: +(91)-(79)-25840556

STORAGE TANKS

Suresh Steel Industries, Mumbai
Farida House, 1st Floor,
Office No. 8, 2nd Panjarapole Lane,
No. 59/61,
C. P. Tank Road,
Mumbai,
Maharashtra - 400 004, India
Phone: +(91)-(22)-66362114
+(91)-(22)-22405460
Fax: +(91)-(22)-22405460
Mobile: +(91)-9833881192
Website: www.steelrailing.in/

Shitla Road Equipment
Address: No. 359, G. I. D. C.,
Dediyasan, Behind Sarvodaya Bank,
Mehsana, Gujarat - 384 001, India
Phone: +(91)-(2762)-224482
+(91)-(2762)-224060
Fax: +(91)-(2762)-224771
Mobile: +(91)-9825308838
9825031838
Website:
www.asphaltdrummixplantindia.com
asphalt-drum-mix-plant.html

Ravi Kiran Industries
Address: No. 213, Mittal Estate,
No. 2,
Marol Naka, Andheri East,
Mumbai,
Maharashtra - 400 059, India
Phone: +(91)-(22)-28506569
+(91)-(22)-28597856
Fax: +(91)-(22)-28506135
Mobile: +(91)-9820478893

STIRRERS

Star Scientific Glass Co.
Mr. Pratham Kaushik
(Export Manager)
E 22, Sardar Estate, Ajwa Road
Vadodara - 390019, Gujarat, India

Mobile: +(91)-9825027834
+(91)-9428402583
Phone: +(91)-(265)-2563472
+(91)-(265)-2563474
+(91)-(265)-2512473
Fax: +(91)-(265)-2514417
Email: info@starscientificindia.com
exports@starscientificindia.com

Teleflo India Private Limited

Mr. Sampath . (Owner)
No. 3, 1st Floor, Uday Building, 70-D, MDS Marg, Chembur (East)
Mumbai - 400071,
Maharashtra, India
Mobile: +(91)-9819626265
+(91)-9821027547
Phone: +(91)-(22)-25285345
+(91)-(22)-25280073
+(91)-(22)-32518991
Fax: +(91)-(22)-25280642

37

SUPPLIERS OF RAW MATERIALS

ACETONE

Shree Sai Chemicals
Mr. Nilesh Mallik (Proprietor)
Plot No. 4793, Near 2nd Water Tank, GIDC,
Ankleshwar, Ankleshwar - 393002, Gujarat, India
Mobile: +(91)-9879245058
+(91)-9974183115

Krishna Chemtech
Mr. Arvind Gevariya (Proprietor)
Office- 205, Shyamal Building, Koninoor Road,
Mini Bazar, Varachha Road,
Surat - 395006, Gujarat, India
Mobile: +(91)-9879655109
Email: krishnachemtech@yahoo.com

ACETIC ACID

Patel Trading
Mr. Mahesh Patel (Proprietor)
C/4, Madhuram Estate,
Behind T. C. I. Transport,
Sachin Palsana Road,
Pardi Kande, Sachin
Surat - 394230, Gujarat, India
Mobile: +(91)-9687613766
+(91)-9825113766
+(91)-9879607428
Phone: +(91)-(261)-6533766

Arihant Chemical
Mr. Nimesh Shah
No. 102, Nahar Complex, First Floor above Amber Hotel, N H No. 8, G.I.D.C.
Vapi - 396195, Gujarat, India
Mobile: +(91)-9825148189
+(91)-9662548189
Phone: +(91)-(260)-2423152
+(91)-(260)-2430849

ACTIVATED CARBON

Air Care Equipments
Dreams Aakruti, C-102, Plot No-1,
Sr. No.-52, Kalepadad,
Near Dhere Concrete Company, Hadapsar,
Pune, Maharashtra - 411 028, India
Phone: +(91)-(20)-24345758
Fax: +(91)-(20)-24345758
Mobile: +(91)-9823050371
9420174854
Website: www.aircarepune.com/

Hindustan Produce Company
No. 7, Clyde Row, Hastings, Kolkata,
West Bengal - 700 022, India

Phone: +(91)-(33)-22230828
+(91)-(33)-22230110
Fax: +(91)-(33)-22230140
Mobile: +(91)-9831484682
Website: www.hindustanproduceco.co petroleum-coke-graphite-powder-flakes-activated-carbon.html

CAUSTIC SODA

B. K. Chemicals
B - 2, Shrushti Apartment, 1st Floor,
Near Century Enka, Colony No. 2,
Pune - Nasik Highway, Bhosari,
Pune, Maharashtra - 411 039,
India
Fax: +(91)-(20)-27111941
Mobile: +(91)-9371020040
+(91)-9881418345
Website: www.bkchemicals.in
industrial-chemicals-powder.html

Triveni Chemicals
No. 135, Pancharatna Char Rasta,
G. I. D. C., Vapi,
Gujarat - 396 195, India
Phone: +(91)-(260)-6618618
Fax: +(91)-(260)-6618624
Mobile: +(91)-9227788155
Website: www.trivenichemical.com
chemicals-by-alphabet-c.html

BENZENE

Shivam Industries, Mumbai
Mr. Chandan Ganguly (CEO)
Shop No. 11,
Arihant Vrindavan Society,
Kasturi Park,
Navghar Road,
Bhayander East
Mumbai - 401105, Maharashtra, India
Mobile: +(91)-9820823043
+(91)-9819991694
Phone: +(91)-(22)-28152328
+(91)-(22)-28152309

Solvo Chem
Mr. Tushar Vora / Nimesh Vora
(Owner)
C- 2/ A/10, Phase-1,
GIDC, Vatva
Ahmedabad - 382445,
Gujarat, India
Mobile: +(91)-9825035989
+(91)-9825479300
Phone: +(91)-(79)-25831940
+(91)-(79)-25831941
Fax: +(91)-(79)-25894700

BUTYL ACETATE

Organo Chem (India)
Mr. Gyanendra K. Vaish (C.E.O.)
G-375-376, Phase-II, M.G. Road,
UPSIDC Industrial Area
Ghaziabad - 201005,
Uttar Pradesh, India
Mobile: +(91)-9810846377
+(91)-8459110412
+(91)-9582555832
Phone: +(91)-(120)-4252742

CHINA CLAY

Ashapura China Clay Private Limited
No. 2, Shiv - Kutir, 5th Road,
Juhu Scheme,
Vile Parle - West,
Mumbai - 400056,
Maharashtra, India
Phone: +(91)-(22)-32929785
Website: www.ashapurachinaclay.co.in

Sri Ramamaruti Vermiculite Mines
310, SIDCO AIEMA Tower,
1st Main Road,
Ambattur Industrial Estate,
Chennai - 600 058,
Tamil Nadu, India
Phone: +(91)-(44)-65475163
Website: www.vermiculitemanufacturers.com/

CASTOR OIL

Shree Uday Oil & Foods Industries
Mr. Vijay K. Thakkar (CEO)
B - 77-78, Maruti Industrial Park,
Opposite Noroda Fire Station,
Memco - Naroda Road
Ahmedabad - 382345, Gujarat, India
Mobile: +(91)-9714611344
+(91)-9377011348
+(91)-9377011342
Phone: +(91)-(79)-22123897

Jyoti Soap Industries
Mr. Jawahar Milani (Proprietor)
Sr. No. 37 Kondhwa Bk.
Behind Angaraj Dhaba,
Next to Monginis Bakery
Pune - 411048,
Maharashtra,
India
Mobile: +(91)-9822033271
+(91)-9822142071
Phone: +(91)-(20)-26930271
Fax: +(91)-(20)-26932219

DEXTRIN

Vijay Chemical Industries
Mr. Saumil Parikh (Partner)
No. 6, Jafferbhoy Industrial Estate,
Andheri - Kurla Road
Mumbai - 400059,
Maharashtra, India
Mobile: +(91)-9820840569
+(91)-9819112161
Phone: +(91)-(22)-28508703
+(91)-(22)-40056663
Fax: +(91)-(22)-28506937

Thirthraj Consolidated Company
Mr. Girish T. Shah (CEO)
No. 15/16, Kamdhenu, 1st Cross,
Opposite L. I. C. Of India, Chamrajpet
Bengaluru - 560018, Karnataka, India
Mobile: +(91)-9844061994
+(91)-9341861994
+(91)-9538383854
Phone: +(91)-(80)-41223981
Fax: +(91)-(80)-26609719

STARCH

Desai Marketing
Mr. Nilesh Desai
Aadeshwar, Opposite Kotecha Girls School, Kotecha Nagar Main Road
Rajkot - 360001, Gujarat, India
Mobile: +(91)-9825072675
Phone: +(91)-(281)-2457099
+(91)-(281)-2478958

Jeecon Foods Private Limited
Mr. Abhishek Mahipal (Director)
1726/205, RITCO Rice Palace, Naya Bazar, Khari Baoli
Delhi - 110006, India
Mobile: +(91)-9210858838

Phone: +(91)-(11)-22344401
Amrut International
Mr. Mukesh Mehta (Director)
45, Shree Ram Industrial Estate,
Opposite Shah Alloys, Santej Char Rasta, Santej, Tal. Kalol
Gandhinagar - 382721, Gujarat, India
Mobile: +(91)-9898982725
Phone: +(91)-(79)-40070018
+(91)-(79)-27544186

ALL FOLLOWING PROJECT REPORTS ARE READILY AVAILABLE

AUTOMOBILES, MECHANICAL, STEEL & IRON & METALLURGICAL

- Agricultral Equipments
- Aac & Acsr Aluminium Conductors (All Aluminium Conductors)
- Agricultral Equipments Including Threshers
- Air Brake Helical Coil
- Air Cooler
- Air Filters (For Scooter Car & Excavators Etc.)
- Aluminium & Aluminium Alloys From Aluminium Scrap To Make Utensils (Induction Furnace Melted)
- Aluminium Alloy Wheels
- Aluminium Alloys From Aluminium Scrap To Make Utensils (Induction Furnace)
- Aluminium Hot & Cold Rolling Mill
- Aluminium Conductors
- Aluminium Bottle Manufacturing (Cold Extrusion Of Aluminium)
- Aluminium/Copper Cable Lugs
- Aluminium Cans For Beer Pkgs.
- Aluminium Cans For Capacitors
- Aluminium Caps For Injection Vials
- Aluminium Extrusion
- Aluminium Furniture & Hardware
- Aluminium Sheet Rolling Mill
- Alloy Steel Casting (Foundry)
- Aluminium Utensils
- Aluminium Utensils & School Boxes
- Aluminium Wire Drawing And Super Enamelling For Winding
- Anodised Aluminium Utensils
- Anodizing Of Aluminium
- Antimony Oxide From Lead Scrap
- Anti Scale Compound For Adding In Sugar Boilers
- Arc Welding Filter Glass
- Aluminium Foil Cutting & Roll Making
- Auto Flaps For Trucks & Buses
- Automobile Workshop (Garage & Service Centre)
- Auto Bulb
- Auto Electrical Parts (Armature)
- Auto Gears
- Auto Horns
- Auto Leaf Spring
- Auto Tubes
- Auto Piston Ring
- Auto Piston
- Auto Parts (Electricla And Electronic)
- Auto Rubber Parts And Turned Components Silent Block Bush And Ceiling Fan Shaft+
- Auto Wire Outer (Outer For Auto Wire)
- Bakery And Biscuits Equipments Fabrication
- Ball Point Pen Refills
- Ball Roller & Taper Bearing
- Band Saw Blades
- Barbed Wire
- Barrels (Oil)/(Metalliic Barrels)
- Bath Fittings, Turned Components (All Type) Sheet Metal (Job Work) And Hdpe/Pp Moulded Articles
- Battery For Car (Dry)
- Battery Operated Three Wheelers
- Benefication Of Chromite Ore Processing Charge Chrome
- Bicycle Spokes
- Bicycle Assembly
- Brake Lining Asbestoes/Resin Based & Asbestoes Free
- Brass Artware/Hollow Ware Casting (With Thehelp Of Phenolic Resin)
- Brass Casting
- Brass Pipes From Brass Sheet With Longitudinally Welding
- Brass Ware By Casting Method (Brass Articles Viz. Brass Pooja Lamps And Other Casted)
- Bright Bars
- Buffing And Polishing Industry (Job Work)
- Butt Hinge (Brass Sheet)
- Carbon Brush Holder & Slip Ring
- Co₂ Welding Wire Electrodes (Copper/Copper Alloy Coated M.S.Wire)
- Carbon Film Resistors
- Car Dealership (Hyundai)
- Carburettors
- Cast Steel Body Valve
- Cast Steel Panes For Melting Furnace
- Ceramic Coated Steel Pipes
- Chemical Etching Of Stainless Steel
- Chemical Resistant Iron & Steel
- Concast Steel Bars
- Cold Form Section Mill
- Cold Rolled Forming Of Section And Other Sections
- Cold Rolling Of Ms Strip
- Cold Twisted De-Formed Ribbed Steel
- Cold Rolling Mill
- Compressor (Hermetic) For Air Conditioners
- Compressed Natural Gas (Cng Kit) For Autovehicle
- Continuously Cast Steel Wire Rods (5 Mm)
- Continuous Casting Copper Wire Rods
- Conveyor Beltings
- Conveyor Belt, Transmission Belt & V Belts
- Cooking Ranges
- Copper/Brass Sheets,Circle & Utensils
- Copper Foil
- Copper Ingots, Rods Making & Wire Drawing
- Copper Products From Copper Scrap
- Copper Smelting Plant
- Copper Wire Rods From Copper Scrap
- Corrugated Box Making Machinery And Other Their Parts
- Cylinder Liner For Automobiles
- Disposable Plastic Razors
- Door Locks/Pad Locks
- Drill Bits & Tool Bits
- Drum Closures
- Erw Steel Pipes And Tubes
- Erw Steel Conduit Pipe
- Earth Moving Eqpt.
- Engine Valves For Automobiles
- Fabrication Of Heat Exchanger
- Fabrication Of Storage Tanks And M.S. Drum
- Ferrous Alloy Ni-Hardy I.V Casting
- Ferrous Mn Alloy Casting By Alumina Thermic Process
- Ferro Alloys
- Ferro Silicon & Ferro Manganese From Dolomite (Sms Grade)
- Fire Extinguishers
- Fire Fighting Equipments And Appliances
- Flip-Tone Cans
- Forged Conecting Rod
- Forging Unit
- Fountain Pen Nibs
- Foundry Sand
- Free Wheels, Free Wheel Bushes And Free Wheel Plates For Autorickshaws
- Fuel Briquettes From Agro Waste
- Fuel Injection System
- Fused Magnesia
- Generator Canopy
- Galvanized M.S.Strips
- Galvanizing Plant
- Galvanized Iron Wire (G.I. Wire)
- G.I. Pipes
- Gas Welding Torches And Nozzles
- Gasket Sheet
- Gate Grills & Window Frames
- Generating Set (Diesel)
- Hard Anodised Aluminium
- High Pressure Cylinder

Market Survey Cum Detailed Techno Economic Feasibility Report on all Projects are available Contact.
"ENGINEERS INDIA RESEARCH INSTITUTE". 4449, Nai Sarak (D), Main Road, Delhi-110006 (India)
Ph.: 09811437895, 91-11-23918117, 23916431, 45120361, 64727385 Fax : 91-11-23916431
E-mail : eiriprojects@gmail.com, eiribooks@yahoo.com • website: www.eiri.in, www.eiriindia.org

ALL FOLLOWING PROJECT REPORTS ARE READILY AVAILABLE

- Steel Furnitures And Electrical Appliances
- Steel Furniture And Fire Fighting Equipments
- Steel Furniture And Room Cooler
- Steel Wire Drawing And Galvanizing
- Steel Wire/Rod
- Steel Wool
- Ston Scrusher And Screening Plant
- Submerged Arc Welded Pipes
- Submersible Pump Manufacturing
- Super Enamelled Copper Wire
- Super Enamelled Copper Wire (From Copper Cathode Rod)
- Three Wheelers
- Tie-Rod Ends
- Tin Containers
- Toolroom And Sheet Metal Products
- Trolley (Shopping) For Carrying Of Stores At Super Market And Ware Houses
- Tractor Trailers
- Transmission Power Fitting
- Tubular Poles
- Tyre Retreading By Cold Process
- Super Enamelled Copper Wires
- Trolley (Shopping) For Carrying Of Stores At Super Market & Ware Houses
- Tmt Bars
- Tubular Poles For Electrical Transmission (By Fabrication Process)
- Tubular Poles Of M.S. & High Tensile Steel
- V- Belt
- Vacuum Cleaners
- Vacuum Flask (Stainless Steel)
- Valves For Refrigeration And Air-Condition
- Vehicle Welding & Painting
- Venetion Blind
- Washing Machines (Automatic & Computerised)
- Water Controller (Automatic)
- Watch Straps/Chains/ Bracelets/Belt Brass & Stainless Steel
- Water Coolers
- Welded Wire Mesh
- Welding Electrodes
- Wheel Barrow
- Wick Stoves
- Wind Mill Window Frame (Ferrous & Non-Ferrous)
- Wrist Watch

CHEMICALS (ORGANIC & INORGANIC) WITH PETROLEUM PRODUCTS

- Acetic Anhydride
- Acetic Acid (Glacial)
- Acetic Acid From Ethanol
- Acetone
- Acetylene Black
- Acetyl Chloride
- Acetylene Gas
- Acetylene Gas & Oxygen Gas (Integrated Unit)
- Acid Black Dye
- Acid Slurry
- Activated Alumina
- Activated Bleaching Earth (Activated Fullers Earth)
- Activated Carbon From Cashewnut Shell
- Activated Carbon From Rice Husk
- Activated Carbon From Rice Husk, Coconut Shell & Coconut Powder
- Activated Carbon From Wood
- Activated Carbon Powder & Granules From Coconut Shell
- Activated Carbon & Sodium Silicate From Paddy & Rice Husk
- Alcohol From Broken Rice
- Alum For Water Treatment
- Adhesive (Fevicol Type)
- Aerosol Insecticides Spray (Baygon, Hit, Mortein Type)
- Agarbatti Synthetic Perfumery Compounds
- Alcohol From Potato
- Alcohol From Rice Grains
- Alcohol From Rice Husk
- Alcohol From Molasses
- Alcohol, Beer, Starch, Liquid Glucose, Dextrose, Sorbitol, Vitamin-C,
- Alcoholic Beverages And Vinegar From Coconut Water
- Germ Oil, Cattle Feed Etc. From Maize
- Alkyd Resin
- Alkylated Phenol Likenonyl Phenol, Dodecyl Phenol
- Alum (Non Ferric)
- Alum (Ferric)
- Aluminium Chloride From Aluminium Ore
- Alum Cake
- Alum From Aluminium Hydrate
- Aluminium Ingot By Bauxite
- Aluminium Phosphide
- Aluminium Phosphate
- Aluminium Sulphate (Non Ferric Alum) 17% - 18% Alumina Content In Granules (2 Mm To 4 Mm) And Flakes
- Amines & Allied Products
- Amino Acid
- Ammonia Gas
- Ammonia Gas Bottling
- Ammonia Liquor
- Ammonium Nitrate
- Ammonium Chloride (Pure & Technical)
- Ammonium Sulphate
- Annato Seed Extraction And Processing
- Anti Corrosion Chemicals
- Anthranilic Acid From Phthalic Anhydride
- Anesthesia (All Types) Used In Hospitals
- Aniline
- Argon Gas
- Ariel Type Detergent Powder
- Anthraquinone
- Antimony Trioxide
- Atenolol
- Auramine "O"
- Azodicarbonamide
- Baking Soda From Ash
- Barium Carbonate
- Barium Compounds
- Barium Nitrate
- Barium Peroxide
- Barium-Thio-Sulphate Banzene
- Baryte Powder
- Bar Soap (All Varieties) Using Soap Noodles
- Beer Plant
- Belt Paste
- Beneficiation Of Chromite Ore Processing Charge Chrome
- Benzyl Acetate, Benzyl Benzoate, Benzyl Alcohol
- Beta Naphthol
- Bentonite Powder
- Benzoic Acid
- Benzidine
- Biofertiliser From Mother Culture
- Bio Oil For Power Generation From Coffee Husk
- Bio Gas Plant
- Bio Gas Filling In Cylinder
- Bio Tech Unit
- Bi-Chromate Of Sodium, Potassium & Ammonium
- Bi-Functional Black Mfgr.Reactive Dye (Dye From Cotton Yarn Dyeing)
- Bio-Fuel (Jatropha Cultivation And Extraction)
- Bituminous Roademulsion
- Black Phenyl
- Black Sulphur
- Bleaching Powder (Stable)
- Blue Detergent Powder
- Bone Crushing Plant
- Bone Meal (Calcined) Enrichment With Calcium & Phosphorus
- Boric Acid
- B.O.N. Acid
- Bromine Gas Plant
- Brandy
- Butanol
- Butyl Rubber For The Manufacture Of Tubes For Truck And Car Tyres
- 1,4, Butanediol
- Butyl Acetate
- Caffein From Tea Waste
- Calcined Lime (Dead Burnt Dolomite)

ALL FOLLOWING PROJECT REPORTS ARE READILY AVAILABLE

- Calcined Petroleum Coke
- Calcining Of Magnesite & Dead Burnt Magnesite
- Calcium Aluminate
- Calcium Based Grease
- Calcium Carbide
- Calcium Carbonate
- Calcium Carbonate (Precipitated) From By Product (Lime Slurry & Carbon Dioxide)
- Calcium Carbonate (Activated & Precipitated)
- Calcium Chloride
- Calcium Gluconate
- Calcium Nitrate
- Calcium Silicate Bricks
- Calcium Stearate By Fusion Process
- Camphor Powder (Synthetic)
- Construction Chemicals (With Detailed Market Survey And Formulae Etc.)
- Carbon Dioxide
- Carbon Black From Fertilizer Waste
- Carbon Black (Petroleum Based)
- Carboxy Methyl Cellulose (Cmc)
- Casein And By Products
- Casein From Milk
- Cationic Softner (Stearic Acid Based)
- Caustic Soda
- Caustic Soda From Soda Ash By Soda Lime Process
- Caustic Soda (Liquid) By Electrolytic Process
- Caustic Soda From Trona
- Caustic Soda, Chlorine And Hydrogen Gas By Electro-Lysis Of Brine Solution
- Cellulose Acetate Moulding Powder
- Cellulose Powder & Micro Crystalline Cellulose Powder
- Cement Admixture
- Cement Colour
- Cement Water Proofing Compound
- Cement From Fly Ash & Lime
- Cement Tiles (Glazed)
- Chlorinated Paraffin Wax (Cpw)
- Citric Acid From Lemon
- Citric Acid From Molasses
- Double Firing (Heating)
- Chelated Zinc (Zn Edta)
- Chemicals From Prawn Head
- Chitin & Chitosan From Prawn Shell Waste
- Chloral Hydrate
- Chloramphenicol
- Chromic Acid (With Pollution Control)
- Chromic Acid (Oxide) & Blue Oxide
- Chlorinated Paraffin Wax (Cpw)
- Chromic Acid
- Cement Paint & Distemper
- Citric Acid From Lemon
- Citric Acid From Molasses
- Cleaning Of Cooling System And Boiler
- Coal Tar Distillation
- Coal Washing Plant
- Cobalt Octoate
- Compost For Mushroom
- Construction Chemicals
- Copper Oxychloride
- Coolant (Engine)
- Copper Phthalocyanine Blue & Green
- Correction Fluid
- Cupric Chloride
- Crude Oil Bleaching For Petroleum Jelly
- Cutting Oil
- Cyanuric Chloride
- Cyanoacrylate Adhesive
- Cutting Oil
- Defoaming Agent For Paper Industry
- De-Nickeling (Electrolytic Process)
- Detergent Cake & Powder
- Detergent Powder
- Detergent Concentrate (Idet 10)
- Dextrose Monohydrate & Dextrose Anhydrous Powder From Tapioca Starch
- Di-Basic Lead Stearate
- Di Calcium Phosphate
- Diclofenal Sodium Slow Release (Sr) Tables 100mg.
- Di Ethyl Oxalate
- Di Methyl Orthophthalate
- Di-Methyl Phthalate
- Diclofenac Gel
- Dioctyl Phthalate (Dop)
- Di Phenyl Glycerine
- Di Phenyl Oxide
- Dinitro-Chloro Benzene
- Distillery
- Distilled Water
- Dodecyl Benzene Sulphonate
- Dustless Chalk
- Edta & Its Salts
- Electroless Nickel Plating On Plastics
- Electrolyte (Like Sulphuric Acid) For Lead Acid Dry Rechargable 5.5.Ah. Battery
- Electropolishing On Gold Jewellery
- Electropolishing On Various Metals
- Endosulfan
- Enzyme Based Detergent Powder
- Ephedrine Hydrochloride
- Epoxy Resin Based Compound
- Ethanol (Biofuel)
- Ethyl Alcohol From Molasses
- Ethyl Acetate
- Ehtyl Ether
- Ethyl Alcohol (Potable Liquor)
- Ethyl Hexanol
- Extra Temperature Lubricating Grease
- Extraction Of Essential Oils By Sugar Critical Fluid (Carbon Dioxide) Method From Flowers, Herbal & Spices
- Fabric Stain Remover
- Fatty Acid
- Ferric Alum
- Ferric And Non Ferric Alum (Aluminium Sulphate)
- Ferro Chrome Ligno Sulphonate
- Ferro Manganese
- Ferro Silicone

Contact EIRI for required Project report apart from this list.

- Ferro Vanadium From Vanadium Sludge
- Ferrous Silicate
- Ferrous Sulphate
- Ferrous Sulphide
- Fertilizer From Animal Blood & Leather Waste
- Fluorescent Tube Light Powder
- Foamed Pvc Compounding & Its Products
- Formaldehyde
- Food Grade Grease Or Lubricant
- Fractional Distillation Of D.M.O (Dementholized Oil)
- Fractional Distillation Of Essential Oil & Medicinalplant Extract
- Friction Dust (Liquid & Powder) From Cnsl
- Fruit Flavours
- Furfural From Rice Husk
- Fumaric Acid
- Gas Filling Of Lpg Cylinder
- Garlic Acid
- Ginger And Garlic Paste
- Ginger Processing
- Gasket Shellac Compound
- Gear Oil
- Gibberellic Acid
- Glass Putty
- Gluconic Acid
- Glucose D- Powder
- Glycerine
- Gossypol (Poly Phenol) From Cotton Seed Oil
- Greases (Lithium Based)
- Guar Gum Powder
- Hair Fixer (Hair Gel Type)
- High Temerature Grease
- Hard Grease
- H - Acid
- Henna Paste Making
- Henna Powder Repackaging
- Heptal Dehyde
- Herbal Beer
- High Carbon Ferro Chrome
- Humid Acid
- Hydrated Calcium Silicate Brick
- Hydrated Lime From Sea Shell
- Hydrochloric Acid
- Hydro Fluoric Acid
- Hydrogen Peroxide (By Auto-Oxidation Process)
- Ice Packs (Solutions Type, White Gel Type, Violet Semi Solid Polymer Type)
- Improving Drop Point Paraffin Wax From 45-50°c To 75-80°c
- Industrial Alcohol

Market Survey Cum Detailed Techno Economic Feasibility Report on all Projects are available Contact.
"ENGINEERS INDIA RESEARCH INSTITUTE". 4449, Nai Şarak (D), Main Road, Delhi-110006 (India)
Ph. : 09811437895, 91-11-23918117, 23916431, 45120361, 64727385 Fax : 91-11-23916431
E-mail : eiriprojects@gmail.com, eiribooks@yahoo.com • website: www.eiri.in, www.eiriindia.org

EDIBLE OILS, ESSENTIAL OILS, LURICATIING OILS, GREASES, VEGETABLE OILS, WAXES, CAMPHOR, PERFUMES & PERFUMERY COMPOUNDS AND REFINED OILS ETC.